THE MAKING OF MODERN POETRY IN CANADA

THE MAKING OF
MODERN POETRY IN CANADA

Essential Articles on
Contemporary Canadian Poetry in English

EDITED BY LOUIS DUDEK AND MICHAEL GNAROWSKI

Toronto
The Ryerson Press

To the memory of John Sutherland

Grateful acknowledgment is made to the Canada Council,
which aided in the publication of this book.

First published 1967. Reprinted 1968
First paperback edition, 1970

SBN 7700 6036 6

Preface

The study of Canadian literature has reached a point of development where conclusions drawn from secondary sources are no longer adequate and a first-hand examination of essential literary documents becomes necessary. Readers who are curious to know literary history in this sense, however, find that the books and magazines in which essential items might be found are often not available in local libraries and collections. The present assembly of articles and background materials for the study of modern Canadian poetry is designed to answer this need in one particular area of interest.

Such a collection, it must be noted, implies a different principle of selection from those anthologies of Canadian literary criticism which have so far appeared. It seeks to offer essays and documents intimately involved in the literary history of the period, rather than exemplary or autotelic show pieces of criticism.

The main purpose, as history, is to present to the reader original texts which are not otherwise easy of access and to make it possible for him to arrive at his own interpretations and to form his own conclusions. To be sure, the arrangement and presentation of this material in the chapter introductions imposes some interpretation on the part of the editors; but this the reader may either challenge or confirm by a close reading of the evidence in question.

The preparation of the book has required the help and co-operation of a number of libraries and individuals. Especially we would like to express our gratitude to Miss Jay Andison of the Reference Department, Sir George Williams University Library; to Mrs. E. Lewis of the Rare Book Room, Redpath Library, McGill University; and for the use of documents, to Mrs. Irene Dawson at the Library of Lakehead University. Also to M. Jean Ethier-Blais for useful insights, and to F. R. Scott for specific details of Montreal literary history. To Diana Gnarowski, as well, for very generous help in the preparation of the manuscript. We are also grateful to The Canada Council for a grant in aid of publication; and to the C. D. Howe Foundation for its fellowship to M. Gnarowski in support of research into little magazines.

THE EDITORS

Preface to the Second Edition

It is reassuring that the increasing study of Canadian literary history through primary documents has confirmed the need for this new edition of *The Making of Modern Poetry in Canada*.

The book was not meant to be, and is not in any sense, a comprehensive history of modernism in Canada; it is a collection of essential source material, together with documents relating to the subject, from which the reader can discover some of the problems and leading ideas of the period.

The question for the critical reader is to understand what has happened in the course of events, and what the nature of the new poetry might be. Modern poetry in Canada must be defined in its own terms, which means that it must be read in the light of its own supporting criticism and theoretical work. 'What is modern poetry?' is a question that applies to Canadian poetry as well as to English and American poetry, and it has its own unique context and meaning.

It may be taken for granted that the poetry itself is the first object of interest, and that the full dimension of its study lies in the compendious literary histories and surveys, the studies of individual writers, and the collections of criticism on movements and periods which have recently appeared.

It is encouraging therefore that books of this kind have become increasingly central. The present work provides primary materials that would not be easily available to confirm or to test more general findings and theories.

THE EDITORS

Contents

Preface v

I THE BEGINNINGS OF THE MODERN SCHOOL   1

The Precursors (1910-1925)

Introduction	3
ARTHUR STRINGER: Foreword to *Open Water*	5
JOHN MURRAY GIBBON: Rhymes With and Without Reason	9
FRANK OLIVER CALL: Foreword to *Acanthus and Wild Grape*	21

The Initiators (1925-1936)

Introduction	24
A. J. M. SMITH: Contemporary Poetry	27
A. J. M. SMITH: Wanted: Canadian Criticism	31
LEO KENNEDY: The Future of Canadian Literature	34
F. R. SCOTT: Preface to *New Provinces*	38
A. J. M. SMITH: A Rejected Preface	38

II THE NEW POETRY: A MANIFESTO

Introduction	45
JOHN SUTHERLAND: Introduction to *Other Canadians*	47

III THE EARLY FORTIES

The New Literary Scene

Introduction	65
JOHN SUTHERLAND: Brief to a Royal Commission	66
ROBERT WEAVER: John Sutherland and *Northern Review*	80

New Critical Currents

Introduction	84
NORTHROP FRYE: Canada and Its Poetry	86
F. R. SCOTT: A Note on Canadian War Poetry	97
NEUFVILLE SHAW: The Maple Leaf is Dying	101
LOUIS DUDEK: Academic Literature	104
JOHN SUTHERLAND: Review of *Poems* by Robert Finch	107
Editorial Board of *Northern Review:* Notices of Resignation	109
P. K. PAGE: Letter to *Northern Review*	110

IV SIGNS OF REACTION, NEW AND OLD

Introduction   113
JOHN SUTHERLAND: The Past Decade in Canadian Poetry   116
LORNE PIERCE: Foreword to *Canadian Poetry in English*   122
V. B. RHODENIZER: Introduction to *Canadian Poetry in English* 124

V RESURGENCE

Introduction   141
LOUIS DUDEK: Où sont les jeunes?   142
LOUIS DUDEK: Preface to *Cerberus*   144
IRVING LAYTON: Preface to *Cerberus*   145
RAYMOND SOUSTER: Preface to *Cerberus*   146
EARLE BIRNEY: Letter of Resignation   147
ROBERT A. CURRIE: Don't Blame This on Bliss   149

VI POINTS OF VIEW

Introduction   155
EARLE BIRNEY: Introduction to *Twentieth Century
   Canadian Poetry*   157
DESMOND PACEY: English-Canadian Poetry, 1944-1954   160
LOUIS DUDEK: The State of Canadian Poetry: 1954   169
IRVING LAYTON: Foreword to *A Red Carpet for the Sun*   173
NORTHROP FRYE: The Keys to Dreamland   178
NORTHROP FRYE: Verticals of Adam   188
JAMES REANEY: Editorial   197
ELI MANDEL: Preface to *Poetry 62*   199

VII THE LITTLE MAGAZINES

Introduction   203
LOUIS DUDEK: The Role of Little Magazines in Canada   205
MICHAEL GNAROWSKI: The Role of "Little Magazines" in the
   Development of Poetry in English in Montreal   212
FRANK DAVEY: Anything But Reluctant:
   Canada's Little Magazines   222

VIII WIDER HORIZONS

Poetry Finds a Public   231

Introduction   231
WILLIAM CARLOS WILLIAMS: A Note on Layton   233

The Private World of Raymond Souster 241
The Purdy Pigment 243
ROBERT FULFORD: On Raymond Souster 245

Relations With French Writing in Canada

Introduction 247
A. J. M. SMITH: From the Introduction to *The Oxford Book
   of Canadian Verse* 250
JEAN-CHARLES BONENFANT: L'influence de la littérature
   canadienne-anglaise au Canada français 256
F. R. SCOTT: The Poet in Quebec Today 265

Modern Poetry Across Canada

Introduction 270
LOUIS DUDEK: Patterns of Recent Canadian Poetry 271
GEORGE WOODCOCK: Editorial 286
MILTON ACORN: Open Letter to a Demi-Senior Poet 287
ALAN BEVAN: Editorial 289
MILTON ACORN: The Montreal Miracle and K. V. Hertz 292
GEORGE BOWERING: The Most Remarkable Thing About *Tish* 293
FRANK DAVEY: Statement 294
FRANK DAVEY: Rime, A Scholarly Piece 295
RAYMOND SOUSTER: Preface to *New Wave Canada* 300

Acknowledgments 303

I

THE BEGINNINGS
OF THE MODERN SCHOOL

The Precursors (1910-1925)

It is often assumed that the modern idiom in Canadian poetry sprang full-blown from the editorial brow of A. J. M. Smith and F. R. Scott, both guiding spirits behind *The McGill Fortnightly Review* (1925-1927). This assumption places the beginning of the modern tradition in the middle of the 1920s, and serves to support the view that literary developments in Canada at that point were a generation behind those of the literary centres of the world. The truth, however, is that a sense of strong modernist individualism is apparent in the work of some Canadian poets before that time. Some writers were thoroughly aware of contemporary trends, and in fact elements of the modern idiom were beginning to operate in the work of these poets even before 1920.

Arthur Stringer published his book of poems entitled *Open Water* in 1914. This book must be seen as a turning point in Canadian writing if only for the importance of the ideas advanced by Stringer in his preface. In a carefully presented, extremely well-informed account of traditional verse-making, Stringer pleaded the cause of free verse and created what must now be recognized as an early document of the struggle to free Canadian poetry from the trammels of end-rhyme, and to liberalize its methods and its substance. Stringer's arguments become even more striking from the point of view of literary history if we recall that in 1914 free verse was still in the experimental stage, and that the famous notes of F. S. Flint and the strictures of Ezra Pound on *imagisme* and free verse had appeared less than a year before this, in the March 1913 issue of *Poetry: A Magazine of Verse* (Chicago).

By 1919 in Canada, arguments about the merits of free verse and the role of imagism had given way to a loud debate on the subject of the future of poetry, showing all the disquieting signs of radical change. The quarrel between the old and the new was carried on in the pages of most periodicals, finding expression in the *Canadian Bookman* in a reasoned article of unusual length by J. M. Gibbon. Here, the man who was to become President of The Canadian Authors' Association, attempted an appraisal of the new poetry by means of comparison and actual illustration drawn from good examples of work being done by the new poets. He quoted from

Pound, Aldington, Eliot and Sandburg, and while he was pointedly critical of the faults and abuses of those whom he termed the *vers librists*— ". . . write too much or at least have too much published . . ." —he responded with acumen and intelligence to the promise of the new poetry.

A year later F. O. Call's *Acanthus and Wild Grape* was published. Once more the reader was treated to something more than he might have bargained for in a preface to a small collection of poetry. Call took up the cudgels in the cause of free verse, and argued with more than passing eloquence and conviction for the rejection of the hackneyed limitations imposed by end-rhyme. His message was identical to that of Stringer and he pleaded for a hearing and a chance to get poetry moving once more in the direction of a technically freed and spontaneous expression. His method was that of comparison, and as evidence of the worth of his experiment Call offered two widely differing types of poetry in his book. He wanted the reader to compare the traditional method as typified in the poetry of the "Acanthus" section of the book with the free verse of the section entitled "Wild Grape".

In addition to the efforts of poets and writers like Gibbon, Stringer and Call, signs of the modern idiom in practice appeared in the earliest published work of W. W. E. Ross, R. G. Everson, Raymond Knister and Dorothy Livesay. Ross and Everson wrote in the new *Imagiste* and *vers libre* style from 1923 on, and their poems appeared in the pages of *Poetry: A Magazine of Verse* (Chicago) and in Marianne Moore's *The Dial*. (Ross first appeared in *The Dial* in April of 1928, and was featured with seven poems in the August issue of that year. Everson appeared in *Poetry: A Magazine of Verse* (Chicago) in 1928 as well). Raymond Knister, who had been publishing from 1922 in *The Midland* (Iowa City), *Voices* (Boston), and *Poetry: A Magazine of Verse* (Chicago), was featured prominently with twelve poems in Eugene Jolas' Paris magazine *This Quarter* in Autumn of 1925. Dorothy Livesay's earliest free verse dates from the same period, with poems appearing not only in magazines like *The Canadian Forum* and *Saturday Night,* but also in newspapers and the American poetry bi-monthly *Voices* (Boston). In short, a scattering of Canadian writers, in no way organized or identified with any Canadian literary magazine, already reflected the changes taking place in the early 1920s.

ARTHUR STRINGER

To even the casual reader of poetry who may chance to turn to the following pages it will be evident that the lyrics contained therein have been written without what is commonly known as end-rhyme. It may also be claimed by this reader that the lyrics before him are without rhythm. As such, it may at first seem that they mark an effort in revolt against two of the primary assets of modern versification.

All art, of course, has its ancestry. While it is the duty of poetry both to remember and to honour its inherited grandeurs, the paradoxical fact remains that even this most convention-ridden medium of emotional expression is a sort of warfare between the embattled soul of the artist, seeking articulation, and the immuring traditions with which time and the prosodian have surrounded him.

In painting and in music, as in sculpture and the drama, there has been a movement of late to achieve what may be called formal emancipation, a struggle to break away from the restraints and the technical obligations imposed upon the worker by his artistic predecessors. In one case this movement may be called Futurism, and in another it may be termed Romanticism, but the tendency is the same. The spirit of man is seen in rebellion against a form that has become too intricate or too fixed to allow him freedom of utterance.

Poetry alone, during the last century, seems to have remained stable, in the matter of structure. Few new forms have been invented, and with one or two rare exceptions success has been achieved through ingeniously elaborating on an already established formula and through meticulously re-echoing what has already been said. This has resulted, on the one hand, in a technical dexterity which often enough resembles the strained postures of acrobatism, and, on the other, in that constantly reiterated complaint as to the hollowness and aloofness of modern poetry. Yet this poetry is remote and insincere, not because the modern spirit is incapable of feeling, but because what the singer of today has felt has not been directly and openly expressed. His apparel has remained mediaeval. He must still don mail to face Mausers, and wear chain-armour against machine-guns. He must scout through the shadowy hinterlands of consciousness in attire that may be historic, yet at the same time is distressingly conspicuous. And when he begins his assault on those favouring moments or inspirational moods which lurk in the deeper valleys and byways of sensibility, he must begin it as a marked man, pathetically resplendent in that rigid steel which is an anachronism and no longer an armour.

Rhyme, from the first, has been imposed upon him. His only escape from rhyme has been the larger utterance of blank verse. Yet the iambic pentameter of his native tongue, perfected in the sweeping sonority of the later Shakespearean tragedies and left even more intimidatingly austere in the organ-like roll of Milton, has been found by the later singer to be ill-fitted for the utterance of those more intimate moods and those subjective experiences which may be described as characteristically modern. Verse, in the nature of things, has become less epic and racial, and more and more lyric and personal. The poet, consequently, has been forced back into the narrower domain so formally and so rigidly fenced in by rhyme. And before touching on the limitations resulting from this incarceration, it may be worth while to venture a brief glance back over the history of what Milton himself denominated as "the jingling sounds of like endings" and Goldsmith characterized as "a vile monotony" and even Howells has spoken of as "the artificial trammels of verse."

It has been claimed that those early poets of Palestine who affected the custom of beginning a number of lines or stanzas with the same letter of the alphabet unconsciously prepared the way for that latter-day ornamental fringe known as end-rhyme. Others have claimed that this insistence of a consonance of terminals is a relic of the communal force of the chant, where the clapping of hands, the stamping of feet, or the twanging of bow-strings marked the period-ends of prehistoric recitative. The bow-string, of course, later evolved into the musical instrument and when poetry became a written as well as a spoken language the consonantal drone of rhyming end-words took the place of the discarded instrument which had served to mark a secondary and wider rhythm in the progress of impassioned recitative.

It must be admitted, however, even in the face of this ingenious pleading, that rhyme is a much more modern invention than it seems. That it is not rudimentary in the race is evidenced by the fact that many languages, such as the Celtic, the Teutonic, and the Scandinavian, are quite without it. The Greeks, even in their melic poetry, saw no need for it. The same may be said of the Romans, though with them it will occasionally be found that the semi-feet of the pentameter constitute what may be called accidental rhyme. Rhyming Latin verse, indeed, does not come into existence until the end of the fourth century, and it is not until the time of the Conquest that end-rhyme becomes in any way general in English song. Layman, in translating Wace's "Le Brut d'Angleterre," found the original work written in rhymed lines, and in following that early model produced what is probably the first rhymed poem written in England.

With the introduction of end-rhymes came the discovery that a decoration so formal could convert verse into something approaching the architectural. It gave design to the lyric. With this new definiteness of outline, of course, came a newer rigidity of medium. Form was acknowledged as the visible presentation of this particular art. Formal variations became a matter of studious attention. Efforts were made to leave language in itself instrumental, and in these efforts sound frequently comes perilously near triumphing over sense. The exotic formal growths of other languages were imported into England. No verbal *tour de force* or *troubadour* or *trouvère* or Ronsardist was too fantastic for imitation and adoption. The one-time primitive directness of English was overrun by such forms as the ballade, the chant royal, the rondel, the kyrielle, the rondeau and the rondeau redouble, the virelai and the pantoum, the sestina, the villanelle, and last, yet by no means least, the sonnet. But through the immense tangle of our intricate lyric growth it can now be seen that mere mechanics do not always make poetry. While rhyme has, indeed, served its limited purposes, it must be remembered that the highest English verse has been written without rhyme. This verbal embroidery, while it presents to the workman in words a pleasingly decorative form, at the same time imposes on him both an adventitious restraint and an increased self-consciousness. The twentieth century poet, singing with his scrupulously polished vocalisation, usually finds himself content to re-echo what has been said before. He is unable to "travel light"; pioneering with so heavy a burden is out of the question. Rhyme and meter have compelled him to sacrifice content for form. It has left him incapable of what may be called abandonment. And the consciousness of his technical impedimenta has limited the roads along which he may adventure. His preoccupation with formal exactions has implanted in him an instinctive abhorrence for anything beyond the control of what he calls common sense. Dominated by this emotional and intellectual timidity, he has attributed to end-rhyme and accentual rhythm the self-sufficiency of mystic rites, in the face of the fact that the fewer the obstacles between feeling and expression the richer the literary product must be, and forgetting, too, that poetry represents the extreme vanguard of consciousness both adventuring and pioneering along the path of future progress.

For the poet to turn his back on rhythm, as at times he has been able to do with rhyme, is an impossibility. For the rhythmising instinct is innate and persistent in man, standing for a law which permeates every manifestation of encrgy. The great heart of Nature itself beats with a regular systole and diastole. But rhythmically, the modern versifier has been a Cubist without quite comprehending it. He has been viewing the world mathematically. He has been crowding his soul into a geometrically designed mould. He has bowed to a rule-of-thumb order of speech, arbitrarily imposed on him by an ancestry which wrung its ingenuous pleasure out of an ingenuous regularity of stress and accent. To succeed under that law he must practise an adroit form of self-deception, solemnly pretending to fit his lines to a mould which he actually over-runs and occasionally ignores. He has not been satisfied with the rhythm of Nature, whose heart-beats in their manifold expressions are omnipresent but never confined to any single sustained pulse or any one limited movement. It is not argued that he should ignore rhythm altogether. To do so, as has already been said, would be impossible, since life itself is sustained by the rise and fall of mortal breasts and the beat and throb of mortal hearts. Rhythm is in man's blood. The ear of the world instinctively searches for cadences. The poet's efforts towards symphonic phrasing have long since become habitual and imperative. But that he should confine himself to certain man-made laws of meter, that he should be shackled by the prosodian of the past, is quite another matter. His predecessors have fashioned many rhythms that are pretty, many accentual forms that are cunningly intricate, but at a time when his manner of singing has lost its vital swing it is well for man to forget these formal prettinesses and equally well to remember that poetry is not an intellectual exercise but the immortal soul of perplexed mortality seeking expression.

To abandon fixed rhythm, or meter, for the floating rhythm of the chant may not be an immediate solution of the problem. To follow the Psalms of David, for example, will not suddenly conjure a new school of verse into the word. But to return to the more open movement of the chant, which is man's natural and rudimentary form of song, may constitute a step toward freedom. The mere effort towards emancipation, in fact, is not without its value. It may serve to impress on certain minds the fact that poetry is capable of exhausting one particular form of expression, of incorporating and consuming one particular embodiment of perishable matter and passing on to its newer fields. Being a living organism, it uses up what lies before it, and to find new vigour must forever feed on new forms. Being the product of man's spirit, which is forever subject to change, verse must not be worshipped for what it has been, but for what it is capable of being. No necrophilic regard for its established conventions must blind the lover of beautiful verse to the fact that the primary function of poetry is both to intellectualize sensation and to elucidate emotional experience. If man must worship beauty only as he has known it in the past, man must be satisfied with worshipping that which has lived and now is dead.

Arthur Stringer, Preface to *Open Water* (Toronto: Bell & Cockburn, 1914).

JOHN MURRAY GIBBON

"Poetry," said Don Marquis once in his column in the *New York Sun*, "Poetry with us is a business; it takes time, muscular effort, nervous energy and, sometimes, thought to produce a poem." In the same vein he said,

> Poetry is something we once got paid
> A dollar a line for;
> But we're not going to tell you the name
> Of the Magazine;
> We're saving it.

A third of his definitions was,

> Poetry is something Amy Lowell says
> Carl Sandburg writes.

While in a more serious mood he gave this definition:

> Poetry is the clinking together of two
>   unexpected coins
> In the shabby pocket of life.

With airy definitions such as these in mind, the classic definition of Theodore Watts-Dunton in an old edition of the Encyclopaedia Britannica seems elephantine. "Poetry," he says (I quote from memory), "is the concrete and artistic expression of the human mind in emotional and rhythmical language." Ponderous, you will say, and yet there are those who take poetry seriously, to whom poetry represents the supreme rendering of beautiful thoughts.

They are not in the majority, I fear—otherwise poverty and poetry would not so often go hand in hand. To quote Don Marquis again, "Publishing a volume of verse is like dropping a rose petal down the Grand Canyon and waiting to hear the echo."

Poverty, however, has not kept the poem from singing—never indeed were poets so numerous and so prolific as today. "Poets," says one editor, "seem as numerous as sparrows through the cool sunshine, and almost as quarrelsome." Their name indeed is legion. A hundred of them are represented in the Anthology of *The New Poetry*, edited by Harriet Munroe and Alice Corbin Henderson, the editors of the

Chicago magazine called *Poetry*, and yet this anthology omits many familiar names—Lawrence Binyon, Katherine Tynan, Francis Thompson, Bliss Carman and Alan Seeger, for instance. These hundred who are apparently the elect are responsible for over two hundred volumes quoted in the bibliography and for vast quantities of stray verse scattered through innumerable magazines. When the editors of *Poetry* not very long ago asked for a poem on a certain subject, over seven hundred manuscripts came in response through the mails.

What is the reason for this apparently irrepressible output? Is it because, as Don Marquis faintly insinuates, there are magazines that pay a dollar a line, or is it because the human race—particularly the race on this side of the Atlantic—is growing more imaginative, more idealistic, more sensitive to the music of words? Or is it—and this is one of the thoughts which have come from recent reading—is it because the discovery or re-discovery of "free verse" removed the barriers of rhyme and let in the multitude? Are there so many poets today because poetry, now that it may be rhymeless and irregular in rhythm and form, looks easier to write?

Rhythm and quantities, indeed, though they may unconsciously tickle the ear, are not very extensively understood [*sic*] of the people. "The public," says Richard le Gallienne, "is a good deal like a pretty girl I was talking to the other day. 'Of course,' I said to her, 'you know what hexameters are, don't you?' 'Sure,' she replied, 'I had a ride in one the other day through the Park.'"

Yet it is only fair to say that the leaders in the free verse movement are scholarly poets—Ezra Pound, for instance, or Richard Aldington—familiar in the original with the literature of Greece, which indeed in the choruses of Aeschylus and Sophocles provides the irrefutable precedent. Aldington belongs to the group known as *Imagists*, whose creed is to use the language of common speech but to employ always the exact word, not the merely decorative word; to create new rhythms as the expression of new words; to allow absolute freedom in the choice of subject; to present an image rendering particulars exactly and not dealing in generalities, however magnificent and sonorous; to produce poetry that is hard and clear, never blurred nor indefinite; to be concentrated.

Typical is Aldington's "Choricos," with the lines . . .

[Aldington's "Choricos" originally quoted here.]

Ezra Pound, in spite of his eccentricities and egoism and postures, has a lyric quality of high order. Here is "The Return" descriptive of the Furies and just as Greek as could be:

[Pound's "The Return" originally quoted here.]

That, you will say, is a Greek subject, but here is a lyric on New York which Sappho might have written:

[Pound's "My City . . ." originally quoted here.]

Ezra Pound has given a new flair to the epigram, as for instance in "The Garden":

[Pound's "The Garden" originally quoted here.]

Born of Greek inspiration also is that volume of free verse poems which is perhaps the only instance in recent years of poetry becoming a best seller—I refer to the *Spoon River· Anthology*. The title is, I take it, an admission of the debt the poet owes to the Sepulchral Epigrams of the Greek Anthology, numbers of which have that ironic vein which is the keynote of their Spoon River offspring. Edgar Lee Masters, of course, has created an entirely new and original work— has merely taken an old idea and applied it with modern methods, and with admirable skill and breadth of vision. One wishes that in his later poems he had attained the same heights. Unfortunately he seems to be concerned now more with quantity than quality, and is endeavouring to prove to the very prolific Miss Amy Lowell that he can write more verse per month than she.

Although free verse or *vers libre*, the unrhymed verse with lines of irregular length, is generally taken to be a modern movement, it is more strictly a revival. Rhyme is a comparatively recent invention— barely known before the tenth century and not accepted into English literature till the days of Chaucer. But most revivals are due to intense emotion which bursts the bonds of moribund rite and tradition, and the revival of free verse is no exception to the rule. It is the expression in literature of the same spirit of unrest which has introduced impressionism into painting, flower masses into the old formal garden, and Debussy, Strauss and Scriabine into music.

Rhyme was definitely established as a suitable form for English verse by Chaucer. It had been used before, but never so happily. Two centuries later it had become so popular that it was even considered vulgar, and some of the more accomplished poets in the days of Elizabeth reacted into blank verse.

In the seventeenth century rhyme came into fashion again, so much so that Dryden in his "Defence of Poetry" could say, "Blank verse is acknowledged to be too low for a poem." The royalist rhymesters of his day were certainly accomplished—daintiest of all being Robert Herrick, as for instance in "To Daffodils":

> We have short time to stay, as you;
>   We have as short a spring;
> As quick a growth to meet decay,
>   As you, or any thing.
>   We die
> As your hours do, and dry
>   Away,
>   Like to the summer's rain;
> Or as the pearls of morning's dew,
>   Ne'er to be found again.

But for 150 years after Dryden rhyme and rhythm became so formal and conventional that poetic expression was stifled, the truly lyric note being almost confined to the less sophisticated poets of Scotland.

The spirit which came into literature about the time of the French Revolution broke down this stiff conventionality—and the nineteenth century opens with more elastic metres. Wordsworth, Byron, Shelley and Keats rang changes on the old iambic pentameter, Byron in particular reverting to the more musical, if more intricate Spenserian stanza, Wordsworth browsing around in blank verse or sonnet form, while Shelley wove rhyme patterns of his own, introducing anapaestic and dactyllic measures.

English metre became still more elastic in the hands of the Victorians — Robert and Elizabeth Browning, Swinburne, Dante and Christina Rossetti, William Morris, Matthew Arnold and Tennyson, while a distinctive rhythm was used by George Meredith in his "Love in the Valley," a rhythm which ignores the old tumti-tum measure, and while using a classical metre follows the stress and rests and time intervals of natural speech:

> Under yonder beech-tree single on the greensward,
>   Couched with her arms behind her golden head,
> Knees and tresses folded to slip and ripple idly,
>   Lies my young love sleeping in the shade.
> Had I the heart to slide an arm beneath her,
>   Press her parting lips as her waist I gather slow,
> Waking in amazement she could not but embrace me:
>   Then would she hold me and never let go?

The American poets of that time were more or less mild echoes of their English contemporaries until Walt Whitman sent an electric shock through the world of rhymes with his *Leaves of Grass*. Nowadays, except to Bostonians and others of that kind who take American literature of the nineteenth century seriously, Walt Whitman is too often a verbose old man whose long-winded lines are a useful soporific just before turning out the lights, but in his time he certainly did good by setting poets a-thinking, and like the curate's egg he is excellent in parts. There are indeed some who claim that as a sleep inducer Walt Whitman must yield place to that other darling of the Bostonian, Sir Rabindranath Tagore.

Rhyme was shocked, but it was not killed, and the poetry of the late nineteenth and early twentieth centuries was still predominantly rhymed. Much of that rhyming was of high technical skill, for the English were becoming a more musical nation, more sensitive to the niceties of metrical harmony.

Now if all English verse in rhyme had been written with equal skill, there might have been no movement in favour of *vers libre*. But rhyme in less inspired poets has led to inversions of phrase which disturb the natural sequence of thought, it encourages the use of obsolete phrases used only because they easily rhyme—such as meseems, bedight, forsooth, and the like—it results in artificial expression, it has been responsible for doggerel-writers like Longfellow or the confused involutions of a thousand Sonneteers.

Hence a new school of poets which declares, "Away with rhyme! —Let us express our emotions without this fetter, in natural language of our own time, with rhythm if you please, but not necessarily in lines of regular length. Let us consider the content rather than the form of our poetry."

"There must," says Ezra Pound, "be no book words, no periphrases, no inversions. There must be no clichés, set phrases, stereotypes, journalese—no straddled adjectives (as 'addled mosses dank') —nothing that you couldn't in some circumstances, in the stress of emotion, say. Every literaryism, every book word fritters away a scrap of the reader's patience, a scrap of his sense of your sincerity. When one really feels and thinks, one stammers with simple speech." Elsewhere he gives as his ideals:

1. Direct treatment.

2. Use absolutely no word that does not contribute to the presentation—use no superfluous word, no adjective which does not reveal something. Avoid abstractions.

3. As regards rhythm, compose in the sequence of the musical phrase, not in sequence of a metronome. The rhythm must correspond exactly to the emotion or shade or emotion to be expressed. Your rhythm structure should not destroy the shape of your words or their natural sound or their meaning.

To illustrate what this prophet of free verse means, take the twenty-third Psalm. The metrical version used in the Scots Kirk is rhymed and runs:

> The Lord's my Shepherd: I'll not want.
> He makes me down to lie
> In pastures green; he leadeth me
> The quiet waters by.

The Authorized Version has no inversions, such as "down to lie," "pastures green," "quiet waters by," but follows the natural sequence of thought. Its lines are of irregular length, but who will say it has not just as much claim to be called poetry? At any rate it is "free verse":

> The Lord is my Shepherd: I shall not want
> He maketh me to lie down in green pastures
> He leadeth me beside the still waters.

One modern, who in certain of his verses practises the direct simplicity and unfettered rhythm which Ezra Pound preaches is Carl Sandburg, a Chicago poet whose chief handicap is that he seems to have read nothing earlier than Walt Whitman. As a result he lacks self-criticism, is too often unmusical, and is therefore best read in anthologies. His "Under the Harvest Moon" has admirable felicity of phrase:

[Sandburg's "Under the Harvest Moon" originally quoted here.]

Read the little nine line word-picture "Lost," and you must admit that rhyme and uniform symmetry of syllables are non-essentials:

[Sandburg's "Lost" originally quoted here.]

Carl Sandburg is not always so inspired. He likes to be thought a roughneck, and prints as poems what might better be classed as indifferent prose. Take for instance "Ice Handler":

[Sandburg's "Ice Handler" originally quoted here.]

A little of this kind of thing at first amuses, but very soon it palls. The truth is that the *vers librists* write too much or at least have too much published. You have to wade through acres of camouflaged prose to find the thrill of sincere emotion. Rhyme at its worst was never so verbose as this. Too many of the *vers librists* fancy that a catalogue of names or epithets is impressive, whereas it is merely dull. Walt Whitman who introduced this fashion, suffers the penalty. Walt is more often praised than read.

Vers libre is too often used as a cloak for slipshod, slovenly writing by a host of charlatans, of whom the most impudent are to be found in the 1917 volume of a publication entitled *Others*, e.g., Walter Conrad Arensberg whose "Axiom" I quote:

[Arensberg's "Axiom" originally quoted here.]

These, however, are but the campfollowers of the movement parading as soldiers, and their Falstaffian braggadocio provokes little more than derision. Yet in spite of the eccentrics, the fact remains that verse of a very high order has been written in the last twenty years without the metrical and rhyming conventions of preceding centuries. Within the last ten years just as fine poetry has been written in free verse as in rhyme, and poets are foolish to deny themselves this freedom from metrical fetters.

Rhyme is the natural refuge of the minor poet. Without its aid he is unable to create a phrase which has much chance of being remembered. Without its aid in many cases he could not write anything at all. It is the rhyme which suggests his thoughts. He makes the throstle sing because it rhymes with spring, his sky is blue because it rhymes with dew. Now, if the thought suggested by a rhyme is really a good thought, there is no harm done. It is a good thing for the race when love is born of a child. The chances are then all the greater that there will be more children to follow.

In the case of Keats, whose manuscripts with all their variant readings and corrections have been at the mercy of Buxton Forman, there is no question that the rhyme was often father to the thought. So that the minor poets do rhyme in good company.

The *vers librists* are also in good company.

Shakespeare's plays are dated by the prevalence or paucity of rhyme; the rhyming plays are for other reasons also proved to be the earlier. Sidney Lanier in his *Science of English Verse* points out that Shakespeare in his later plays such as Measure for Measure uses so many run-on lines and phrase groups which insert pauses within the body of the line, that the line group is practically obliterated for the ear. Were it obliterated for the eye also by the typesetter, Shakespeare would admittedly belong to the *vers librists*. Collins in his "Ode to Evening" discards rhyme successfully in a metre which is not blank verse although it retains a symmetry of lines.

Such, however, was the charm of carefully handled rhyme that it could not be killed. It was well suited to the English temperament, which always has preferred melody to orchestration and tunes to tone pictures.

In the hands of certain poets of rich vocabulary rhyme has proved an added charm to fine thought. The most ardent champions of free verse admit the magic of John Keats. Take the "Ode on a Grecian Urn," for instance, the second verse:

> Heard melodies are sweet, but those unheard
> Are sweeter; therefore, ye soft pipes, play
> on;
> Not to the sensual ear, but, more endear'd
> Pipe to the spirit ditties of no tone:
> Fair youth, beneath the trees, thou canst not
> leave
> Thy song, nor ever can those trees be bare;
> Bold Lover, never, never canst thou kiss,
> Though winning near the goal—yet, do not
> grieve;
> She cannot fade, though thou hast not
> thy bliss,
> For ever wilt thou love, and she be fair!

Yet so far from being a necessary quality of poetry, rhyme is at the best a convention. It is possible to write real poetry in rhyme just as it is possible to express real grief while wearing a top hat and frock coat at a funeral, but there are other ways also both of writing poetry and of expressing grief.

Of all the forms of rhyme, familiar to English verse of the last fifty years, the most severely conventional is probably the Sonnet, and particularly the Petrarchan form. This form of Sonnet requires the poet to find four rhyming words twice over within eight lines, a strain on vocabulary which was too much for Shakespeare who appropriated an easier form of Sonnet for his particular use. However, the minor poet of to-day revels in this Petrarchan form. The result has been an appalling output of distorted language and twisted thought. Such a metre is as fatal to natural movement of thought as the average corset is to the female figure. Of course if you are used only to the corsetted figure, you may think the Venus of Milo indecent.

Rhyme is essentially an appeal to the ear, but the ear is not the only avenue of approach to the human intelligence. In the days of the ballad monger, poetry was more spoken than read, but in these days of the printed page, verse is read a hundred times to once when it is said aloud.

Free verse which in practised hands allows a line to a phrase, however short or long that may be, presents the thought in the form which most easily gets home to the reader. The writer of free verse who chops his lines irregularly, without any method or reason except to be eccentric, is merely a poor craftsman who does not understand his tools. But the skilful writer of free verse, to use the phrase of a printer, "makes type work," and "making type work" is just as legitimate an aid to the poet as the repetition of a note in rhyme.

There are, of course, slaves who become so used to their servitude that they would be unhappy as freemen, and so there are rhyming poets who shudder at the thought of free verse. It savours to them of licence. And yet if they only take courage and brave an ignorant ridicule, how much could they accomplish? I think, for instance, of Sara Teasdale, whose *Love Songs* was voted by a committee of the Poetry Society of America the best book of poems published in 1917. Sara Teasdale is the most skilful and dainty of rhymers— rather thin in thought but perfect in technique. Of her *Love Songs* there is only one in free verse, but how much higher it stands than the others in intensity. "But Not to Me" is typical of her rhyme:

[Teasdale's "But Not To Me" originally quoted here.]

Compare with this her unrhymed poem "Summer Night, Riverside":

[Teasdale's "Summer Night, Riverside" originally quoted here.]

Between the formal symmetrical rhymed verse and the irregular free verse there are certain poems with lines of irregular length, but still rhymed, which may be called transition. Notable among these are poems by T. S. Eliot, Ford Madox Hueffer and Conrad Aiken. T. S. Eliot has a curious skill in suggesting atmosphere, the atmosphere particularly of English middle class life—least inspiring of subjects to the ordinary poets—as for instance in the "Portrait of a Lady," the opening of which runs:

[Eliot's "Portrait of a Lady" originally quoted here.]

Conrad Aiken who is technically one of the most expert of the younger American poets, and who is a critic rather than a defender of unrhymed verse, is particularly happy with this transition form in his poem "Disenchantment." The most impressive use of this form is however that by Ford Madox Hueffer, who with unconventional rhythms and unexpected rhymes keeps the mind alert to music of extraordinary charm. Here for instance are the closing lines of that wonderful poem called "Antwerp":

[Hueffer's "Antwerp" originally quoted here.]

In this Chicago anthology of *The New Poetry,* edited by these leaders of the modern poetry, I find only one poem ascribed to a Canadian, and that Canadian does not appear in the Valhalla erected by Mr. John Garvin in his encyclopaedic volume of Canadian poets. Bliss Carman is dismissed by the Chicago editors as belonging to the nineteenth century—the one ewe Canadian lamb who apparently counts in the twentieth century being a lady of the name of Constance Lindsay Skinner. Born in British Columbia, this lady was brought up among a tribe of Indians and the poems cited are her interpretation into English of the Indian spirit and romance. They are "free verse," and to me are fine verse—even though they do not rhyme like Mr. Garvin's galaxy of the stars. Here is one called "The Song of the Search:

[Lindsay's "The Song of the Search" originally quoted here.]

Bliss Carman is discarded by these Chicago anthologists probably because of his recent verse, which certainly seems to have lost the original fire. Yet his unrhymed verses in the cycle entitled *Sapho* [*sic*] belong to this century, and are better than many of those printed. Take for instance these two:

[Two poems from Carman's *Sapho* cycle originally quoted here.]

These two poems are frankly inspired by Greek spirit and follow Greek rhythms. Yet they are simple and direct, and belong to today just as much as to two thousand years ago. Had the later Bliss Carman developed on such simple forms of expression, Canadian poetry might well have been the richer.

Although the output of poetry by Canadians is considerable, so far it has been only minor poetry—in certain cases of admitted charm and in many cases of technical excellence. There is, however, no strong vigorous voice of individual note whose message arrests attention from the whole English-speaking world. There is nothing in Canadian poetry on as impressive a scale as Canadian landscape or commensurate with Canada's vast forests, great rivers and tremendous distances.

I wonder whether this is not due in part at least to the shackles of rhyme, to the metrical conventions which Canadian poets have almost without exception blindly accepted. How can the spirit of a half-tamed new continent be expressed in a courtly seventeenth-century jingle?

In the case of one of the finest of the young Canadian singers, I find that these shackles chafe—Arthur Stringer, who in spite of a recent lapse into purely commercial movie melodrama has given evidence of great literary ability and is a lyrical poet of no mean order. I remember how six years ago I was thrilled by a few lines of verse ascribed to him by a Canadian paper. They were headed "One Night in the North West," and ran:

[Stringer's "One Night in the North West" originally quoted here.]

You will find that verse in his volume of poems entitled *Open Water*. Now listen to what Arthur Stringer says in his preface to that book:—

Modern poetry is remote and insincere, not because the modern spirit is incapable of feeling, but because what the singer of today has felt has not been directly and openly expressed. His apparel has remained mediaeval. He must still don mail to face Mausers, and wear chain-armour against machine-guns. The one-time primitive directness of English was overrun by such forms as the ballade, the chant royal, the rondel, the kyrielle, the rondeau and the rondeau redouble, the virelai and the pantoum, the sestina, the villanelle, and last, yet by no means least, the sonnet.

The twentieth century poet, singing with his scrupulously polished vocalisation, usually finds himself content to re-echo what has been said before. He is unable to "travel light"; pioneering with so heavy a burden is out of the question. Rhyme and metre have compelled him to sacrifice content for form. It has left him incapable of what may be called abandonment.

Unable to express himself adequately in the conventional tradition of end-rhymes, Arthur Stringer therefore takes to free verse. In this mode he is not always successful—it is not so easy as it looks—a certain monotony due, I think, to too great regularity of line lengths, weakens the effect of some of his experiments. But on the whole he gives an impression of intense and sincere emotion which comes refreshingly after so much conventional rhyming. Here are two typical verses:

[Stringer's "The Nocturne" and "Autumn" originally quoted here.]

Duncan Campbell Scott is another established Canadian poet who has experimented with free verse, though not so extensively or with such success as Arthur Stringer. . . .

[Scott's "New Year's Eve, 1916" originally quoted here.]

You will find the poem in the volume called *Lundy's Lane*—and such as it is, it seems to me the best in the book.

A few months ago Isabel Ecclestone MacKay sent me a book of her verses called *Between the Lights* on the flyleaf of which she wrote, "I think that 'Indian Summer' is almost the only one that's any good." Now is it a coincidence that "Indian Summer" is the only poem in that book in which the rhyme is almost negligible?

[MacKay's "Indian Summer" originally quoted here.]

In the last few months Mrs. MacKay has come under the spell of free verse, and although she has not yet discarded rhyme, she finds an ease of expression in this newer mode which comes as a relief after the old hunt for rhymes. Arthur L. Phelps is another Canadian poet who is very nearly a convert. The most perfect thing in Marjorie L. C. Pickthall's *The Lamp of Poor Souls* is her free verse "Improvisation on a Flute."

Put yourself in the place of the writer whose soul is burning with a great message. What would the Songs of David or the Song of Solomon have been if they had had to conform to the rules of the rhyming dictionary? Job had many grievances, but the Lord never asked him to reply only in sonnet form. It is a great thing for English literature that this "chain mail," as Arthur Stringer calls it, is being laid aside—an admirable costume for a fancy dress ball but no longer suited for this freer world. It would be a great thing for Canadian literature if it kept pace with the times instead of lingering in the drawing rooms of the early Victorians. The times are moving. Dynasties are falling, are being swept away. The whole world is aflame with a war against the over-bearing tyranny of military caste. The voice today is the voice of the people, not the voice of a special caste. So too with poetry, where metrical rhyming forms are only the shibboleth of imaginary rank, of imaginary finish and style, of imaginary caste. They are a fashion which for seven hundred years has dominated certain languages of Europe, a fashion, however, which shows every sign of passing away, and being relegated like the harpsichord and the crinoline into the domain of the museum and of history.

J. M. Gibbon, "Rhymes With and Without Reason," *Canadian Bookman*, January 1919.

FRANK OLIVER CALL

Poetry has been defined as "Thought touched by Emotion," and I know no better working definition, although no doubt more scientific and accurate ones could be found. The best poets of all ages seem to have had this ideal plainly before them, whether consciously or unconsciously, and I cannot see how modern poets can dispense with either thought or emotion if they are to write real poetry. For one is not enough without the other. Take for example the first lines of Masters' *Spoon River Anthology*.

[Masters' "Where are Elmer, Herman, Bert . . ." originally quoted here.]

This sounds tragic indeed, but seems to have aroused no emotion on the part of the poet and excites none in his readers. In fact, through the whole poem, emotion is held in check with a strong hand, and only allowed to show itself in some distorted cynicism.

Let us take an example of the opposite extreme where emotion, whether real or fancied, has stifled thought.

O World! O Men! O Sun! to you I cry,
I raise my song defiant, proud, victorious,
And send this clarion ringing down the sky:
"I love, I love, I love, and love is glorious!"

The definition chosen need not hamper the most "modern" poet nor restrict his choice of subject, for there are few things that cannot awaken both thought and emotion if looked at in the right way. An iron foundry and a Venetian palace have immense possibilities of arousing both elements, and perhaps the foundry has the greater power.

The modern poet has joined the great army of seekers after freedom, that is, he refuses to observe the old conventions in regard to his subjects and his method of treating them. He refuses to be bound by the old restrictions of rhyme and metre, and goes far afield in search of material on which to work. The boldest of the new school would throw overboard all the old forms and write only in free verse, rhythmic prose or whatever he may wish to call it. The conservative, on the other hand, clings stubbornly to the old conventions, and will have nothing to do with vers libre or anything that savours of it.

But vers libre, like the motor-car and aeroplane, has come to stay whether we like it or no. It is not really a new thing, although put to a new use, for some of the greatest poetry of the Hebrews and other Oriental nations was written in a form of free verse. At the present time the number of those using it as a medium of expression is steadily increasing. In France, Italy, the United States, and even in conservative England, the increase in the number of poems recently published in this form has been remarkable. The modernists hail this tendency as the dawn of a new era of freedom, while the conservatives see poetry falling into decadence and ruin. The right view of the case probably lies, as it generally does, between the extremes. There is much beauty to be found in walking in beaten paths or rambling in fenced-in fields and woods, but perhaps one who sails the skies in an aeroplane may see visions and feel emotions that never come to those who wander on foot along the old paths of the woods and fields below.

But it seems to me that it matters little in what form a poem is cast so long as the form suits the subject, and does not hinder the freedom of the poet's thought and emotion. And I am old-fashioned enough to expect that beauty will be revealed as well. Out of this union of thought, emotion and beauty, we could scarcely fail to get strength also, which term many modern poets use to cover an ugliness that is often nothing but disguised weakness. But form alone will not make even a semblance of poetry as the following lines, unimpeachable in form, from Sir Walter Scott plainly show:

> Then filled with pity and remorse,
> He sorrowed o'er the expiring horse.

Nor can I conceive of more beautiful poetry than the following, by Richard Aldington, although rhyme and regular metre are absent:

> [Aldington's "And we turn from the music of old . . ."
> originally quoted here.]

And this brings me to the real purpose of this Foreword—the explanation of the title of this book. On the hills and plains of Southern Europe there grows a plant with beautiful indented leaves— the Acanthus. The Greek artist saw the beauty of these leaves, and, having arranged and conventionalized them, carved them upon the capitals of the columns which supported the roofs and pediments of his temples and public buildings. Since that time, wherever pillars are used in architecture, one does not have far to look to find acanthus leaves carved upon them. In the Roman Forum, in Byzantine churches like Saint Sophia or Saint Mark's, in the Mediaeval Cathedrals of France, England and Spain, in the Renaissance buildings scattered throughout the world, and even in the most modern office-buildings of our great cities, this decoration of acanthus is to be found. And the reason is not far to seek.

> A thing of beauty . . . will never
> Pass into nothingness.

I recently saw a picture of a Corinthian column of a ruined Greek temple standing against the sky, and broken fragments of its fellows lying at its foot, with wild vines climbing over them. And who could say that one was more beautiful than the other? The carved acanthus leaves upon the column were beautiful because of their symmetry, harmony of light and shade and clear-cut outline, but the wild grape was perhaps more beautiful still in its natural freedom.

So in this little book will be found some poems in the old conventional forms and some others in free rhythms, in which the author has tried in a humble way, to mingle elements of thought, emotion and beauty.

F. O. Call, Preface to *Acanthus and Wild Grape* (Toronto: McClelland & Stewart, 1920).

The Initiators (1925-1936)

A more fully-developed and coherent program of renovation in poetry, along modernist lines, appeared in Canada in the late 1920s and early thirties. The chief spokesman for this new literary orientation was A. J. M. Smith, and the chief satirist in the Eliotic vein was F. R. Scott. A. M. Klein followed soon after, writing poetry in an exuberant satiric style that had similar relations to T. S. Eliot and the modern tradition.

It all began in 1925 in the environs of McGill University in Montreal. From October eighth, 1924 to March eleventh, 1925, Smith edited a special "Literary Supplement" of the college newspaper *The McGill Daily. The McGill Daily Literary Supplement* was published on Wednesdays as an independent tabloid of four pages. On November twenty-first, 1925 a periodical was launched which was called *The McGill Fortnightly Review,* and which continued until April twenty-seventh, 1927. These were college publications in most respects very much in the *genre* of student publications on other campuses. McGill had had the *University Gazette,* the *McGill Outlook* (originally also named *McGill Fortnightly,* 1892-1898), *The Martlet, The Scratch, The Critic,* a sequence of student magazines. *The McGill Fortnightly Review* followed these closely in tradition and format, offering campus information, sports news, and items of literary edification. Its distinction, however, lay in the originality and authority of one of its editors, A. J. M. Smith, and in the vitality and promise of one of its editor-contributors, F. R. Scott.

Smith, a graduate student at the University (M.A. '26), possessed those rare gifts which make successful editors and initiators of literary movements—a precocious knowledge of the literary situation, and an uncanny intuition of the most pressing needs. His first two articles reproduced here, one written at the age of twenty-four, the other two years later, show him as a critic of unusual maturity, providing a masterful diagnostic of Canadian literary conditions.*

In earlier issues of *The McGill Fortnightly Review* Smith had announced the importance of symbolism and mythology for the new poetry, and in November 1926 he had written an analysis of T. S. Eliot's "The Waste Land" that stands up well today as a critical interpretation of this difficult poem. His article on "Contemporary

---

*Smith was also making his mark as a poet: his earliest publication includes three poems in *The Measure* (1925-26); poems in *The Dial* (1925-29) notably "The Two Sides of a Drum" (December 1926) and "The Lonely Land" (June 1929); and "Shadows There Are" in *The Nation* (June 1927).

Poetry," which appears here, senses a spirit of change; it looks to new approaches in technique and new subject matter; it predicts a deeper probing of the subconscious sources of poetry, and favours formal aesthetic intensification in the use of "every-day speech." The article on Canadian criticism (1928) prophetically calls for a work in Canada which will be "successful and obscene"; it prescribes "realism," "irony . . . and cynicism," and "aesthetic harmony" as the coming requirements for poetry. The search for the "militant critic" as well as "the critic contemplative" describes the new arbiters of taste and the task before them. These two articles, long buried in the Canadian periodical archives, define better than any later history the programme of the new literature.

"Wanted—Canadian Criticism" was one of the high points in what proved to be a growing sense of dissatisfaction with the state of criticism as applied to Canadian writing. In the 1920s, before modern poetry was properly established in Canada, and before there was any critical understanding on the part of the public as to what modern poetry should be like, a demand was raised for a set of firm critical standards for Canadian literature. The general public was accused of shoddy taste, and of a sentimental and patriotic preference for the second-rate, while reviewers and critics alike, were condemned for their weak partiality for the same kind of cultural pabulum. *The Canadian Bookman* (1919-1939) was especially open to criticism for such literary "boosterism" chiefly because of the magazine's close connections with The Canadian Authors' Association.

It was, however, in the pages of *The Canadian Forum,* that the issue was brought out into the open, and the old guard of Canadian criticism found itself under attack. Douglas Bush was one of the early skirmishers in what proved to be a long and drawn-out action in which even the reputations of the likes of Carman and Lampman came under fire. In an article entitled "Making Literature Hum" in the December 1926 issue of *The Canadian Forum* Bush was painfully trenchant:

This happy conviction [that Canada is taking its permanent seat in the literary league of nations] is not at all disturbed by the fact that most of the few Canadian books which find their way to American or English reviewers are at best dismissed as negligible; a very few receive tempered praise—as good for Canada. This attitude of competent foreign judges (if not mere jealousy) might, one would think, lead to some sort of self-examination, some wonder if we are so good as we say we are. But self-reverence survives self-knowledge, and the only result of occasional deflations is that certain domestic critics become unpopular.

The trouble is that, born to hew wood and draw water, we are trying desperately to be literary, to have a real renaissance. In the literary way Canada is probably the most backward country, for its population, in the civilized world, and the quickest way to get rid of this unpleasant family skeleton is to abolish critical standards and be a booster. We don't know what to write, but by jingo if we do we have the pen, we have the ink, we have the paper too. And so we have bulky histories of Canadian literature appraising the product of every citizen who ever held a pen; bulky anthologies preserving almost everything metrical that has sprung from a Canadian brain; little books celebrating the genius of people who in another country would not get beyond the poetry corner of the local newspaper; reprints of Canadian "classics" which not even antiquity can render tolerable; respectful consideration of inferior Zane Greys as literature—in short, an earnest and sincere desire to establish a completely parochial scale of values.

This attitude may serve to win repute at home, for a time, but it is not likely to carry conviction abroad. Its vicious results have been sufficiently evident for years; in the dearth of Canadian anthologies one might make a very pretty collection (it would need to be in two or three volumes) of the more fantastic critical comments of the last decade—the most patriotic soul would be surprised at the number of Shakespeares in our midst. Our standards of judgment not only lead us to worship the small but to neglect the big.*

The other three articles in this section, that by Leo Kennedy and the two prefaces, enlarge the perspective for this period. The 1936 Preface to *New Provinces,* actually written by F. R. Scott, appeared without a signature. It was modest and overly reticent, yet it defined the modern direction of six Canadian poets—Pratt, Scott, Smith, Finch, Klein and Kennedy—succinctly and clearly. Of these poets, only Kennedy and Pratt managed to publish books during the Depression decade of the Thirties. *New Provinces* was therefore both a manifesto and the first book-publication for the others, the chief modernists in Canada.

The original preface to *New Provinces* by A. J. M. Smith did not appear in 1936. It was vetoed by E. J. Pratt who "objected to its contents," and it only came to light recently as a result of conversations with A. J. M. Smith (one of the editors of the present book, M. Gnarowski suggested the re-examination of the "vetoed preface") appearing for the first time in the Spring 1965 issue of *Canadian Literature*.

Leo Kennedy's article from *The Canadian Mercury,* another magazine in which Scott and Smith were the moving spirits, further clarifies the new directions of poetry: the rejection of Victorianism, the

*Douglas Bush, "Making Literature Hum," *The Canadian Forum*, December 1926, pp. 72-73.

direct assault on Canadian parochialism, the search for a large, all-embracing modern vision in poetry. A good example of the militant critic in action, it is an incisive statement of the radical modernist position as it appears newly-adapted and translated to the Canadian scene.

A. J. M. SMITH

Our age is an age of change, and of a change that is taking place with a rapidity unknown in any other epoch. Science has altered not only the character of our everyday life, but has had its influence on the philosophies by which we interpret that life. If the Victorian Age was one of solid, gradual progress from precedent to precedent, with a growing confidence in the applications of science and in the stabilizing effect of business, our own age has known the disaster which is bound to occur when a respectable philosophy makes terms with an acquisitive society. In our case, however, the problem has been vastly complicated by the sudden acceleration of the change which had hitherto only been gradually making itself felt. In less than three decades came the motor car, the steam turbine, the aeroplane, the telegraph and wireless, and the electric light. The result was that the standard of living was very quickly raised, business corporations were formed to exploit the new discoveries, and the whole world contracted almost visibly under the tightening bands of closer communications. Things moved faster, and we had to move with them.

It is not, however, only in the realm of everyday life and commonplace death that progress has been suddenly accelerated. Our way of living has changed; so too have our religious and philosophical ideas. Science, again, has been the catalyst. The discovery that the atom is not a single, solid whole, but a miniature solar system in itself; the principle of relativity which affirms the curvature of space and the limitations of the universe; the anthropological discoveries systematized by Sir James Frazer in *The Golden Bough,* which traces Christian creed and ritual back through folk lore to the pagan rites of the older civilizations and finally to those of savagery: all these have had their influence upon contemporary thought. Our universe is a different one from that of our grandfathers, nor can our religious beliefs be the same. The whole movement, indeed, is a movement away from an erroneous but comfortable stability, towards a more truthful and sincere but certainly less comfortable state of flux. Ideas are changing, and therefore manners and morals are changing. It is not surprising, then, to find that the arts, which are an intensification of life and thought, are likewise in a state of flux. Those who attended the concert given by the Boston Symphony Orchestra a few weeks ago will have noticed the influence of our changing age upon music, while Post-Impressionism, Cubism, Vorticism and half a dozen other isms indicate its effect upon painting. Contemporary poetry reflects it as clearly as any other art.

Poetry today must be the result of the impingement of modern conditions upon the personality and temperament of the poet. Some have been awakened to a burning enthusiasm by the spectacle of a new era; others are deeply disturbed by the civilization of a machine-made age. Some have heard music in the factory whistle; others have turned aside into solitude that they might the better hearken to the still small voice.

But however much contemporary poets may differ in their estimate of the value of our civilization, the peculiar conditions of the time have forced them all to seek a new and more direct expression, to perfect a finer technique. In a preface to James Stephens' *Collected Poems* published just the other day, occurs the following excellent summary of the situation: "The world interest today differs notably from that which gave it enthusiasm in the past, for, within the last thirty years, the tempo of the whole world has been enormously accelerated. It is still accelerating, and the technique that we inherited, in whatever art, from a leisured society is not equal to the demands that are now made upon it, and which demands are still incoherent if not unconscious. We must evolve a new technique, or we must continue to compose and paint and write in the only form that can deal with an interim situation, or with speed—the lyrical form. We are at the beginning of an era, and who creates a new world must create a new art to express it."

Here we have an explanation of why there is being written what has been called, and what may very conveniently be called, the New Poetry. It remains to ask, What is the new poetry and wherein does it differ from the old? The difference is not solely one of form, for though some contemporary poetry is written in *vers libre,* by far the greater amount infused with the new spirit is written in the traditional metres and with the traditional rhyme schemes. It is not solely one of diction, though this, indeed, is an extremely important question: the *deems, forsooths, methinks,* the inversions for the sake of a rhyme, the high sounding pomposities and all the rhetorical excesses which make so much Victorian poetry seem overdressed and slightly vulgar

—all these have been ruthlessly removed from the diction of contemporary poetry. The result was that the new work spoke to people in their own language, and the difference between the new poetry and that to which it is a reaction, though most obvious as a change in form, is something at once deeper and more fundamental. As Miss Harriet Monroe has put it, "The new poetry strives for a concrete and immediate realization of life; it would discard the theory, the abstraction, the remoteness found in all classics not of the first order. It is less vague, less verbose, less eloquent than most poetry of the Victorian period and much work of earlier periods. It has set before itself an ideal of absolute simplicity and sincerity—an ideal which implies an individual, unstereotyped rhythm."

Now this contemporary poetry is divided by the war into two clearly marked epochs. In the earlier it was the work of the poets to overthrow an effete and decadent diction, and to bring the subject matter of poetry out of the library and the afternoon-tea salon into the open air, dealing in the language of present-day speech with subjects of living interest. This is the task that W. B. Yeats, John Masefield, Robert Frost, E. A. Robinson and Carl Sandburg have performed, each in his own manner, so successfully. But besides this there has been a turning back to the seventeenth century, a renewed interest in the poems of John Donne, an attempt to recapture and exploit in a new way the poetics of the Metaphysical poets. Rupert Brooke was one of the pioneers in this movement. Such a poem as "Dining Room Tea" describes a trance-like state of super consciousness that is akin to the Platonic ecstasy described by Donne in his poem, "The Ecstasy." From Donne to Brooke, and from Brooke to Eliot: it is a long stretch, but the curve is continuous. An advantage which the very latest poets of this school have had over their predecessors in that they have been able to make use of the various psychological theories of the subconscious, and to forge from them what is almost a new form of expression—a form which has found so far its culmination in the prose of James Joyce and poetry of T. S. Eliot. Poets, such as Eliot, the Sitwells, Wallace Stevens, E. E. Cummings, whose widely divergent characteristics may be all included in the term ultra-modern, have been hurled into poetry under the compulsion of a bitter and poignant disillusionment, and they have,—most of them—turned aside from the world, concerned themselves with abstruse questions of technique, probing with the best instruments they can forge the wounds in their own subconsciousness. It is perhaps dangerous to group the poets I have just named together in this way. Certainly, however, they are all poets of disillusion. Eliot and Cummings have delved deeply into the subconscious; while Edith Sitwell and Wallace Stevens have constructed their own artificial, beautiful and cubist world; and they have all emphasised the importance of form.

This preoccupation with form has led some critics to see in the works of the ultra moderns the symptoms of a deep decadence. The dislike exhibited by these poets, they say, for didacticism, for the moral aim has led them to take the safe course, and to keep not only morality but meaning out of their poems. If you read some of Eliot's Sweeney poems, or Edith Sitwell's *Bucolic Comedies* you may at first think that there is a good deal in the charge. If, however, you have had any experience as a reader of poetry, and you come to the test with an open mind, I think you will find it easier to admit that there is beauty in such poetry than to discover in it a logical meaning. More than once someone has spoken to me of a poem. "I don't understand altogether what it means—but I like it; it sounds well; there is beauty in it." Perhaps they were only being polite. But if that is the case, the fact that such a remark is considered to be a compliment rather than an insult shows that even in the popular mind Beauty, (that is, form), is considered to be more important than the idea or the logical meaning, (that is, than subject matter). In other words, though most people loudly disclaim it, in their hearts they really think that what you say is less important than how you say it. A fallacy, of course, but if they did not think thus when wishing to be complimentary they would say: "I don't think there is any *beauty* in your poem, but I understand and admire its *sentiments* very much." This, however, would be considered an affront.

Now this popular idea that form is more important than content, of course, is just as absurd as the professorial conception of the supreme importance of right-thinking and the comparative insignificance of right-expression; and, as a matter of fact the discussion of the relative value of form and subject matter is one, that should never have arisen; because, in poetry, at least, these two things should be merged into one—a single and complete artistic whole—form the body, and content the soul: the one but the visible manifestation of the other.

But what, then, are we to say when the beauty of a poem appeals to us, while its meaning is somehow hidden? Simply that our faculty of aesthetic appreciation is more fully developed than our understanding—that we are become, God help us!—by natural right, a member of that despised sect—the Aesthetes.

A. J. M. Smith, "Contemporary Poetry," *The McGill Fortnightly Review*, December 15, 1926.

A. J. M. SMITH

One looks in vain through Canadian books and journals for that critical enquiry into first principles which directs a new literature as tradition guides an old one. Hasty adulation mingles with unintelligent condemnation to make our book reviewing an amusing art: but of criticism as it might be useful there is nothing. That this should be so at a time when we are becoming increasingly "Canada-conscious" may seem strange, but the strangeness disappears when we examine the nature of the consciousness in question. This, judging from its most characteristic forms of expression, is a mixture of blind optimism and materialistic patriotism, a kind of my-mother-drunk-or-sober complex that operates most efficiently in the world of affairs and finds its ideal action summarized in the slogan "Buy Made in Canada Goods." There is, perhaps, something to be said for this state of mind if cultivated within certain very definite limits, if it be regarded solely as a business proposition and with due regard for economic laws; but when duty and morality are brought in and the above mercantile maxim is held to apply to things of the mind and spirit: that is an altogether different matter.

The confusion is one between commerce and art, an error which a society such as ours has some difficulty in escaping. A small population engaged in subduing its environment and in exploiting the resources of a large new country may very easily develop an exaggerated opinion of the value of material things, and has some quite understandable doubts as to the necessity of artists. Indeed, most of our people are so actively engaged in tilling the soil or scrambling to the top of the tree in the industrial and commercial world that they have neither the time nor the inclination for reading poetry on the back porch—unless it be inspiration stuff or He-man Canadiana. The result is good for business but bad for poetry and, if you happen to think that poetry is the more important, you are tempted to ask what is to be done about it.

To the serious Canadian writer this is a vital question, for to him the confusion between commerce and art presents itself in the light of a temptation to effect a compromise. If he chooses to work out his own salvation along lines which cannot be in keeping with the prevailing spirit of pep and optimism he finds himself without an audience, or at least without an audience that will support him. The one Canadian magazine, it must be noted, for which such an artist would care to write is at present unable to pay contributors, while poor imitations of the *Saturday Evening Post* are ready to pay him handsomely if he will cease to be an artist and become a merchant.

This is the temptation with which the devil has assailed the Canadian Authors' Association, and the whole communion has succumbed in a body. There would be little harm in this if everyone knew the nature of the compromise that has been made, if, for instance, the Canadian Authors had the honesty to change the name of their society to the Journalists' Branch of the Canadian Manufacturers' Association and to quit kidding the public every Christmas that it (the public) has a moral obligation to buy poor Canadian, rather than good foreign books.

So far, it is true, literature as an art has fought a losing battle with commerce, but the campaign as a whole has barely begun. Reinforcements are on the way. Young writers like Morley Callaghan and Raymond Knister have contributed realistic stories of Canadian life to foreign radical journals. Mazo de la Roche, having won an important literary prize in the United States, has a firmly established reputation in her native land. E. J. Pratt and Edward Sapir are demonstrating that Canadian themes are improved by modern treatment. All these examples are definite, if modest, successes, but reverses are encountered too. A good poet such as Wilson Macdonald is praised for the wrong things, and seems likely to succumb to the blandishments of an unfortunate popularity, the sort of popularity that appears to be at the command of any poet who hammers a vigorous rhythm out of an abundant assortment of French and Indian place-names. If you write, apparently, of the far north and the wild west and the picturesque east, seasoning well with allusions to the Canada goose, fir trees, maple leaves, snowshoes, northern lights, etc., the public grasp the fact that you are a Canadian poet, whose works are to be bought from the same patriotic motive that prompts the purchaser of Eddy's matches or a Massey-Harris farm implement, and read along with Ralph Connor and Eaton's catalogue.

The picture, on the whole, is one of extreme confusion. There are little skirmishes, heroic single stands: but no concerted action. Without a body of critical opinion to hearten and direct them Canadian writers are like a leaderless army. They find themselves in an atmosphere of materialism that is only too ready to seduce them from their allegiance to art, and with an audience that only wishes to be flattered. It looks as though they will have to give up the attempt to create until they have formulated a critical system and secured its universal acceptance.

What are the tasks that await such a criticism?

First and foremost, as a sort of preliminary spade-work, the Canadian writer must put up a fight for freedom in the choice and treatment of his subject. Nowhere is puritanism more disastrously prohibitive than among us, and it seems, indeed, that desperate methods and dangerous remedies must be resorted to, that our condition will not improve until we have been thoroughly shocked by the appearance in our midst of a work of art that is at once successful and obscene. Of realism we are afraid—apparently because there is an impression that it wishes to discredit the picture of our great Dominion as a country where all the women are chaste and the men too pure to touch them if they weren't. Irony is not understood. Cynicism is felt to be disrespectful, unmanly. The idea that any subject whatever is susceptible of artistic treatment, and that praise or blame is to be conferred after a consideration, not of its moral, but of its aesthetic harmony is a proposition that will take years to knock into the heads of our people. But the work must be done. The critic-militant is required for this; not a very engaging fellow, perhaps, but a hard worker, a crusader, and useful withal.

It is the critic contemplative, however, the philosophical critic, who will have the really interesting work. It will be the object of such an enquirer to examine the fundamental position of the artist in a new community. He will have to answer questions that in older countries have obvious answers, or do not arise. He will follow the lead of French and English critics in seeking to define the relation of criticism and poetry to the psychological and mathematical sciences, and will be expected to have something of value to say as to the influence upon the Canadian writer of his position in space and time. That this influence, which might even become mutual, be positive and definite seems desirable and obvious: that it should not be self-conscious seems to me desirable; but not to many people obvious. Canadian poetry, to take a typical example, is altogether too self-conscious of its environment, of its position in space, and scarcely conscious at all of its position in time. This is an evident defect, but it has been the occasion of almost no critical comment. Yet to be aware of our temporal setting as well as of our environment, and in no obvious and shallow way, is the nearest we can come to being traditional. To be unconscious or overconscious—that is to be merely conventional, and it is in one of these two ways that our literature today fails as an adequate and artistic expression of our national life. The heart is willing, but the head is weak. Modernity and tradition alike demand that the contemporary artist who survives adolescence shall be an intellectual. Sensibility is no longer enough, intelligence is also required. Even in Canada.

A. J. M. Smith, "Wanted: Canadian Criticism," *Canadian Forum*, April 1928.

LEO KENNEDY

Creative minds in Canada are rapidly bringing the literary powers of this country to the attention of the world: John Mebourne Elson, "The Canadian Literary Scene."

Nothing is more conducive to diatribe than poppycock of the above order. Mr. John Mebourne Elson, writing in the *Canadian Bookman* of last January . . . rather fails to endorse his statement, and that, in view of the patent mediocrity of most of the Authors catalogued in his article, is in no way extraordinary. The world at large is *not* being made aware of the literary powers of this country, because there are *no* literary powers; with rare exceptions the best prose and poetry hitherto produced in Canada compares unfavourably even with the eyewash poured annually from third-rate British and United States presses. Practically all Canadian writing in English is negligible as literature, and this fact is one against which the shrill vociferations of every Canadian Author registered will not avail. The Canadian literary scene of 1929 is dominated by the Frank L. Packards, the Howard Angus Kennedys, the Ralph Connors; the Robertses and the Campbells. In a word, by the Canadian Authors' Association. And the linotyped opera of these gentlemen, so far from being enduring literature, are fit for immediate consumption only, and that by persons of their own casual aesthetic taste, and restricted outlook.

What is the cause of this, and what, precisely, may be done about it?

In the first place the least attractive aspects of Victorianism still hold licensed Canadian creative writers firmly by the gullet. In poetry the Tennysonian and Wordsworthian traditions still rule, and are bolstered by none of the genius and technical ability of those poets; and Canadian novelists when not writing detective stories are catering with might and main to the namby pamby. The highly respectable protestantism of a past era, coupled with a firm belief in Empire and the indelicacy of sex psychology and human anatomy; a credo based on the apothegms that all is not gold that glitters, a still tongue makes a wise head, and an Englishman's home is his castle; a pronounced Anglo-Saxon self-approval, a distrust of Latin influence (the naughty Frenchmen!) and new ideas . . . the prevalence of these evils may be partly responsible. In our gum-shoeing among the possible causes of the great Canadian calamity—the dearth of inspired and intelligent authorship—we are brought again and again, by one path or another, to the Canadian Authors' Association. They have foisted themselves on the local public, creating a market at home for their product, and from their Philistine entrenchment direct their Canadian Book Weeks—one with Fish Week, Music Week, and Mother's Day—their Afternoon Teas, their Inspired Committees formed for the reception of lecturing English and United States literati, and similar happy diversions. All to their profit and self-gratification, no doubt, but scarcely likely to benefit our purely hypothetical literature.

Such an organization as this is legitimate and permissible up to a certain point. It is good for tradesmen and manufacturers to bind themselves together, for the purpose of disposing of their goods at an even price. But when a number of writing persons consolidate, and advertise their ill-constructed detective stories, their adventure thrillers and prosy encomiums on the western farmer as literature, and Canadian literature at that, some action must be taken.

That action is ridicule.

The Canadian Authors' Association, that pillar of flim-flam, is a stumbling block over which the aspiring younger Canadian writer must first climb before approaching his local Parnassus. Occasionally the country does produce an original youngster, but due to the existing reprehensible conditions, the country does not keep him long. Moving self-consciously among fatheads, his nationalism is severely chastened, and he invariably loses it. He is afraid of being called a Canadian Author, and invariably becomes an American novelist. No one can blame him.

With these points in mind it is difficult to consider Canada's literary future unaskance. It is apparent that Canadian literature—and by that I mean books from Canada which will be definitely recognised by Europe and the United States—will not readily be written by Canadian Authors. I have already alluded to the younger writers, and now shift my focus to them, since it is to these restless, dissatisfied and on the whole sceptical young people, that we must necessarily look.

The Duke of York Hotel, within easy walking distance of a certain university, is primarily an undergraduate pot-house, a refuge for the ragged and the raccoon-coated. It is in the pleasant atmosphere of such taverns that the doctors and lawyers, architects and engineers of tomorrow forgather, drinking cold beer, talking about their mistresses and their work. Frequently there is a gathering of the elect, the poets and prosodists whose badgering of the eminently respectables was regarded with mild disapproval and the invariable shrug, but due to the agreeable dearth of such men at well-regulated Canadian universities, these groups are few. Each year, however, a small number of such originals contrive to band together, and filling a corner, they talk of Joyce and Hemingway, Arthur Machen, Shaw, Pound, and Aldous Huxley.

It is significant that they do not talk of Lampman, Campbell, Robert W. Service or Charles G. D. Roberts. It is noteworthy that they do not mention the innumerable haphazard imitators of these Canadian Authors. And it is vitally important to ask why.

In a recent paper on Canadian Poetry, Mr. S. I. Hayakawa declared: "The bulk of poems written in Canada may be briefly classified under four heads. They are, Victorian, Neo-Victorian, Quasi-Victorian, and Pseudo-Victorian. We find the Indian of Canadian poetry represented as one of Nature's Noblemen; the French Canadian virtues are metamorphosed by English hands into qualities characteristically Wordsworthian. Our poets carol (regrettably) in Victorian English."

Well, Victoria was tucked away long ago. There was nothing particularly wrong with Victorian English, beyond that it took literary giants to write in it enduringly, but even the English have put it by for good. The Victorian tradition was transplanted here in the flower of its youth, and has by now outgrown its usefulness. This is a reality of which the majority of Canadian Authors of any merit are tragically unaware.

Having as yet no worthwhile tradition of their own, the young men are inclined, and wisely, to look abroad for that which will influence them. After a three- or four-year apprenticeship to the English classics, they are concerned usually with the work of moderns ... of men who unchronologically are little older than themselves, and whose writing reveals their own wounds and echoes the cry which they have not yet managed to utter. James Branch Cabell and Sherwood Anderson, Hergesheimer, Lawrence and Willa Cather influence their style; Wyndham Lewis, T. S. Eliot, Arthur Schnitzler and Barbusse affect their philosophy. They will discourse creditably on the work of Mann, Werfel, Gide and Valéry; they have read Verhaeren and Duhamel; while unfortunately their knowledge of the better English contemporaries tends to be slight, and casually gleaned in tabloid-form book reviews. *The Monthly Criterion, The Dial, The Forum,* and odd copies of *transition* are their immediate text books, and they occasionally appear (with much fluttering in the dove cotes) in some one or another of these and similar journals.

They are distrustful of the dignified cultural stupidities of their elders, and of the injustice and polite barbarism synonymous with state and industrial administration; they have investigated social and economic theories as well as theories of aesthetics. Their acceptance of orthodoxy and the conventional formula for decorous living is

seriously weakened by a smattered acquaintance with behaviourism, some persistent aspects of biology, and the not-wholly-to-be-depreciated outcome of their own observations. Having neither fears nor taboos, and recognising no cause for such, they are inclined to be distressingly frank; their preoccupations are idealistic, and a grave menace to humbug.

Concerned then with writing something which is true and enduring, desiring to declare what is fine and not necessarily best-selling, they will commence, and come in time to express themselves with gratifying clarity. They will approach the task of expression fortified by new ideas and original conceptions; they will learn the lesson of all precursors, discovering in a western grain field, a Quebec *maison,* or in a Montreal nightclub, a spirit and a consciousness distinctly Canadian. Just as the writers of the United States today are inclined to segregate, with Frost expressing New Hampshire and Sandburg exploiting Chicago, so I believe these younger Canadians when properly fledged will embrace this practice, and write each of the soul and scene of his own community. Only Whitman has comprehensively surveyed the whole American scene, and what is better the whole American consciousness. Only a Canadian Whitman, and by that I mean a man of his genius and spiritual breadth, will correctly interpret the whole Canadian consciousness. Since Whitmans are purely accidents of birth, and may not be specifically begotten, these younger Canadians will continue their work of enlightenment and propagation, each striving at all times to be the national literary *obermensch*, and in due course will serve as a fitting background for this inevitable man. The emancipation of Canadian letters will have been contrived; Canada, in effect, will assume position among those nations contributing to the universal betterment, but as it is, Gentlemen, very certainly there may be no future for Canadian literature until Canadian literature as such, is recovered from its present affliction of infantile paralysis.

Leo Kennedy, "The Future of Canadian Literature," *The Canadian Mercury*, December 1928.

F. R. SCOTT

What has been described as the "new poetry" is now a quarter of a century old. Its two main achievements have been a development of new techniques and a widening of poetic interest beyond the narrow range of the late Romantic and early Georgian poets. Equipped with a freer diction and more elastic forms, the modernists sought a content which would more vividly express the world about them.

This search for new content was less successful than had been the search for new techniques, and by the end of the last decade the modernist movement was frustrated for want of direction. In this, poetry was reflecting the aimlessness of its social environment.

In confronting the world with need to restore order out of social chaos, the economic depression has released human energies by giving them a positive direction. The poet today shares in this release, and contemporary English and American verse as a consequence shows signs of regaining the vitality it had lost.

The poems in this collection were written for the most part when new techniques were on trial, and when the need for a new direction was more apparent than the knowledge of what that direction would be. *New Provinces* contains work which has had significance for the authors in the evolution of their own understanding.

F. R. Scott, Preface to *New Provinces* (Toronto: Macmillan, 1936).

A. J. M. SMITH

The bulk of Canadian verse is romantic in conception and conventional in form. Its two great themes are Nature and Love—nature humanized, endowed with feeling, and made sentimental; love idealized, sanctified, and inflated. Its characteristic type is the lyric. Its rhythms are definite, mechanically correct, and obvious; its rhymes are commonplace.

The exigencies of rhyme and rhythm are allowed to determine the choice of a word so often that a sensible reader is compelled to conclude that the plain sense of the matter is of only minor importance. It is the arbitrarily chosen verse pattern that counts. One has the uncomfortable feeling in reading such an anthology as W. W. Campbell's *The Oxford Book of Canadian Verse* or J. W. Garvin's *Canadian Poets* that the writers included are not interested in saying anything in particular; they merely wish to show that they are capable of turning out a number of regular stanzas in which statements are made about the writer's emotions, say "In Winter," or "At Mont-morenci Falls," or "In A Birch Bark Canoe." Other exercises are concerned with pine trees, the open road, God, snowshoes or Pan. The most popular experience is to be pained, hurt, stabbed or seared by Beauty—preferably by the yellow flame of a crocus in the spring or the red flame of a maple leaf in autumn.

There would be less objection to these poems if the observation were accurate and its expression vivid, or if we could feel that the emotion was a genuine and intense one. We could then go on to ask if it were a valuable one. But, with a negligible number of exceptions, the observation is general to these poems and the descriptions are vague. The poet's emotions are unbounded, and are consequently lacking in the intensity which results from discipline and compression; his thinking is of a transcendental or theosophical sort that has to be taken on faith. The fundamental criticism that must be brought against Canadian poetry as a whole is that it ignores the intelligence. And as a result it is dead.

Our grievance, however, against the great dead body of poetry laid out in the mortuary of the *Oxford Book* or interred under Garvin's florid epitaphs is not so much that it is dead but that its sponsors in Canada pretend that it is alive. Yet it should be obvious to any person of taste that this poetry cannot now, and in most cases never could, give the impression of being vitally concerned with real experience. The Canadian poet, if this kind of thing truly represents his feelings and his thoughts, is a half-baked, hyper-sensitive, poorly adjusted, and frequently neurotic individual that no one in his senses would trust to drive a car or light a furnace. He is the victim of his feelings and fancies, or of what he fancies his feelings ought to be, and his emotional aberrations are out of all proportion to the experience that brings them into being. He has a soft heart and a soft soul; and a soft head. No wonder nobody respects him, and few show even the most casual interest in his poetry. A few patriotic professors, one or two hack journalist critics, and a handful of earnest anthologists—these have tried to put the idea across that there exists a healthy national Canadian poetry which expresses the vigorous hope of this young Dominion in a characteristically Canadian style, et cetera, but the idea is so demonstrably false that no one but the interested parties has been taken in.

We do not pretend that this volume contains any verse that might not have been written in the United States or in Great Britain. There is certainly nothing specially Canadian about more than one or two poems. Why should there be? Poetry today is written for the most part by people whose emotional and intellectual heritage is not a national one; it is either cosmopolitan or provincial, and, for good or evil, the forces of civilization are rapidly making the latter scarce.

A large number of the verses in this book were written at a time when the contributors were inclined to dwell too exclusively on the fact that the chief thing wrong with Canadian poetry was its conventional and insensitive technique. Consequently, we sometimes thought we had produced a good poem when all we had done in reality was not produce a conventional one. In Canada this is a deed of some merit.

In attempting to get rid of the facile word, the stereotyped phrase and the mechanical rhythm, and in seeking, as the poet today must, to combine colloquialism and rhetoric, we were of course only following in the path of the more significant poets in England and the United States. And it led, for a time, to the creation of what, for the sake of brevity, I will call "pure poetry."

A theory of pure poetry might be constructed on the assumption that a poem exists as a thing in itself. It is not a copy of anything or an expression of anything, but is an individuality as unique as a flower, an elephant or a man on a flying trapeze. Archibald MacLeish expressed the idea in *Ars Poetica* when he wrote,

A poem should not mean, but be.

Such poetry is objective, impersonal, and in a sense timeless and absolute. It stands by itself, unconcerned with anything save its own existence.

Not unconnected with the disinterested motives that produce "pure" poetry are those which give rise to imagist poetry. The imagist seeks with perfect objectivity and impersonality to recreate a thing or arrest an experience as precisely and vividly and simply as possible. Mr. Kennedy's "Shore," Mr. Scott's "trees in ice," my own "Creek" are examples of the simpler kind of imagist verse; Mr. Finch's "Teacher," tiny as it is, of the more complex. In "Shore" and "Creek" the reader may notice that the development of the poem depends upon metrical devices as much as on images; the music is harsh and the rhythm difficult.

Most of the verses in this book are not, however, so unconcerned with thought as those mentioned. In poems like "Epithalamium," "the Five Kine," "Words for a Resurrection" and "Like An Old Proud King" an attempt has been made to fuse thought and feeling. Such a fusion is characteristic of the kind of poetry usually called metaphysical. Good metaphysical verse is not, it must be understood, concerned with the communication of ideas. It is far removed from didactic poetry. What it is concerned with is the emotional effect of ideas that have entered so deeply into the blood as never to be questioned. Such poetry is primarily lyrical; it should seem spontaneous. Something of the quality I am suggesting is to be found in such lines as

> The wall was there, oh perilous blade of grass
> This Man of April walks again

In the poems just mentioned thought is the root, but it flowers in the feeling. They are essentially poems of the sensibility, a little bit melancholy, perhaps a little too musical. A healthier robustness is found in satirical verse, such as Mr. Scott's much needed counter-blast against the Canadian Authors' Association, or in the anti-romanticism of Mr. Klein's.

> And my true love,
> She combs and combs,
> The lice from off
> My children's domes.

The appearance of satire, and also of didactic poetry that does not depend upon wit, would be a healthy sign in Canadian poetry. For it would indicate that our poets are realizing, even if in an elementary way, that poetry is more concerned with expressing exact ideas than wishy-washy "dreams." It would indicate, too, that the poet's lofty isolation from events that are of vital significance to everybody was coming to an end.

Detachment, indeed, or self-absorption is (for a time only, I hope) becoming impossible. The era of individual liberty is in eclipse. Capitalism can hardly be expected to survive the cataclysm its most interested adherents are blindly steering towards, and the artist who is concerned with the most intense of experiences must be concerned with the world situation in which, whether he likes it or not, he finds himself. For the moment at least he has something more important to do than to record his private emotions. He must try to perfect a technique that will combine power with simplicity and sympathy with intelligence so that he may play his part in developing mental and emotional attitudes that will facilitate the creation of a more practical social system.

Of poetry such as this, there is here only the faintest foreshadowing —a fact that is not unconnected with the backwardness politically and economically of Canada—but that Canadian poetry in the future must become increasingly aware of its duty to take cognizance of what is going on in the world of affairs we are sure.

That the poet is not a dreamer, but a man of sense; that poetry is a discipline because it is an art; and that it is further a useful art; these are propositions which it is intended this volume shall suggest. We are not deceiving ourselves that it has proved them.

A. J. M. Smith, "A Rejected Preface," *Canadian Literature*, No. 24, Spring 1965.

II

THE NEW POETRY: A MANIFESTO

The New Poetry: A Manifesto

By the early 1940s the development of modernism in Canada had reached the point of "cell division," showing a conflict of generations within the modern movement and a clearly marked diversification of trends.

Out of the ferment of little magazines in this period—*Preview, First Statement, Direction, Contemporary Verse*—came the anthology edited by John Sutherland, *Other Canadians* (1947), published by First Statement Press. (Sutherland was editor of *First Statement* and later of *Northern Review*.) His argumentative Introduction to *Other Canadians* is a buried milestone in our literary history. Its importance will be readily appreciated.

The essay has been misunderstood and neglected apparently because critics have been put off by Sutherland's explicit Marxist or socialist position, by his rude polemic against A. J. M. Smith, and perhaps by his later conversion to Catholicism, which seemed to disqualify some of his arguments. Actually, it is a brilliant and prophetic piece of polemical writing, containing a sound core of critical argument, and it will no doubt become, with time, a standard reference in Canadian criticism.

Sutherland in this essay launched an attack on A. J. M. Smith's recently-published anthology *The Book of Canadian Poetry* (1943). Smith had written a capable and well-balanced Introduction—a progress report on Canadian poetry, when to his surprise he found that he had unwittingly wandered into the middle of a battlefield. Poetry in Canada had moved forward since 1926, and Smith, living in East Lansing, Michigan, was unaware that in Montreal at the moment two divergent parties were contesting the field. His Introduction had touched on several fighting issues.

The features of Smith's book which irritated Sutherland should be made clear. Smith had divided his poets into Sections under such titles as "The Rise of a Native Tradition" to describe the romantic nature poets, and "Modern Poetry: The Cosmopolitan Tradition" to describe the moderns. He had treated the present situation in such a way that a preference seemed to be indicated in favour of the metaphysical and cosmopolitan poets in the existing alignment. But for Sutherland, as for others in his group, the true "native" poetry was that of direct realism and simple language, and not the poetry of nineteenth-century romanticism. The "modern" school was not "metaphysical" or "cosmopolitan," but essentially local and particular.

The crucial paragraphs in Smith's Introduction (1943)—much amended and revised in later editions—deserve to be quoted in full to show precisely what provoked Sutherland's angry response:

The modern revival began in the twenties with a simplification of technique. Following the lead of the "new poets" in the United States and the Georgians in England, Canadian poets turned against rhetoric, sought a sharper, more objective imagery, and limited themselves as far as possible to the language of everyday and the rhythms of speech. These reforms were largely the work of younger poets whose outlook was native rather than cosmopolitan and whose aims were those of realism. These poets sought to render with a new faithfulness much that had been passed over as "unpoetic" by previous generations. Some of the lyrics of Dorothy Livesay, the farm poems of Raymond Knister, Charles Bruce's stirring "Words Are Never Enough," the cadenced "laconics" of W. W. E. Ross, and Anne Marriott's fine example of proletarian poetry, *The Wind Our Enemy* (1939), are representative of this aspect of the modern movement.

But it was not in the simplification of style and the emphasis upon the harsher aspects of reality that the new poets made the most significant departure from the school of Roberts, Carman and Lampman. The older masters had sought a spiritual nourishment in the beauty of their natural surroundings. For them, the challenge of environment strengthened both the moral virtues and the aesthetic sensibilities and led ultimately to a powerful feeling of communion with the Divine Spirit, more or less pantheistically conceived. The poets of today, inheritors of what I. A. Richards has called the "neutralization of nature," have turned away from all this. They have sought in man's own mental and social world for a subject matter they can no longer find in the beauty of nature—a beauty that seems either deceptive or irrelevant. Their early simplicity, assumed in reaction to the overloaded diction of much Victorian verse, has been replaced by a variety of individual and subtle rhetorics derived in part from Pound or Eliot, the later Yeats, or the seventeenth-century metaphysicals.*

Thus modern poetry is divided into two lines of development, one of "simplification . . . and realism," the other containing "individual and subtle rhetorics" related to the "metaphysicals." The first of these is somewhat confusingly represented by earlier poets—Knister and W. W. E. Ross—combined with later poets like Anne Marriott

*A. J. M. Smith, *The Book of Canadian Poetry* (Toronto: Gage, 1946), pp. 28-29.

and Charles Bruce. (In later editions of the anthology Dudek and Souster have been added to this list, indicating that Smith had in mind a general type of poetry, not a chronological view of development.) Subsequently, this entire section contrasting the schools has been much revised, and generous treatment has been given to Irving Layton (not included in the 1943 and 1948 editions) and others of this group.

But controversy is sometimes more instructive than peace without lively distinctions. Forgetting John Sutherland's "Marxism" and his militant "anti-religious" stance—really quite irrelevant to his main argument—we should note that in this important essay *cum* Introduction he took a stand for Canadian "realism" and for "Americanism," in contrast to Smith's "metaphysical" bias and preference for aestheticism and eighteenth-century elegance; and also that he singled out three poets, out of a score or so then appearing in the pages of the magazines, to represent a continuing tradition which flourishes to this day.

JOHN SUTHERLAND

Mr. Smith and The "Tradition"

The critical theory advanced by A. J. M. Smith in *The Book of Canadian Poetry* has aroused what we would describe in relative Canadian terms as "considerable speculation." Mr. Smith argues that Canadian poetry has been the product of two schools—the native and the cosmopolitan: "One group has attempted to describe whatever is essentially and distinctively Canadian . . . the other, from the very beginning, has made a heroic effort to transcend colonialism by entering into the universal civilizing culture of ideas." The "extra-Canadian" tradition arose first; the age of nationalism was a regrettable interlude which is even now being superseded by a re-birth of the cosmopolitan ideal: "the poets of today are bringing back to Canadian verse . . . an intellectualism unknown since Heavysege and a merging of personality into a classicism of form that might find its exemplar in Cameron." I believe that the confusion of those who have attempted to discuss this theory might be cleared up if we defined the words "national" and "cosmopolitan" in Canadian terms.

The nationalism of which Mr. Smith appears to speak, and which is still vocal and powerful in present-day Canada, is not of the simple nature that we immediately assume. Its double character was adequately described a long time ago in those verses of Professor Scott's entitled "Canadian Authors Meet." Those artists and their friends who are busy chanting the old refrain—

> O Canada, O Canada, O can
> A day go by without new authors springing
> To paint the native maple, and to plan
> New ways to set the self-same welkin ringing—

ask ourselves in a chorus questions of another kind:

> . . . shall we
> Appoint a poet-laureate this fall,
> Or shall we have another cup of tea?

We can assume that their zeal for Canada depends upon their getting permission to appoint a poet-laureate, and upon their being offered another cup of tea: their chief allegiance is to God and King and Country, and what country it is we do not need to say. Always to be taken into account in any discussion of nationalism and the native tradition, is the Canadian oedipus complex which enables us to praise Canada and her independence even while we are fattening our self-interest by strengthening the ties with the motherland. It will be dangerous if, in our anxiety to attack nationalism we fail initially to define its nature in Canada, and begin discharging our heavy artillery before we know or say what we are aiming at. Must not a critic, who, after all, is in possession of some powerful weapons, be asked to proceed with more caution? Is there not a danger that he will cut down some of his friends quite by accident?

Mr. Smith's criticism is directed at impulses which have been dead in the creative sense ever since the beginning of the century and are no doubt dead for good; and at a powerful body of opinion which is the social and political heir of the so-called national school and finds its focus in the Canadian Authors' Association. The view-point of this association is just as blunt and crude as we are told. I find in a review of Patrick Anderson's *A Tent for April* in the official publication of the group the following statement:

His verse contains many ideas which are essentially Canadian, and that is good, for he may stimulate other Canadian poets to choose their homeland as subject for their verse. If this is accomplished Mr. Anderson will have made a valuable contribution to Canadian literature.

One can only say of such criticism that it is consistent with itself. The incredible absurdity which can find "essentially Canadian" ideas in the poetry of Patrick Anderson harmonizes with the declaration that a man who chooses his homeland as his theme will make a valuable contribution to Canadian literature. The point of view, though it is well known and familiar to everyone, is nevertheless evil, and it is a good thing to find Mr. Smith critical of it. I can only regret that he has never referred to the CAA by name, not just because it is healthy to call a spade a spade, but because a consideration of the CAA can help to clarify this question of the national or native tradition in Canadian poetry.

We must assume that those writers and critics whom Mr. Smith has dragged from the shades of the past—the O'Learys, the O'Gradys, and all the rest—would only fail to make good members of the CAA because they retained their individual freedom and possessed charming and attractive personalities. That gentleman who, in a fit of poetic frenzy aroused by the national scenery, walked over a cliff in some wild and inaccessible region of the land must have been a tourist at heart whether he was in Canada on a visit or had come to stay. The evidence shows that he was not properly adjusted to his environment, and doubtless after his accidental fall he harboured a life-long grievance against it. But is there any difference between the Canadianism of the O'Learys and of the Roberts entourage? In the case of the nature poets one is ready to acknowledge a superior poetic ability; but will one refer to this restricted colonial off-shoot of English romanticism as a native or national school? Smith supplies us with a qualified and incomplete answer: "The claim of this poetry to be truly national . . . must on the whole be denied to a body of work which ignored on principle the coarse bustle of humanity in the hurly-burly business of the developing nation." With that remark, it seems to me, native tradition and national school go out the window. What is significant about the nature poets is their isolation in the midst of an alien environment, and their inability to express the environment except with borrowed instruments and from a colonial point of view. Smith continues: "The theme was narrow; (but) it was nothing less than the impingement of nature in Canada upon the human spirit." Naturally we feel a little bit abashed when we meet a concept like "the human spirit" face to face; we are suspended for a moment by a breathless religious awe, and feel a sudden impulse to remove our hats. But we must break the church-like silence long enough to ask whether, as this implies, there is so absolute a division between the life of the people in Canada and the human spirit? Were we not practically told a moment ago that this poetry ignored humanity on principle? Then how does it get on such familiar terms with the human spirit?

Our first question will be as follows: Have there been any poets in Canada whom one could call native or national?

We will notice that Mr. Smith, too, speaks of "the real or supposed nationalism" of Canadian poetry. I believe that he would readily come to the conclusion that the nationalism was only suppositional, if it were not for the advantages to be gained by dividing Canadian poetry into the cosmopolitan and native traditions. His ambiguity can only be explained by saying that the critic has a penchant for the word tradition, and welcomes the wide field of speculation which it throws open to him. At the back of Mr. Smith's mind there is no doubt that the "cosmopolitan" is the only tradition of Canadian poetry; that it is the direction in which the future is tending as well as the established fact of the past. What he tells us about the nature school in the *The Book of Canadian Poetry,* for example—where he freely applies the labels native and national—and what he says about their cosmopolitanism in "Nationalism and the Canadian Poets," are not really two different things: they only look as if they were different. The traditional bias of Mr. Smith's criticism means that his allegiance to the Good—i.e. the cosmopolitan—is fixed and irrevocable but it also means that a Bad must be invented over which the Good can duly triumph. If cosmopolitan Good is to be victorious in the accepted manner, then a devil—i.e. the native tradition—must be conjured up to challenge it: the hoax must be perpetrated, even though Mr. Smith knows it is utter nonsense to talk about a "tradition" of Canadian poetry. We could only use the word tradition if we believed that the poetry was so blended with the life of the country that it was able to reach into the present and influence its course. Mr. Smith knows this cannot be said of Canadian poetry, but he is reluctant to admit it. Here is his comment on the barren middle period of Canadian poetry: "None of these poets who explored the variations of individual romanticism provide any link between the poets of the nineties and the younger experimentalists of the world between the wars." The case looks pretty hopeless until he pulls E. J. Pratt out of the hat: "Such a link . . . is provided by the narrative poet E. J. Pratt". Pratt "points to some of his younger contemporaries" (or does he point the finger?) "because of the richness and variety of his diction and his willingness to experiment with new forms." But—and what a "but" this is—"he has had little direct influence on them. Indeed the very expansiveness of his good nature and the exuberance of his energy serve as something of a barrier . . ." The strangely compromising and ambiguous quality which these sentences have—arguing a likeness on falsely abstract grounds of technique; coupling "direct influence" with the modifier "little"; introducing half-relevant factors like exuberance and good nature; employing seemingly conservative phrases like "something of a barrier"—all this may show how extravagant and involved are the critic's wishful efforts to find a tradition in Canadian poetry.

Mr. Smith, like his spiritual father, T. S. Eliot, is a traditionalist and classicist in literature. Regarding with trepidation the example of America, he flies to European fields, and to those sheltered haunts where the "classical" tradition still maintains itself. Mr. Eliot has not taken more glances at the classical world than he could manage over the shoulder of Dante; but Mr. Smith has slipped past the colossal statue by night and come to anchor in the bay of Virgil. The critic is here to remind us that Canadian poetry is more truly Roman than we could ever have imagined in our wildest dreams. With his classical microscope he is able to find in one poet what he calls a "hint of Virgilian rectitude"; he discovers that an ode of D. C. Scott's will "bear comparison" with Virgil et cetera.; and considering the matter as a whole, we may say that Canadian poetry is more sober and restrained, more firm and pure, indeed more "right" and more "true," than it was a few short years ago, or before it felt the healing touch of the critic. Mr. Smith—in spite of the fact that he is dealing with a predominantly romantic poetry, and in the face of Mr. Eliot's own difficulties—goes whole hog with the latter in upholding the metaphysical school as the last solid phalanx of the English classical tradition. He has dug up a number of mud-caked relics: some of them quite imposing, and some not so even at the best of times. He has divided the sober, restrained and classical poetry of D. C. Scott and Archibald Lampman from the suspiciously heady lyricism of Carman and the barnyard regionalism of Sir Charles Roberts; and he has announced that the future will behave more sensibly than the disappointing, if distinctly manageable, past. The romantic Charles Mair is disposed of in Eliotian terms in the *Book of Canadian Poetry* as, "reflective and sentimental, not imaginative and intellectual"—but in "Nationalism and the Canadian Poets" attention is fastened almost exclusively upon "the sobriety and patience of Mair's description of characteristic aspects of nature. . . . When he turned to the western plains, and the vast stretches of the untamed wilderness, Mair's imagination caught fire, and his writing took on an intensity and power which anticipates the more fervid spirit of the later poets." Mair, however, was not on fire so much of the time that he did not achieve "a solidity and directness, a firmness and clarity . . . that represent the universal and truly classical way of looking at things."

The raging passion which we can detect in Mair's poetry was evidently under the control of a master spirit who combined the zeal of an arsonist with the efficiency of a fire-chief.

Arsonist emotion and fire-chief intellect are asked to beget a child, which will combine the better qualities of both, and possess something else entirely new. This "something else" is comprehended by the term "metaphysical," the use of which has always given Eliot and his followers special advantages over other critics. Able to use the word in either the literary or the religio-philosophic sense, or able to use it in both ways at once, they have the happy choice of meaning sometimes less and sometimes more than they say. It is a delight, surely, to see Mr. Eliot moving with so much tact and skill through so many different lands and times. Romantic poetry, with its fatal atheistic tendency, is put in its place, while the recalcitrant Donne gets the glad hand on his return to bliss; non-conformist Tennyson and Browning do not seem to be poets at all compared with Herbert and Crashaw. Milton is allowed to keep his musical ear, but is shorn of all other faculties; Blake's lack of stature as compared with Dante is due to an embarrassing habit of philosophizing, which prevents him from accepting automatically the principles of Catholicism. So many changes are rung upon the same old theme, sometimes in the name of history and tradition, and sometimes in the name of that pure aestheticism which, properly understood, is nothing less than the history and tradition of the human spirit wrapped in a papal bunnyhug. Bishop Smith, operating in the Canadian diocese, is faced with what are still frontier conditions. There are so many diverse, recalcitrant elements that no matter how one tars and feathers them they cannot all be made to look the same. Margaret Avison is a definite find; the intellectual and moral interest of Ronald Hambleton is promising; W. W. E. Ross and Dorothy Livesay can be turned around until they are useful for church decoration. But the outlook would be pretty bleak and hopeless were it not for that tower of strength, Charles Heavysege, the greatest figure of pre-Confederation times. Heavysege is good in "Count Filippo," with its "curiously intuitive understanding of evil" (how one loves that "curiously intuitive"!); he is even better in "Jephtha's Daughter," where power is demonstrated in "the growth of the young girl's soul as she moves from the first natural weakness of fear and resentment to her final exalted acquiescence in the Divine decree." (How one loves that "natural weakness" and that "exalted acquiescence"!) It is in "Saul," however, that Heavysege is really superb; Smith quotes from a remarkable review of the poem which ends thus: "Seldom has art so well performed the office of handmaiden to religion as in the extraordinary character of Malzah, in whom we have the disembodiment of the soul of the faithless, sophisticated, brave, and generously disposed king of Israel, and a most impressive poetical exposition of the awful truth, that he who is not wholly for God is against Him." And, for the final prize, take the critic's comment on the review: "This is perhaps an old-fashioned kind of criticism, but it is none the worse for that. Its value is due to the fact that it supplies something better than a capricious or arbitrary explanation of the source of our interest in the characters of Malzah and Saul." Oh, how we love that "perhaps old-fashioned," that "capricious and arbitrary explanation"! Anyway, who the devil would be interested enough in Heavysege's "Saul" to start offering "explanations"?

Now it is time that we asked question number two: where has this hilarious catholicism of Mr. Smith's landed us? Are we really located somewhere abroad, busy improving our minds, or are we sitting in a remote section of the Canadian backwoods? Is the native dust shaken off our shoes or not? A while ago we quoted from *The Canadian Author and Bookman,* the organ of the CAA, to get Mr. Smith straight on the question of nationalism: we can go to the same place to clear up this other point. We pick up the same issue of the magazine and happen to turn to a little article on the "pornography" in the novels of Hugh MacLennan. "To Human Flesh," by Elsie Fry Laurence, contains in cruder form everything that Mr. Smith's cosmopolitanism contains. Ingredient No. 1 is expressed as "a tendency to copy the literal bluntness of certain American types rather than the delicate subtlety of the better European masters." Ingredient No. 2 —Mr. Smith's pure and unsullied aestheticism—pops up everywhere like the spots on a leopard: we are told that Mr. MacLennan is "chiefly inartistic"; that "his aesthetic sense is undeveloped," et cetera. Ingredient No. 3 is summed up in this manner: "If they (our novelists) would read Professor Brown's chapter on our literary problems in his *On Canadian Poetry,* and then *explore the recess of the human spirit . . . ."* (Italics are mine; dots are hers). Must we not wonder at this spectacle of the noisy organ of "nationalism" turning out Mr. Smith's cosmopolitanism with such a homey, familiar air? Must we not ask, if cosmopolitanism has made such inroads on parochialism, whether the opposite process has not also taken place?

Mr. Smith is a classicist by inclination, a Catholic by intention, and a Royalist by virtue of what he will certainly achieve. Why this Eliotian stand is so harmful today can only be understood if we consider the persistent colonialism of Canadian poetry in the light of the new developments of the forties.

New Necessities

That phrase which is bandied about everywhere by the critics and reviewers—"the younger poets"—is badly in need of a definition. The Canadian critic uses it in a way different from the English or American critic; indeed, he uses it as it has never been used by anyone else before. I am thinking of that "analysis of a dozen younger poets" by Henry Wells, so called by Mr. Ralph Gustafson and quoted by him in a recent article. There were clipped comments upon the work of Birney, Scott and Livesay; the essence of Ross, Kiein and Hambleton was conveyed to us in the stripped phrase of the hack reviewer; and heading the whole parade of names was a reference to Dr. E. J. Pratt! No disrespect is intended to Dr. Pratt, but surely to describe as a younger poet a man of sixty who has evidently most of his best work behind him, is to reduce our criticism from absurdity to something still more absurd? In these terms, "younger" can only mean younger than Carman, Lampman and Roberts, who are already dead, or younger than D. C. Scott who has reached eighty years. How can we explain this nearly total lapse of memory on the part of the Canadian critic? Has he been so infected by eternal values that he has lost all sense of time?

What is involved, of course, is not one critic's use of a particular phrase, but the relation of what is called Canadian criticism to poetry in Canada. Our criticism cannot have a living function, because it is entirely concerned with Canadian writing of the last century, or with movements of the twenties and thirties which have either proved abortive or been superseded by something else. It can say nothing, except by an indirection, that does not make the past seem more significant and more complicated than it is; that does not distort the nature of the present; that does not confuse the general picture of what is called Canadian literature. It is concerned with the past only for the sake of the past, and therefore it is meaningless and dead. Now a fresh start must be made and the Canadian critic must steel himself to the facts of the situation. He must accept the primary fact that there is no tradition of Canadian poetry; that, however, in this century and the last traditions of English poetry have been transplanted to Canada, which are native only in the sense of being smaller and more cramped than the home plant. The advent in Canada of English romanticism produced a movement in the post-Confederation period, which reached and passed its peak in the early 1900s; the prominence of the contemporary English poets, W. H. Auden and Stephen Spender, Dylan Thomas and George Barker, stimulated in this country the new social poetry of the forties. The pre-Confederation period is of historic interest, insofar as it developed the nature theme that was to play a dominant role in the Roberts school; similarly the poetry of the late 1920s and the 1930s helped to develop the social theme which has become of prime importance in the new movement. Canadian critics will not free themselves of stupidity, but will go on evading the issue, wasting time and energy on theories of a poetry whose existence is largely illusory. But the significant question today is the antipathy of the two main schools, and the effect it has on the colonialism of poetry in Canada.

We can best understand the nature poets if we consider them in the light of Mr. Smith's "perhaps old-fashioned principle" that "art is the handmaiden of religion." The Roberts school are in agreement with Mr. Smith as to the validity of this idea: they would only quarrel when they proceeded to crystallize their vage immanences into definite form. The critic's love of hell and hellish suffering would not endear him to a Bliss Carman or a Charles Roberts. The romantic poet seeking his god has obstacles to surmount, but his profound despair is always counteracted by an exalted cheerfulness. He is always just failing to touch something which cannot be touched, to hear a voice which cannot be heard, or to see a face which cannot be seen: these coquettish delays serve to heighten the pleasurable agony, suggesting that the embrace beyond the grave will be the more ecstatic and prolonged. The firm of Roberts are not so conventially religious nor so enchanted by suffering as Mr. Smith. But they share with him responsibility for maintaining that decayed faith, that shoddy and outworn morality, which blends in Canada with the colonial's desire to preserve the status quo. If we sought an explanation of the extraordinary narrowness of Canadian poetry—the deadening singleness of aim which persists in the face of every change—would not the first cause be this general acceptance of the art-religion hypothesis? If we wanted to explain the close air and the literary smell of our poetry—our sensation of being on the inside of a jar of preserves—would not the same reason come to mind? This idea has done more than anything else to intimidate the Canadian poet, and prevent him from relating his poetry to his environment.

Our critics have spent all their energies emphasizing the distinction between poetry and reality, arguing as if the half-truth were infallible when it was only quite true of poetry in Canada. It is time we began stating the other half-truth—that the poet retains human attributes in spite of being a poet, that his materials are tangible often in spite of appearance, and that he has something to say which frequently has meaning for the ordinary man. We accept the value of this idea where prose is concerned, and often judge it with regard to its relevance to reality. Why then, do we regard poetry in a totally different way? May it not be that the actual environment is even more essential in the case of poetry? Does not the poet work upon everyday things so as to extract their essence and give them back to us in more concentrated, meaningful form? Does he not, therefore, have more to tell us about common ideas and feelings than the prose writer possibly can? Our romantic poets have misled us because they have started with one reality—nature—and used it only as a door of escape or as a pulpit in which to make meaningless but high-sounding affirmations. Nature, the most malleable reality they could find, would put no check on their eloquence because it could not answer them back. And so wearied were they by its perpetual acquiescence that when they turned to ideas and feelings of significance to people, they had absolutely nothing to say, their poetry simply dissolved and faded away. Their failure in this respect is the same as that of our prose writers and is just as relevant to a discussion of Canadian poetry as of Canadian prose.

Surely the fact that the poets of the forties are never mentioned except anonymously is caused by their indifference to the art-religion hypothesis of our escapist writers and critics. For, while our colonialism is exaggerated by the turn of events, it is exaggerated in such a way that the seeds of decay are visible in it: it is threatened by a movement which utterly repudiates the old idea, and whose creative energy exceeds that of the romantic school. Poets such as James Wreford and Ronald Hambleton; the Preview group of P. K. Page, Patrick Anderson, Neufville Shaw and Bruce Ruddick; First Statement writers such as Irving Layton, Louis Dudek and Raymond Souster—all are concerned with the individual and the individual's relation to society, and adopt an attitude which might seem well-nigh blasphemous to conventional people. If God still talks to these poets in private, he carries less weight than Karl Marx or Sigmund Freud. The seven-day fireworks of the world's creation matter less than the creation of the socialist state; the cure of earthly ills is to be achieved by economics or psychology rather than by divine intervention. These poets are interested in events and ideas whose importance is neither ephemeral nor imaginary to the living and thinking individual; they *intend* at least to speak to the average man of everyday realities and of the principles which operate in them. They are determined on principle *not* to ignore the coarse bustle of humanity, and their purpose is surely healthier than that of Roberts and Co. It lets in fresh air at a time when we were almost stifling, and suggests that Canadian poetry may become something other than a chamber music. It creates a base for operations and broaches the possibility of a poetic tradition.

But the movement of the forties does not alter the colonial basis of our poetry. We have found it difficult to admit this because we are faced with some rather paradoxical facts. One of them is the deceptive front of the new poetry, which, being Marxist in outlook, is committed to a society in which colonies, like colonial attitudes, will cease to exist. Another fact is the poetic achievement of the new school, which taken as a whole, reaches a level attained only by isolated figures in the past. There are half a dozen poets writing in Canada today whose work compares favorably with English and American poetry, if it is not as good as that of the best English and American poets. But we should not make the mistake on the one hand of identifying "colonial" with what is bad in the literary sense, or on the other of assuming that poetry in Canada has achieved an individuality of its own and that the impediment to its free development has now been removed. The poets of the forties are English by origin and birth, and the new poetry is predominantly English in tone. James Wreford, Ronald Hambleton, P. K. Page, Patrick Anderson, were all born in England or educated there: what they produce must seem strange and alien to those who, in a way still undefined, feel themselves Canadians. Show the intelligent Canadian even a poem as good as Patrick Anderson's "Poem on Canada," and the response is immediate and emphatic. He will tell you that the poem is not Canadian; that it is not even about Canada, though it may be about anything else in the world. There is no doubt that the English poet will find it difficult to deal with Canadian themes and Canadian material, certainly to deal with them in a way that is felt to be Canadian; he will lack the convincing reality which is increasingly demanded of our poets as Canada begins to grow up. It is this division between the poet and his audience which is of crucial importance today.

Our poetry is colonial because it is the product of a cultured English group who are out of touch with a people who long ago began adjusting themselves to life on this continent. The lack of all rapport between the poetry and the environment is one of the factors accounting for the incredibly unreal and ethereal quality of some of the new poetry. One reads a poem which purports to be written from the socialist point of view, and is reminded more of the work of Lewis Carroll than of Karl Marx. The air of make-believe is due partly to the fact that the middle-class Marxist poet comes from England into an environment doubly alien because it is passing through a period of special change.

His position is complicated by the nature of socialism in Canada. Socialism must take a somewhat different form in every country, and in Canada it cannot be separated from a healthy national point of view. We cannot proceed to the setting up of a socialist society before we greatly weaken or break our colonial ties, which in the economic sense are important and in the spiritual sense are well-nigh crippling. Social change in this country means that the power of changing our constitution must pass from the hands of a British governing body to the Canadian people; that the economic rights and privileges of the mother country must be abolished; that the middle class with its British sympathies must be changed at its base; and—very important politically—that a fusion of viewpoint must take place between French and English Canada, which is impossible while the allegiance of one is owed to another country. Just at the time when socialism has become the most important national issue, one would expect to find poets who would express the aims of the people, and to see a new life and freedom enter into Canadian poetry as a whole. But such freedom exists only in the limited sense described above, and our literary colonialism tends to be heightened by this political development.

Socialism entails something else which is of leading importance for the Canadian writer. We cannot embark on an effort to find Canadian solutions for our problems without at the same time emphasizing our connection with this continent and playing a more unqualified part as a member of the North American group of nations. In this regard Canadian politics can only be catching up with the Canadian people. "A Canadian," says Arthur Lyon Phelps, "is a fellow who has become a North American without becoming an American." That is a negative but true way of saying that the Canadian people, in a way neither clearly defined nor as yet perhaps positively evident, are a distinct entity among the North American peoples. We could also define the typical Canadian poet of the forties as an Englishman trying hard to stop being one, but so far not succeeding. Yet there is abundant evidence that forces are at work from south of the border which must produce a drastic change in him.

As a sign of the times one would instance a contradiction in the nature of the English intellectual in Canada. His personality is not whole-heartedly English, but is divided between an English half and a half that is, or would like to be, American. His poetic self is English; his intellectual habits are borrowed from the mother country.

But he is no longer quite satisfied with his poetic self, and is no longer certain that it represents him as he really is. There are ideas and attitudes, feelings and forms of expression, that sometimes cannot be conveyed by means of the polished and symmetrical vehicle of English poetry, but which attract him, because they seem more easy-going and natural—in short, more American. There is apt to be a struggle between the English and American ideal, though of course the struggle never gets out of hand. The poet may yearn to talk and feel like a bum from Brooklyn, but he never lets the urge get the better of him. His Brooklyn-bum self must make his bow to the tradition; he is to be allowed in over the threshold only if he comes on his knees. That quality of his which seems so racy and vigorous, so healthy and masculine, is to be subdued to the sound of the spheres crossing the polished floor of time. He must be caught up into a lighter air, taught to breathe the aesthetic aether, before he is fully acceptable. But the important thing is that he has somehow been included.

Still more important is the growth of the American influence on Canadian poetry. Not that it was ever absent. As Mr. Smith can show us, the first attempts at creative expression were made by settlers from the United States. But the influence has grown during the present century. The American Imagists were admired and frequently imitated by Canadians, and their example is still being followed today. Sandburg and Kenneth Fearing, Cummings and Marianne Moore, Karl Shapiro and even at this belated date, Walt Whitman, have served individual poets as models or had some effect on the course of Canadian poetry. If the influence is still sporadic, and has no genuine focus, it is wide-spread enough to justify our saying that Canadian poetry struggles to follow the American example even while its dominant bias remains English. One could even venture a prediction, spread a "rumour" that will seem "savage and disastrous" to very many ears. It is quite apparent that the American example will become more and more attractive to Canadian writers; that we are approaching a period when we will have "schools" and "movements" whose origin will be American. And perhaps it is safe to say that such a period is the inevitable half-way house from which Canadian poetry will pass towards an identity of its own.

Among the poets of the forties one will find writers whose work is of special interest and significance. Judged by the pure aesthetic standard, the English colonial poets are producing the best work: the writers I refer to are achieving something of more significance for the future. They are not middle class but proletarian in origin—this fact alone makes them unique among poets in Canada. They have followed American literary models rather than English ones, and they are the first poets of more than passing interest of whom this is true. In their work one finds a more Canadian point of view, a greater interest in themes and problems of a Canadian kind, and a social realism which distinguishes it from the political make-believe of other poets. The poetry of Louis Dudek belongs in some ways in this category and is significant of the impending change. The work of Irving Layton—especially in poems like "Newsboy," "De Bullion Street" and "Words Without Music"—is distinguished by a hard-fisted proletarianism which makes it potential dynamite in the closed chamber of Canadian letters. And of special interest is the writing of Raymond Souster, a young poet who is still in his early twenties. Souster has a freedom of form, and an ability to handle colloquial language, which will not be liked by those perfectionists who can do so much damage to a young and developing poet. He has a way of calling a spade a spade, of saying what he thinks and feels in the most uncompromising terms, which must be positively embarrassing not only to members of the CAA, but to those who go around assuming deliberate disguises. Most important of all, Souster's poetry becomes the embodiment of the common man, completing in poetic terms what the average Canadian thinks and feels. It is poetry on a high creative level which remains perfectly communicative and full of meaning for readers who have not succumbed to spiritual old age.

We can state the whole problem of colonialism in terms of the poet's relation to his audience. The nature poets found a natural audience in the middle class, whose sympathies and values were English, like their own. But this detour is closed to the poets of the forties. Obviously, they cannot appeal to the same class of readers, or hope that they ever will appeal to those Canadians whose traditional viewpoint becomes more frozen and immoveable every day. Yet they are in the unhappy position of being unable to accept the only alternative and seek their audience among a people whom they cannot understand. And that is why we attach such significance to poets like Souster, Layton and Dudek. They give hope that the dividing wall between the author and the people is gradually being broken down, and that our poetry is coming into contact with the Canadian environment.

Our critics are not without ulterior motive in their discussions of Canadian poetry. They make concessions to the new movement now and then, to persuade us that they are on our side, but actually they want to find us a nice little cul-de-sac where we can bury our noses until they cool off. But there are many indications that this last-minute effort to turn back the clock will be of no avail. No amount of gabbling about "European masters" can remove that pressure which focuses Canada's attention on her North American future, and which must draw Canadian literature willy-nilly in its train. Mr. Smith's oxygen tent with its tap to the spirit will keep a few remnants breathing for a while, but can hardly impede the growth of socialism in Canada, or prevent the radical consequences which must follow for the Canadian writer. The future in this country is already beginning to move.

John Sutherland, Introduction to *Other Canadians* (Montreal: First Statement Press, 1947).

III

THE EARLY FORTIES

The New Literary Scene

The two articles that follow tell their own story and require little comment. They serve as an introduction to the poetry and ideas of the early 1940s in Canada. Other essays contained in Section VII, "The Little Magazines," provide further background and interpretation of the publishing scene and the importance of dedicated enterprise on the part of the poets in getting the new poetry into print in books and magazines.

Robert Weaver's article illustrates certain contrasts between the present period and that of the forties. From this point of view, it is both a retrospective criticism and an evaluation of Sutherland's work. It is, however, faulty on some minor points: the chronology and facts are sometimes incorrect—*Other Canadians* appeared in 1947, not in 1949 as implied, nor did the little magazines become an "anachronism"; after 1945, they showed a continuing vigour and steady proliferation. The article illustrates very well the difference between the viewpoint of *Tamarack Review*, of which Robert Weaver is the editor, and the little magazines of the forties. For example, Weaver misreads the so-called "anti-academicism" of the early magazines; it would not be so much "courses" in Canadian literature, or a scholarly interest in Canadian writing, which these angry critics opposed, as the premises of academic criticism grounded in conservative tradition and divorced from life values. (For a further discussion of this issue, see page eighty). Weaver clearly disparages Canadian literature as a serious study, and with the detachment of literary hindsight undervalues the drift of John Sutherland's critical argument. The article was written in 1957; but to make Sutherland a good textual critic and no more, and to discount "the group of writers with which he was first associated," is to miss, surely, the historical importance of *Northern Review* and its ill-starred editor. However, this article records a genuine appreciation of Sutherland's sense of dedication and his profound seriousness as a critic of Canadian literature.

While Sutherland's contribution to the struggle of Canadian poetry in the Forties is known in general terms, the intimate details of this effort are not part of common knowledge. The Brief to the Massey Royal Commission which is here reproduced is a little-known document which casts much light on the activities of the Forties. As E. K.

Brown notes in the passage quoted by Sutherland in his submission, there were only two publishers in Canada providing a steady outlet for the poets of the new school in the 1940s: these were the Ryerson Press under the editorship of Lorne Pierce, and First Statement Press under John Sutherland. Since that time, with the establishment of the Canada Council, and with the widespread recognition of the new poetry (see Section VIII of this book), other reputable publishers have become actively interested—the Oxford University Press, Macmillan's (which had earlier published Pratt), the University of Toronto Press, and especially McClelland & Stewart Limited.

The situation is very much changed for the better, just as the economic life of Canada in every department is richer and bigger than it was thirty years ago. Whereas in the early 1940s the poets struggled in a virtual wasteland of public indifference and isolation, today they are often subsidized, well-placed, and enshrined in anthologies and beautifully printed books. The young are finding readier acceptance and easier publication. There are dozens of little and not-so-little magazines in Canada in which current poetry is published, discussed and reviewed. Even the newspapers, especially the large, metropolitan ones, have instituted literary sections, and have opened their pages to the discussion of new poetry. The old struggle of course exists, but it too has moved beyond "early beginnings" to a more confident resourcefulness and diversity. The comparison between past and present is one of the benefits of reading these documents.

JOHN SUTHERLAND

Origin of the First Statement Press

The origin and purpose of the First Statement Press are best understood in relation to those movements in modern Canadian writing which had their beginnings in the late 1920s and which have found so rich and full an expression during the present decade.

Our literary criticism has gradually recognized that the present decade has seen a development of Canadian writing more significant than that at any period since the 1880s when the nature school of Bliss Carman, Archibald Lampman, D. C. Scott and Charles G. D. Roberts first became known. At no time previously has such a wealth and diversity of talent simultaneously appeared. While this has been especially true of our poetry, which has always been in advance of

Canadian writing as a whole, our prose has also shown signs of maturity.

In some respects a close comparison exists between the intense activity of the decade just past and that of the 1880s. As the school of Carman and Roberts brought into sharp focus tendencies evident earlier in the work of Isabella Crawford, Charles Mair and others, giving a vivid new expression to the nature theme, so the new poetry developed other tendencies already announced in the early writing of E. J. Pratt and in the writing of the so-called "Montreal Poets" and the Western Group of the 1930s. The nature poets arose in the period of expansion following Confederation and these later poets in the new era created in Canada by the Second World War. Today, as in the 80s, Canadian poetry shows a sharpened awareness of Canada itself.

But, while similarities exist between the two periods, there are also marked differences. Canadian poetry in the present decade, and, in fact, since 1925, has caught something of the experimental temper of twentieth-century literature everywhere, and, in form and expression, it has reacted against the more conservative techniques of the romantic nature poets. It has ranged further for its themes than the nature poetry and has never sought to ignore but instead has sought to interpret its social environment. While not indifferent to the Canadian landscape, it has shown less interest in nature itself than in nature as related to people. In part its emphasis on the human world reflects the increasing urbanization of Canadian life.

The same concern with people and with the inhabited landscape is apparent more directly in recent Canadian prose. In general, in the last two decades and a half a vital contact has been established between Canadian literature and Canadian society.

The Public Response to the New Writing

The public response to modern writing in Canada has been a tardy one. Many developments in Canadian literature during the modern period have proved abortive, and part of the blame must be placed on the critics and publishers and on the reading public.

Recently a well-known student of the Canadian novel warned against attributing the limitations of Canadian writing to the meagre public response or to the economic difficulties of the writer. He expressed the opinion that a book "which . . . merits publication will, at the present time, find a publisher in Canada." Perhaps this is almost true in the Canada of the late 1940s. But whether it will remain true may be questioned on the evidence of the recent past.

An example from the period of the 30s is provided by the so-called "Montreal Poets"—A. J. M. Smith, Leo Kennedy, F. R. Scott and A. M. Klein. These promising poets first attracted attention with their publication in *The McGill Fortnightly Review* (1926). Yet no poet in this group was able to attain the dignity of book publication until ten years later,* and two did not publish a first volume of verse until the mid-forties or approximately two decades later. When *New Provinces*, an anthology of their work and of the work of E. J. Pratt and Robert Finch, was issued by private printing in 1936 it sold less than 100 copies.

With the notable exception of A. M. Klein, the Montreal Group have ceased to be practising poets. Ironically, they are now widely regarded as active leaders of the modern poetry movement in Canada. In our criticism they have been recognized and embalmed.

Our student of the novel also remarked that, because of the existence of "literary cliques," "in the cities of the east the writer can always find a few of his own kind . . . thereby satisfying his need of communication." But literary cliques, Canadian and cosmopolitan brand, are generally formed by writers in their nonage. What happens when the clique disbands and they have no way of satisfying their "need for communication"? The denouement of the Montreal Group seems to suggest an answer.

Even the most talented writer would have found the situation in Canada in the 30s formidable. Publication in book form was only possible at long odds. The magazines provided the scantiest avenues of communication with the public. Criticism was either non-existent or pre-occupied with Canadian writing of the last century.

In the established writers' body, the Canadian Author's Association, the same static condition was reflected. Whatever its virtues, this association has always been lacking in awareness of the great contemporary movements in literature. As a result it has alienated a very large number of the talented writers in Canada today.

The "Little Magazine" in the 40s

Virtually the same situation existed at the beginning of the 40s. But now, with the development of so many new talents, a tentative solution was found. The writers formed themselves in groups and issued publications of their own.

In the modern literature of many countries the so-called "little magazines" have exerted an influence out of all proportion to the small impression they have been able to make on the general public.

*Leo Kennedy's *The Shrouding* appeared in 1933.

An outstanding example is the famous *Poetry: A Magazine of Verse,* which since 1931 has played a leading role in the development of American poetry. Resisting the commercialization of literary taste, such magazines have provided an eventual entrance to public attention for many deserving writers and have encouraged the production of informed and intelligent criticism. Indigenous to the cosmopolitan, they were a relatively new phenomenon in Canada in the 40s.

Contemporary Verse in Caulfield, B.C., was first published in 1939*; *Preview* followed in Montreal in 1941. *Reading* in Toronto, and *Direction* in Cape Breton, appeared in the early forties, while recent editions have been *Here and Now* and *Canadian Life* in Toronto. None of these magazines found more than a small number of readers, and most of them have been short-lived. But during the 40s, they have been almost the only vehicle of expression for most of our best poets and for many of our best prose writers. Although they have been edited by regional groups, they have all attracted contributors from many parts of Canada. It would be difficult to overestimate the service rendered to Canadian literature by these "little magazines."

The First Statement Press and its Aims

But the existence of the little magazine could not by itself solve the difficulties of the new writer. Was it not possible to create a more ample medium of expression for the individual author than he could find in the magazines? An answer was found when a group of young writers established the First Statement Press in Montreal in 1942. Non-commercial in purpose like the little magazines, here was a press that showed at once its willingness to publish good writing wherever it might be written in Canada.

The aims of the Press, since faithfully adhered to, were as follows:

(a) To maintain the highest possible literary standards without regard to any consideration of any other kind.

(b) To provide expression for writers of merit denied publication elsewhere.

(c) To give special encouragement to the young writer and to the experimental writer.

(d) To help sharpen the awareness of Canadian writing both past and present.

*Contemporary Verse first appeared in September of 1941. *Preview* first appeared in March of 1942.

(e) To employ only strict standards of criticism, but to emphasize the importance of the developing native sensibility in Canada.

(f) To establish wherever possible a liaison with the French-Canadian writer.

Organization of the Press

Since the basis of the Press was one of voluntary co-operation among writers and other interested persons, no strict organization was either possible or desirable. Those who were able to contribute their time and labour did so freely. Others helped defray the costs of publication.

From 1940 to 1944, those most immediately concerned were the so-called First Statement Group of Audrey Aikman, Louis Dudek, Irving Layton and John Sutherland. But in Montreal a much larger group attended regular meetings and gave assistance in many ways. In Toronto, Halifax, Winnipeg, Vancouver and other cities, meetings of writers were held at which First Statement publications were discussed and distributed.

At present the First Statement Press is the responsibility of John Sutherland, one of the original editors, in whose name it is registered. As its "editor," he has done much of the work involved not only in the selection of material, but in the typesetting and the printing and in the sale and distribution of the publications. But the Press still depends heavily on the voluntary assistance of persons in Montreal and in many parts of Canada.

Its ability to flourish since 1942, without formal organization and without assured funds, is in itself a proof of the vitality of this Press.

Mechanical Equipment and Production

In 1945 in the annual Letters in Canada section of the University of Toronto Quarterly, Professor E. K. Brown wrote: "Another reason for satisfaction in the existence of the new series"—of First Statement books—"is rather a reason for dissatisfaction concerning the general relation between poets and publishers in Canada at present. The four collections so far noticed have all been from one house, The Ryerson Press; and aside from them, and from the First Statement publication, there is but one significant book to notice . . . ." In 1945, before others awoke to what was happening, the publication of poetry in Canada was shared by one long-established and wealthy house and by the First Statement Press described in the preceding paragraphs.

A series of significant Canadian books was produced on an ancient platen press (still the only capital equipment of the First Statement Press), bought with an accumulation of voluntary contributions and operated by a group of young writers who had to teach themselves how to print. Without benefit of modern linotypes, these books were set in type by hand, word for word and letter for letter, with type purchased in the same manner as the press by the same group of amateur printers. They were distributed by these writers and their friends with no personal expectation of monetary return.

Yet the books so produced were so attractive in format that they were widely regarded as an innovation in Canadian taste in book design. While their sale was very small, never exceeding five hundred copies, and insufficient to defray the costs of printing and distribution, it was nevertheless larger than the sale of comparative publications by the established publishers.

Magazine Publication

The magazine produced by the First Statement Press was founded in 1942 under the name of *First Statement* and, is now the bi-monthly publication entitled *Northern Review*. Some forty-five issues of this magazine have appeared in seven years of publication. During this period it has been the only magazine of creative prose and poetry of a non-commercial nature to appear continuously in Canada.

There has been a steady growth in the size of the magazine as there has been a gain in the scope and standard of its contents. As *First Statement* it was published for one year as a mimeographed sheet of eight pages and for three subsequent years as a printed magazine of thirty-two pages. In 1945 it began to be issued as *Northern Review*, again considerably increased in size and with additions to its contents. Besides poetry, fiction and criticism, *Northern Review* has published reproductions of new Canadian painting and reviews of Canadian film, painting and radio.

Its editorial board at present consists of Audrey Aikman, R. G. Simpson and John Sutherland, the managing editor, all founding editors of First Statement Press, and John Harrison.

The members of its Business Committee are Jean Robertson, A. E. Farebrother and Howard Gamble.

Its regional editors and representatives include Roland Penner (Winnipeg), Donald Clark (Halifax), Guy Glover (Ottawa), Louis Dudek (New York), and Colleen Thibaudeau and Douglas Hall (Toronto).

Magazine Contributors

Northern Review has provided a medium of expression for many of the leading writers and artists in Canada. The contributors to previous issues have included these names:

Ralph Gustafson, Dorothy Livesay, Arthur Lismer, Goodridge Roberts, A. M. Klein, Francois Hertel, Frederick Philip Grove, Anne Marriott, Ronald Hambleton, James Wreford, Patrick Anderson, Louis Dudek, Irving Layton, Raymond Souster, Louis Muhlstock, John Lyman, Guy Glover, Kay Smith, Gordon Webber, F. R. Scott, A. J. M. Smith, Robert Ayre, P. K. Page, James Reaney and many others.

While *Northern Review* has published many established writers it has always been receptive to any writer of promise. A number of talented younger writers have appeared in print for the first time in *Northern Review*.

Magazine Production and Distribution

Like other First Statement publications, the issues of *Northern Review* have been hand-set and printed at the First Statement Press. The managing editor has done much of this work of production, while valuable assistance has been lent by the editors and interested persons.

A Guarantors Fund has helped materially to defray printing costs and to maintain the magazine. Those who have contributed to the Fund include: Senator A. K. Hugessen, Mr. J. W. McConnell, Dr. E. J. Pratt, Mr. Hugh MacLennan, Miss Gwethalyn Graham, Mr. Lawrence Frieman, Mr. Ralph Gustafson, Miss Ellen Ballon and others.

Like all magazines too small in circulation to interest the commercial distributor, *Northern Review* has had to depend for distribution entirely on its own resources. In Montreal, it has been distributed by the managing editor, and in various other cities by friends on a voluntary basis. There has been a small but steady growth in circulation from the original one hundred fifty copies to the present six hundred. Although the readers for any magazine of writing and the arts are never numerous, the editors of *Northern Review* are confident that, with some reasonable facilities for publicity and distribution, the audience for the magazine could be very considerably enlarged.

Aims and Future Plans of Northern Review

The aims of the editors of *Northern Review* in regard to both creative work and criticism correspond with those of the First Statement Press as outlined above. The editors believe that the logical development of the little magazine movement of the 40s is a national magazine of writing and the arts, sufficiently comprehensive in size and scope to interest intelligent readers everywhere in Canada. Their ultimate goal is such a magazine embodying their editorial aims.

With this goal in mind they are planning the following changes in *Northern Review*, beginning with the issue for October first, 1949:

(a) An increase in page-length to approximately sixty pages with improvements in the format to increase the attractiveness and readability of the magazine.

(b) A new art section containing reviews of music and stage, painting, film and radio. Contributors to this section will include: James Scott, literary editor of the *Toronto Telegram* and radio critic on the CBC program, "Critically Speaking," Guy Glover of the National Film Board and of *The World Today* (New York), Neufville Shaw, author of poetry and short stories, and a former editor of *Preview*, and other well-known Canadian critics of the arts. In these reviews, and elsewhere in the new magazine, the effort will be made to employ more strict standards than are customary in Canadian criticism, while emphasizing the development of the native sensibility in the arts.

(c) A more comprehensive review of past and current Canadian books. A number of leading Canadian critics will contribute to this page.

(d) Publication of French-Canadian work and of comment on the arts in Quebec.

(e) An award of one hundred dollars for the best poem or group of poems published in *Northern Review* during the six issues beginning October first. The judges will be Dr. H. G. Files, head of the Department of English at McGill University, L. A. MacKay, professor of classics at the University of British Columbia and Alan Crawley, editor of *Contemporary Verse.* By giving the award the editors hope to compensate, however modestly, for the almost total lack of material recognition of the poet in English-speaking Canada.

Everything possible is being done to ensure the success of this new magazine and to bring the dream of a national magazine of writing and the arts one step nearer.

Book Publication

Since 1944 the First Statement Press has endeavoured whenever possible to issue in chapbook form in its New Writers Series the works of individual authors. Most of these publications have been devoted to poetry, and, in accordance with the editorial aims, special consideration has been given to the young and to the experimental writer. Four of the titles in the series represent the first volumes of the writers concerned. These chapbooks have been designed in an attractive format in the belief that the importance of type and design demanded greater acknowledgement from the book publisher in Canada. The following titles have appeared to date:

> *Here & Now*, by Irving Layton. Poems.
> *A Tent for April*, by Patrick Anderson. Poems.
> *Green World*, by Miriam Waddington. Poems.
> *When We Are Young*, by Raymond Souster. Poems.
> *Other Canadians: An Anthology of the New Poetry in Canada,*
>   1940-46.
> *Now is the Place*, by Irving Layton. Poems and Short Stories.

Of special significance, the anthology *Other Canadians* represented the first comprehensive collection of the new poetry in Canada in the forties. In a critical introduction the importance of this new poetry in the development of Canadian writing, its aims and its tendencies, were described and evaluated for the first time.

Distributed by friends of the First Statement Press on a voluntary basis, these books have necessarily been limited in their sale. But they were widely and favourably reviewed, and their influence on critical opinion was considerable.

Influence and Achievements

The last few years have altered the situation which faced the writer in Canada in the thirties and at the beginning of this decade. If the audience of the modern writer is still very small, at least the publishers have been partially placated and the critics in many cases won over.

It would be difficult to analyze exactly the many factors contributing to this change. But there can be no doubt that the First Statement Press has exerted an important influence.

It has been the pioneer and has frequently done the spade work for the commercial publisher. The poetry of Louis Dudek was first introduced in the pages of the First Statement magazine, while the work of Patrick Anderson and Raymond Souster was first published in book form in the New Writers Series. It is notable that all three of these writers found their way by the mid-forties into the publishing list of one of the best-known Canadian publishers.

In the numerous anthologies published in Canada during the forties there has been a steadily growing recognition of the younger Canadian writers. The most comprehensive and most respected anthology of Canadian poetry devoted approximately half its 1948 edition to the work of this decade, although its first edition in 1944* gave relatively few pages to the same period. It seems not unfair to assume that the appearance in the interval of *Other Canadians*, the only comprehensive collection so far published devoted exclusively to the work of the forties exerted some influence on this large-scale revision of contents.

In 1948 a well-known commercial house published an anthology of the Canadian short story from its earliest beginnings to the present time. As representative of modern work the anthology included a story by P. K. Page, who contributed to early issues of the First Statement magazine, and a story by William McConnell who was first introduced to Canadian readers in the same magazine.

These and many other instances indicate that the First Statement Press has not only influenced the commercial publishers, but played a part in developing critical opinion.

Conclusion

In view of the facts outlined in this memorandum it seems evident that an organization such as the First Statement Press can render a service not easily performed by any other means. There is a task to be performed on the publishing heights, and there is this other task which can only be accomplished by organizations such as this press at the grass roots. Guided by the common denominators of taste the commercial publisher is often reluctant to publish the experimental writer and slow to accept the young writer. If he must produce cash results he must sometimes reject, perhaps against his own wishes, work of merit that promises no large sale. The very size of his organization and the diversity of his interests prevent him from establishing the immediate, continuous contact with young writers that is so essential to their full development.

Poetry cannot receive the attention that it deserves from the commercial publisher because its publication is seldom profitable. Poetry in Canada demands greater attention than it has received because it is, and remains, our most valid literary achievement.

*This refers to A. J. M. Smith's *The Book of Canadian Poetry*, the first edition of which was published in September of 1943.

Down below the level of the established publisher there must be a listening post responsive to vibrations of many kinds, to the strong and the less strong, to the familiar and to those that are unexpected. Such a listening post has in effect existed in Canada in the forties with the First Statement Press. Through literally thousands of contacts with young writers, and by encouraging talent wherever it was found, it was able to relay valuable messages to the enthusiast, to the critic, and eventually to the publisher.

Projects for which the First Statement Press Seeks Assistance

The First Statement Press seeks a grant of $4,000 a year to be used for the purposes outlined below, for a period of at least five years. It is suggested that the grant be administered by a committee of five members, consisting of John Sutherland, the editor of the First Statement Press; an editor chosen from the present editorial board of *Northern Review*; and three members acquainted with and sympathetic to the aims of the First Statement Press, whose selection should be approved by the Government.

Of the total of $4,000 a year, $2,000 a year is asked for *Northern Review*, to build from this magazine a national medium for creative literary expression and criticism, and to be administered each year in the following manner:

$250 to supplement the present prize of $100 offered by *Northern Review*, to create an annual prize of $350 for poetry.

$250 for a prize for the best short story published in *Northern Review* during the year. It is suggested that the judges for both awards be appointed by the administering committee.

$500 for small regular payments to all contributors to the magazine.

$400 for publicity, and for the purpose of enlarging the audience of the magazine.

$600 to help defray regular printing costs and to allow for a greater page length and for improvements in the format of *Northern Review*.

Of the grant of $4,000 a year for five years, $2,000 is asked for the First Statement Press, for the publication annually of two new volumes in its New Writers Series, one of them to be by a writer previously unpublished in book form. The selection of titles should be made by the editor of the First Statement Press subject to the approval of the administering committee.

It is respectfully submitted to the members of the Royal Commission that the implementation of these recommendations would stimulate a new and adventurous development of creative writing in Canada.

APPENDIX TO THE MEMORANDUM ON THE FIRST STATEMENT PRESS TO THE MEMBERS OF THE ROYAL COMMISSION ON THE ARTS, LETTERS AND SCIENCES

The brief previously presented has dealt with the activities, the organization and the aims of the voluntary, non-commercial association known as The First Statement Press. The publications of The First Statement Press include a series of book publications called The New Writers Series, which has provided a means of expression especially for younger Canadian poets, and a magazine publication now called *Northern Review*. In the following we would like to present some additional remarks on *Northern Review* and its relation to Canadian literary criticism.

It is assumed in the brief that Canadian writing cannot exist in a healthy state in the absence of any adequate outlet of expression for the best contemporary writing. Such an outlet does not exist in the newspaper publications, nor in the popular magazines nor in the quarterlies published by the universities in Canada. The one type of publication which can provide this outlet in Canada is the "little magazine" such as *Northern Review*. The Royal Commission is asked in the brief to recommend support specifically for *Northern Review* for several reasons. It is the only Canadian "little magazine" publishing both fiction and poetry. Originally produced under the name of *First Statement,* and since 1945 as *Northern Review,* the magazine is now beginning its eighth year of publication. In the past seven years it has grown from a mimeographed sheet of eight pages to its present printed format of nearly sixty pages, and has recently been enlarged and broadened in scope. It has sought to acknowledge the bond between the English-Canadian and French-Canadian writer, and it looks toward their closer relationship. In its new, enlarged format it is fulfilling its purpose of providing a medium for contemporary writing of value wherever it is written in Canada.

Nevertheless the position of a magazine such as *Northern Review* is necessarily tenuous. The response to any non-commercial publication must be very limited. We know that the life of the "little magazine" in every country is likely to be erratic and brief, and this is especially true of the "little magazine" in Canada. We have only three publications of this kind in Canada at present, two magazines of verse and *Northern Review,* and we have no assurance that these magazines will continue to appear or be in a position to provide the medium for contemporary writing that is so necessary.

The reasons why *Northern Review* has been able to persist for seven years, and continued to grow, are outlined in the brief. The issues of the magazine are hand-set and printed by the editor himself with the printing equipment of The First Statement Press which he owns, and the whole work of production and distribution is done on a voluntary basis. But a magazine cannot be produced in a fully satisfactory manner by these means, nor can it be so produced with the assurance of continuance.

There is another and even more important reason why support is asked for *Northern Review*: It is the only magazine of any kind in Canada which has consistently provided from issue to issue through the last decade a medium for criticism of the work of our contemporary poets and prose-writers. It is, in addition, the only publication which has consistently focussed attention on the state of our literary criticism, and sought to examine its limitations and provide it with a direction.

The development of a literature is linked in the closest possible way with that of its criticism. We cannot have a healthy or growing literature except in the climate of an intelligent and informed opinion, and we cannot have such a climate of opinion without direction from criticism itself. Any review of English-Canadian criticism must perforce be a review of the criticism concerned with poetry. So lacking are we in awareness of our own literature, that criticism of the Canadian novel is almost non-existent. Although the body of criticism concerned with poetry is insufficient in quantity, it demonstrates certain limitations in the attitude of English-speaking Canadians to their own literature.

These are some of the relevant facts regarding this criticism:

1. It is generally lacking in any determined spirit of enquiry. It has usually limited its field of enquiry to a narrow area, and has failed to realize that the whole field of a literature is relevant to critical discussion especially where a relatively undeveloped literature such as our own is concerned. It has therefore left almost untouched the work of some of our most important writers.

2. Our criticism has been almost totally unable to supply us with any definition of the characteristics peculiar to Canadian literature, and indeed it has made no serious effort to do so. In effect therefore, it has been left without even the elementary assurance that it has a subject-matter. For unless it is clear that Canadian literature forms a distinct entity, the motive for criticism of this literature rather than the more highly-developed literatures of other countries must be lacking.

3. Our criticism, which has generally been based on the wrong kind of patriotism, or been conducted by persons polishing Ph.D.s, has consistently and harmfully over-estimated the achievement of Canadian literature. The words "major" and "great" have been liberally bestowed by critics who were complacent enough to suppose that Canadian writing could be judged by merely local standards rather than by the standards which apply to writing everywhere. They have been more concerned with boosting our writers than with cultivating an objective point of view.

4. Our critics have always been reluctant to engage in the detailed criticism of the individual writer which should be the main task of criticism in any country. They have been ready to suppose that an innocuous generalization, or a few fitting words of introduction, could be a substitute for genuine criticism. Thus, while they are in haste to make flattering judgments, they have generally deprived themselves of the basis from which to make judgments of any kind.

5. Finally, there is a time-lag so marked in Canadian criticism that it is customarily concerned with Canadian writing only when it is already a matter of history. It has totally failed to provide contemporary writing with the kind of response that is so necessary to its full development.

Generally speaking, there is insufficient recognition of the importance of and need for criticism in Canada. While it is necessary to encourage the Canadian writer in every possible way, for his position is often desperate, we must provide encouragement that is strengthened by informed and courageous opinion. The indefinite distribution of favours and bounties in the absence of criticism will only serve to depress the quality of our literature in the long run.

The First Statement Press and *Northern Review* have made constant efforts to provide a medium for the contemporary Canadian writer over the past seven years. Nevertheless the main purpose of both has been to encourage by the means available to them the development of a more serious criticism in Canada.

John Sutherland, *Brief to the Royal Commission on National Development in the Arts, Letters and Sciences,* submitted by *Northern Review* and First Statement Press, November 1949.

ROBERT WEAVER

It must have been in 1946 that I first saw a copy of *Northern Review*. And it must have been soon afterwards that John Sutherland and I began a fairly steady correspondence. I thought of writing some essays about the younger short-story writers, and he offered to publish them in his magazine; but somehow they were never written. Then we met a few times in Montreal, and one night we were going to run off copies of F. R. Scott's *The Canadian Authors Meet* and distribute them secretly the next morning at the annual convention of the CAA. But the party went on too long. Sutherland liked a drink, he smoked little cigars, and—rankest heresy in the literary world—he occasionally played golf. (We never had the game we said we must play together.)

When John Sutherland died in Toronto on Labour Day weekend, his study of E. J. Pratt, *The Poetry of E. J. Pratt: A New Interpretation,* had just been published, and a final issue of his magazine *Northern Review* had only recently appeared. He was thirty-seven, yet he had been an editor and critic for nearly fifteen years. He knew that he was going to die, and it was typical of his sense of dedication that he spent the last summer of his life working on his book and on the last issue of his magazine.

As a critic and editor, Sutherland was frank and outspoken, and we ought to pay him the compliment, even now, of writing about his career with some of his own honesty. His beliefs changed radically over the years, and *Northern Review* disappointed or alienated some of its early supporters. I was among those who were disappointed. He was always intense and dedicated, but in the last years of his life he grew increasingly sombre and his literary opinions hardened. He often showed a surprising lack of curiosity about writers who did not obviously fit in with his immediate interests, but like any good editor he published work in *Northern Review* which certainly didn't always reflect his own prejudices.

John Sutherland was an editor, a critic, occasionally a poet. He was also a kind of literary patron, for *Northern Review* was able to survive as a forum for writers simply because he and his wife Audrey were willing to make continual sacrifices for the magazine. It's doubtful whether *Northern Review* ever had five hundred subscribers, and for a number of years it kept going by appealing to its readers to contribute to a sustaining fund. But its influence was much greater than its circulation, and in the files of the magazine are poems and short stories which are bound to be reprinted in discriminating anthologies of contemporary Canadian writing. As Sutherland once wrote of magazines like *Northern Review:* "They are in perpetual search of money, yet they continue to appear without it. For them the economic problem is either everything or nothing." Yet the difficulty wasn't that the field was so crowded: for most of its existence *Northern Review* was the *only* general literary magazine being published in English Canada.

It all began in 1941. In Vancouver Alan Crawley brought out the first issue of his poetry quarterly *Contemporary Verse,* and a few months later two mimeographed "little magazines" appeared in Montreal: *Preview* and Sutherland's *First Statement.** The Montreal writers who were associated with the two magazines were mostly poets who had read W. H. Auden, Stephen Spender, and the other English poets of the thirties. Most of them had leftist political views and a vision of a better world after the war. The magazines were founded to do battle for writers who expected short shrift from the Toronto commercial magazines and publishers. In 1945 *Preview* and *First Statement* were combined to form *Northern Review,* whose editors and regional editors included almost all the new poets. But not long afterwards, John Sutherland wrote a bitter review of a book of poems by Robert Finch, who had had the misfortune to win the Governor-General's Award for Poetry in a year when two or three of the *Northern Review* poets were eligible. When the review appeared, half a dozen of the poet-editors took to the woods.

Sutherland tried to capture the mood of those years with a book, *Other Canadians,* which had the sub-title "An Anthology of the New Poetry in Canada 1940-1946." He contributed a long introduction, in which he attacked the poet and editor A. J. M. Smith for his views on Canadian writing, ridiculed the Canadian Authors' Association, poked fun at Mr. Smith's religious sympathies, forecast the probable effect on Canadian writing of the (inevitable) coming of socialism to Canada, and (most significantly, I think) suggested that in the future, Canadian writers were more likely to be influenced by their American contemporaries than by literary developments overseas.

It was a ringing manifesto, and it had a curious aftermath. I believe that *Other Canadians* was intended to appear in 1946, but that an accident delayed its publication for three years. Two years after that, in 1951, Sutherland published an essay on "The Past Decade in Canadian Poetry" in *Northern Review,* and ruefully confessed that a number of the poets he had included in *Other Canadians* had stopped writing; that others had abandoned politics for a vaguely defined religious commitment; and that the social and political beliefs of the whole movement of new poets now seemed to him to have had

---

*Preview and *First Statement* appeared not just ". . . a few months later . . ." but, more accurately, in March and September of 1942 respectively, which makes it a *year* later in the case of *First Statement.*

shallow roots. Today much of the poetry in *Other Canadians* and much of Sutherland's introduction seems naïve and out of date even for the early forties. (There seems to be about a ten-year lag before new literary tendencies filter into Canada.) But Sutherland's willingness to write off so much of his own past was admirable.

Eventually Sutherland began to make *Northern Review* a more general and a more national literary magazine. In the next few years he published a number of good short stories, more critical essays and reviews, and comment about painting, music, radio, and the movies. This was sensible, since it is clear that in the post-war world the embattled "little magazine" is becoming an anachronism, and that in Canada we need magazines to fill some of the space that yawns between, say, the university quarterlies and *Maclean's*. Finally Sutherland became a Roman Catholic, and Roman Catholic and neo-conservative writers from England and the United States began to fill much of his magazine.

While I was re-reading *Northern Review* this fall I noticed two omissions from the magazine that seemed not only to reflect Sutherland's own attitudes but also the limitations of the group of writers with which he was first associated. An outsider meeting the Montreal poets notices at once that they show little interest in other writers who happen not to be poets, and as far as I can discover, *Northern Review* published in a decade only one substantial critical article about a Canadian novelist—or any novelist, for that matter. Even more surprising is the discovery that in those ten years *Northern Review* seems to have published no work from French Canada and no comment on writing by French Canadians with the exception of a small group of poems by Anne Hebert translated by F. R. Scott. Montreal is supposed to be the Canadian city where French and English-speaking writers and intellectuals are able to meet, but most translations of French-Canadian writing have been made and published in New York and—of all places—Ontario.

As I re-read *Northern Review* it was also plain to what extent its editor was also its most interesting critic and commentator on the literary scene. It is his critical essays and reviews (often published as "Canadian Comment") that give the magazine its real character. (One of the paradoxes of literary magazines is that they are generally most interesting because of their critical articles and reviews, and that it takes the exceptional poem or short story to capture the reader's imagination.) Sutherland's criticism forms the only serious and sustained discussion we have of the poets who emerged in Canada in the dozen years after 1941. He was at his best when he was doing a detailed, specific reading of the texts; he was not nearly as convincing,

I think, when an ideology took over. He did the sort of homework not many Canadian critics bother to attempt: for example, his review of James Reaney's *The Red Heart*, for which he took the trouble to compare specific poems with earlier and different versions that had appeared in the literary magazines. Sutherland's argument was that in most cases the rewritten poem was inferior to the original, and I think he made his case.

Sutherland's great virtue as critic and editor was that he remained free of the official entanglements that bedevil literary men in this small country. His economic insecurity as publisher of *Northern Review* had its compensations. His misfortune was that lack of sympathy and curiosity kept him from using his freedom to the full. Right up to the final issue of his magazine he shows a suspicion of the academic world's tendency to move in on Canadian writing, and in a country where most serious critics are university teachers he stands as one of the few exceptions. It's a pity he didn't write a polemic about the increase of university courses on Canadian literature, the emergence of young academics whose Ph.D.s are granted for a thesis on some aspect of Canadian writing, and what this is likely to do to a literature that has still the shakiest of foundations. Sutherland could be an infuriating critic, he could be wrong, he could be narrow; but he couldn't have written a book like E. K. Brown's *On Canadian Poetry,* which is also often wrong (see the comments on Morley Callaghan), as well as cautious, pallid, and alas, the likely progenitor of a whole school of Canadian criticism.

I have left my comment* about Sutherland's study of E. J. Pratt* to the end. It is a book that we must admire for its detailed and loving analysis of a writer to whom the critic became in the end wholly committed. But it belongs to Sutherland's ideological criticism, and unless one shares his views it isn't convincing. It tells us more about the critic's emotional and intellectual journey than about the poet who became the focal point of that journey. Even if Sutherland had lived, this book would have had no successor: his disillusionment with Canadian writing was profound. We cannot tell what caused that disillusionment (too much faith in the beginning? too many years of dreary manuscripts? some private torment?), but it was a fitting end to John Sutherland's dedicated career that he should believe he had discovered in this country one writer he cared to number among "the few significant poets of the time."

*John Sutherland, *The Poetry of E. J. Pratt: A New Interpretation* (Toronto: Ryerson, 1956).

Robert Weaver, "John Sutherland and *Northern Review,*" *Tamarack Review,* No. 2, Winter 1957.

New Critical Currents

A. J. M. Smith in 1928 had called for "the militant critic." By 1947 his prophecy had not only been fulfilled but he himself had come to feel the lance of one such critic in John Sutherland's Introduction to *Other Canadians*. The period of the forties was one of polemics and militant writing; poets as a body were doctrinaire, aggressive, and in revolt against society to an extent never seen before in Canadian literature (though not as much in revolt as the next generation was to be): the beginnings of several significant lines of thought about our literature were opened up and partly developed in this period.

The article by Northrop Frye reviewing Smith's anthology *The Book of Canadian Poetry* (1943) may be contrasted with Sutherland's critique. What may not be obvious at first sight is that Dr. Frye in this article holds a position directly opposed to that of John Sutherland. The question whether "poets should be original . . ." or "aboriginal" is in effect aimed against the school of realism and of American orientation in poetry as represented by Sutherland and his group, although Dr. Frye was probably not conscious of this opposition. He describes the devotees of "Tarzanism" as those who "have sought for the primitive and direct and have tried to avoid the consciously literary and speak the language of the common man." The later development of our poetry in writers like Souster, Layton, Purdy, Nowlan, Acorn and the *Tish* poets (see Section VIII) would argue that Dr. Frye's essay underestimated the possibilities of this kind of poetry; while others, Reaney, Jay Macpherson, Le Pan, Watson and Mandel may well represent the traditionalist line of descent so much approved by A. J. M. Smith and Dr. Frye. The controversies of the 1940s therefore lay the ground for the pattern of development in our poetry since that time.

Dr. Frye, however, applies to Canadian poetry a serious and impressive philosophical interpretation. This is an important venture in that it is the first attempt at a theory of Canadian literature on large comprehensive lines. The view that a particular conception of nature —nature as cruel, indifferent, or violent—is recurrent in our poetry presents a significant and daring hypothesis. The same idea, of course, can be treated historically and related to central currents of modern thought. It then appears as a stage in the disillusionment of modern man with the romantic idea of nature—from romantic "pantheism" to existentialist "meaninglessness"—and the idea can be carried further to possible forms of reconstruction.

The article by F. R. Scott is a good example of the political focus of writing in the little magazines at this time. He confirms the charges against the CAA that we have already seen in Leo Kennedy, and defines the needs of poetry in terms of the historical moment. But perhaps most striking of all is Scott's affirmation of Canada's independent national status and his rejection of colonialism in literature.

Neufville Shaw was an editor and contributor to *Preview* as well as a poet. One should note the ironic tone, the bitter of discontent, in this essay so characteristic of the period: the poetry of the past is treated with curt dismissal. Shaw also differs with Smith in the evaluation of Pratt, a judgment that Smith himself revised in later editions of his anthology (in the 1957 edition Pratt becomes a "unique" poet where he had formerly been "the greatest of contemporary poets"). Finally, despite the characteristic political orientation, a note of caution is sounded about "political sloganry." The poetry of this period has often been disparaged for its simplistic political bias. It may be that the real situation contained more complex mixtures of ideas and social attitudes than this kind of criticism allows.

The article on "Academic Literature" written in 1944 struck a chord which has since resounded frequently, with pros and cons, in Canadian criticism and poetry. On the international level, *Partisan Review* has carried a full scale debate on the question, while in Canada Phyllis Webb made an investigation of the poet's profession (*Queen's Quarterly*, Winter 1955), and the Humanities Association of Canada published a symposium on "The Poet and the University" in its *Bulletin* of January 1957. But the subject was still new in 1944. The modern poets—Yeats, Eliot, Pound, Cummings, Crane, et cetera —were not attached to universities; but in the 1940s it became clear that the "homelessness" of the modern intellectual was being replaced by the doubtful comforts of the university. It was a subject for debate, confused by "anti-academic" attitudes, and accusations of "anti-intellectualism"—but the real issue was poetry and the vitality of the poet's imagination. The easy jibe that even poets most critical of the academies frequently become teachers in universities misses the point. Poets in the university are just as likely in the long run to transform the academy in the interests of creative scholarship and good writing as they are to be influenced by the academic routines. The only question is whether good poetry results.

The final selections here, a review by John Sutherland and other items from *Northern Review* require a note of explanation. In 1945 the magazines *Preview* and *First Statement* were merged to form *Northern Review*, a new magazine with a large editorial board consisting of the two branches of the poetry movement in Montreal. Sutherland's review of Robert Finch's Governor-General's Award-winning book created a rift in the editorial board, and ended in the resignation of the majority of its members. The result of this was that the Montreal situation reverted to the earlier "two-camp" alignment, with the exception that the *Previewites* were now without a magazine, while John Sutherland was left to edit *Northern Review* largely on his own.

NORTHROP FRYE

The appearance of Mr. A. J. M. Smith's new anthology* is an important event in Canadian literature. For instead of confining his reading to previous compilations, as most anthologists do, he has made a first-hand study of the whole English field with unflagging industry and unfaltering taste. A straightforward research job is simple enough to do if one has the time: but Mr. Smith has done something far more difficult than research. He had to read through an enormous mass of poetry ranging from the lousy to the exquisite, the great bulk of which was that kind of placid mediocrity which is always good verse and just near enough to good poetry to need an expert to detect its flat ring. He had to pronounce on all this not only with a consistent judgment but also with historical sense. He had to remember that a modern poet may hold deeply and sincerely to the more enlightened political views and become so gnarled and cryptic an intellectual that he cannot even understand himself, and still be just as conventional a minor poet as the most twittering Victorian songbird. In dealing with many of the older writers, Campbell for instance, or Carman, he had to trace the thin gold vein of real imagination through a rocky mass of what can only be called a gift of metrical gab. He had to remember that occasionally a bad poem is of all the greater cultural significance for being bad, and therefore should go in. In judging his younger contemporaries he had to remember both that a flawed talent is better than a flawless lack of it and that still it is performance and not "promise" that makes the poet, of whatever age.

*A. J. M. Smith, *The Book of Canadian Poetry* (Toronto: Gage, 1943), 452 pp.

It is no easy job; but Mr. Smith has, on the whole, done it. Of course there are omissions, of which he is probably more acutely aware than his readers. In any case anthologies ought to have blank pages at the end on which the reader may copy his own neglected favourites. In my judgment, a few people are in who might well have been out, and a few out who might well have been in: some dull poems are included and many good ones are not; and one or two poets have been rather unfairly treated—including, I should say, one A. J. M. Smith. But no kind of book is easier to attack than an anthology; and in any case the importance of this one is not so much in the number or merits of the poems included as in the critical revaluations it makes. Mr. Smith's study of the pre-Confederation poets is the only one that has been made from anything like a modern point of view. In Charles Heavysege he has unearthed —the word will not be too strong for most of his readers—a genuine Canadian Beddoes, a poet of impressive power and originality: and he has given Isabella Crawford enough space to show that she is one of the subtlest poets that Canada has produced. The more famous writers of the so-called Maple Leaf school come down to a slightly more modest estimate, and though Mr. Smith is scrupulously fair to them, he cannot and does not avoid saying that they talked too much and sang too little, or sang too much and thought too little. In any case the supremacy of Lampman over the whole group comes out very clearly. In the next period Pratt gets his deserved prominence, and the younger poets are generously represented. Here is, in short, what Canada can do: the reader who does not like this book simply does not like Canadian poetry, and will not be well advised to read further. Of course, as Mr. Smith says in his Preface, French-Canadian poetry is a separate job—still to be done, I should think, for Fournier's *Anthologie des Poètes Canadiens* is, as its editor Asselin frankly admits, more a collection of poets than of poems. But we cannot leave the French out of our poetry any more than we can leave Morrice or Gagnon out of our painting, and one can only hope for some French-speaking philanthropist to produce a companion volume.

The thing that impresses me is the unity of tone which the book has, and to which nearly all the poets in various ways contribute. Of course any anthologist can produce a false illusion of unity by simply being a critic of limited sympathies, responding only to certain kinds of techniques or subject matter. But Mr. Smith is obviously not that: his notes and introduction show a wide tolerance, and his selections, though bold and independent, are certainly not precious. No: the unity of tone must come from the material itself, and the anthology thus unconsciously proves the existence of a definable Canadian genius (I use this word in a general sense) which is neither British nor American but, for all its echoes and imitations and second-hand ideas, peculiarly our own.

Now admittedly a great deal of useless yammering has been concerned with the "truly Canadian" qualities of our literature, and one's first instinct is to avoid the whole question. Of course what is "peculiarly our own" is not what is accidentally our own, and a poet may talk forever about forests and prairies and snow and the Land of the North and not be any more Canadian than he will be Australian if he writes a sonnet on a kangaroo. One of F. R. Scott's poems included by Mr. Smith notes a tendency on the part of minor poets to "paint the native maple." This is like saying that because the quintuplets are Canadian, producing children in litters is a Canadian characteristic. Nevertheless, no one who knows the country will deny that there is something, say an attitude of mind, distinctively Canadian, and while Canadian speech is American, there is a recognizable Canadian accent in the more highly organized speech of its poetry. Certainly if a Canadian poet consciously tries to avoid being Canadian, he will sound like nothing on earth. For, whatever may be true of painting or music, poetry is not a citizen of the world: it is conditioned by language, and flourishes best within a national unit. "Humanity" is an abstract idea, not a poetic image. But whether Canada is really a national unit in any sense that has a meaning for culture I could not decide myself until I saw Mr. Smith's book; and even then one has misgivings. The patriotic avarice that claims every European as "Canadian" who stopped off at a Canadian station for a ham sandwich on his way to the States, is, no doubt, ridiculous; but apart from that, does not any talk about Canadian poetry lead to some loss of perspective, some heavy spotlighting of rather pallid faces? Every Canadian has some feeling of sparseness when he compares, for example, Canada's fifth largest city, which I believe is Hamilton, with the fifth largest across the line, which I believe is Los Angeles. And the same is true of poetry. Every issue of the *New Yorker* or *New Republic,* to say nothing of the magazines which really go in for poetry contains at least one poem which is technically on a level with five-sixths of Mr. Smith's book. With so luxuriant a greenhouse next door, why bother to climb mountains to look for the odd bit of edelweiss? The only answer is, I suppose, that in what Canadian poets have tried to do there is an interest for Canadian readers much deeper than what the achievement in itself justifies.

The qualities of our poetry that appear from this book to be distinctively Canadian are not those that one readily thinks of: a fact which was an additional obstacle in Mr. Smith's path. For Canada is more than most countries a milieu in which certain preconceived literary stereotypes are likely to interpose between the imagination and the expression it achieves. What a poet's imagination actually can produce and what the poet thinks it ought to produce are often very different things. They never should be, but they sometimes are; and it is hard to judge accurately the work of a man who is a genuine poet but whose poetry only glints here and there out of a mass of verse on conventional themes he has persuaded himself he should be celebrating. If a poet is a patriot, for instance, there may be two natures within him, one scribbling ready-made patriotic doggerel and the other trying to communicate the real feelings his country inspires him with. If he is religious, the poet in him may reach God in very subtle ways; but the man in him who is not a poet may be a more commonplace person, shocked by his own poetic boldness. If he is revolutionary, the poet in him may have to argue with a Philistine materialist also in him who does not really see the point of poetry at all. This is at least one reason why so much patriotic, religious and revolutionary verse is bad.

Now this creative schizophrenia is, we have said, common in Canada, and the most obvious reason for it is the fact that Canada is not only a nation but a colony in an empire. I have said that culture seems to flourish best in national units, which implies that the empire is too big and the province too small for major literature. I know of no poet, with the very dubious exception of Virgil, who has made great poetry out of what Shakespeare calls "the imperial theme": in Kipling, for instance, this theme is largely a praise of machinery, and of the Robot tendencies within the human mind. The province or region, on the other hand, is usually a vestigial curiosity to be written up by some nostalgic tourist. The imperial and the regional are both inherently anti-poetic environments, yet they go hand in hand; and together they make up what I call the colonial in Canadian life.

This colonial tendency has been sharpened by the French-English split, the English having tended to specialize in the imperial and the French in the regional aspects of it. The French are on the whole the worse off by this arrangement, which has made Quebec into a cute tourist resort full of ye quainte junke made by real peasants, all of whom go to church and say their prayers like the children they are, and love their land and tell folk tales and sing ballads just as the fashionable novelists in the cities say they do. True, I have never met a French-Canadian who liked to be thought of as an animated antique, nor do I expect to: yet the sentimental haze in which the European author of *Maria Chapdelaine* saw the country is still quite seriously accepted by Canadians, English and French alike, as authentic. A corresponding imperial preoccupation in English poets leads to much clearing of forests and planting of crops and tapping vast natural resources: a grim earnestness of expansion which seems almost more German than British. The more naïve expressions of this do not get into Mr. Smith's book. Instead, he sets Isabella Crawford's song, "Bite Deep and Wide, O Axe, the Tree," in its proper context, a viciously ironic one; and Anne Marriott's "The Wind Our Enemy" and Birney's "Anglo-Saxon Street" are also there to indicate that if we sow the wind of empire with too little forethought we shall reap a dusty whirlwind of arid squalor.

The colonial position of Canada is therefore a frostbite at the roots of the Canadian imagination, and it produces a disease for which I think the best name is prudery. By this I do not mean reticence in sexual matters: I mean the instinct to seek a conventional or commonplace expression of an idea. Prudery that keeps the orthodox poet from making a personal recreation of his orthodoxy: prudery that prevents the heretic from forming an articulate heresy that will shock: prudery that makes a radical stutter and gargle over all realities that are not physical: prudery that chokes off social criticism for fear some other group of Canadians will take advantage of it. One sees this perhaps most clearly in religion, because of the fact that the division of language and race is approximately one of religion also. Mr. Smith has included a religious poem called "Littlewit and Loftus," which, though in some respects a bad poem, is at any rate not a prudish one in the above sense: it ends with the authentic scream of the disembodied evangelical banshee who has cut herself loose from this world and who has the sense of release that goes with that, even if she is not wholly sure what world she is now in. It is a prickly cactus in a desert of bumbling platitude and the pouring of unctuous oil on untroubled waters; or else, as in Bliss Carman, prayers of a stentorian vagueness addressed to some kind of scholar-gypsy God.

I wish I could say that the tighter grip of religion on the French has improved matters there; but it has done nothing of the kind. In French poetry too one feels that the Church is often most vividly conceived not as catholic but as a local palladium to be defended for political reasons: as a part of the parochial intrigue which is given the title of "nationalism." The type of prudery appropriate to this is a facile and mawkish piety. In short, the imperial tendency may call itself "Protestant" and the regional one "Catholic"; but as long as both are colonial, both will be essentially sectarian. Similarly, the imperial tendency may call itself British and the regional one French; but as long as both are colonial, these words will have only a sectional meaning. It is an obvious paradox in Canadian life that the more colonial the English or French-speaking Canadian is, and the more he distrusts the other half of his country, the more artificial his relation to the real Britain or France becomes. The French-Canadian who translates "British Columbia" as "Colombie canadienne" and flies the tricolor of the French Revolution on holidays, and the English-Canadian who holds that anything short of instant acquiescence in every decision of the British Foreign Office is treason, are the furthest of all Canadians from the culture of what they allege to be their mother countries.

But even when the Canadian poet has got rid of colonial cant, there are two North American dragons to slay. One is the parrotted cliché that this is a "new" country and that we must spend centuries cutting forests and building roads before we can enjoy the by-products of settled leisure. But Canada is not "new" or "young": it is exactly the same age as any other country under a system of industrial capitalism; and even if it were, a reluctance to write poetry is not a sign of youth but of decadence. Savages have poetry: the Pilgrim Fathers, who really were pioneers, started writing almost as soon as they landed. It is only from the exhausted loins of the half-dead masses of people in modern cities that such weary ideas are born.

The other fallacy concerns the imaginative process itself, and may be called the Ferdinand the Bull theory of poetry. This theory talks about a first-hand contact with life as opposed to a second-hand contact with it through books, and assumes that the true poet will go into the fields and smell the flowers and not spoil the freshness of his vision by ruining his eyesight on books. However, practically all important poetry has been the fruit of endless study and reading, for poets as a class are and must be, as an Elizabethan critic said, "curious universal scholars." There are exceptions to this rule, but they prove it; and it is silly to insist on them. In looking over Mr. Smith's book one is struck immediately by the predominance of university and professional people, and it is in the classical scholarship of Lampman, the encyclopaedic erudition of Crémazie which is said to have included Sanscrit, and the patient research and documentation of Pratt's *Brébeuf* and sea narratives, that Canadian poetry has become most articulate. There is nothing especially Canadian about this, but one point may be noted. To an English poet, the tradition of his own country and language proceeds in a direct chronological line down to himself, and that in its turn is part of a gigantic funnel of tradition extending back to Homer and the Old Testament. But to a Canadian, broken off from this linear sequence and having none of his own, the traditions of Europe appear as a kaleidoscopic whirl with no definite shape or meaning, but with a profound irony lurking in its varied and conflicting patterns. The clearest statement of this is in that superb fantasy *The Witches' Brew*, Pratt's first major effort, a poem of which apparently I have a higher opinion than Mr. Smith. It is also to be found, I think, in the elaborate Rabbinical apparatus of Klein.

American even more than Canadian poetry has been deeply affected by the clash between two irreconcileable views of literature: the view that poets should be original and the view that they should be aboriginal. Originality is largely a matter of returning to origins, of studying and imitating the great poets of the past. But many fine American poets have been damaged and in some cases spoiled by a fetish of novelty: they have sought for the primitive and direct and have tried to avoid the consciously literary and speak the language of the common man. As the language of the common man is chiefly commonplace, the result has been for the most part disastrous. And here is one case where failing to achieve a virtue has really warded off a vice. There has on the whole been little Tarzanism in Canadian poetry. One is surprised to find how few really good Canadian poets have thought that getting out of cities into God's great outdoors really brings one closer to the source of inspiration. One reason for this is that there has been no revolution in Canada and less sense of building up a new land into what the American Constitution calls a more perfect state. A certain abdication of political responsibility is sharply reflected in our poetry, and is by no means always harmful to it. We can see this clearly if we compare Bliss Carman with his American friend Hovey, who sang not only of freedom and the open road but also of America's duty to occupy the Philippines and open up the Pacific. The Canadian likes to be objective about Americans, and likes to feel that he can see a bit of Sam Slick in every Yankee: as a North American, therefore, he has a good seat on the revolutionary sidelines, and his poetic tendencies, reflective, observant, humorous, critical and quite frankly traditional, show it.

The closest analogy to Canadian poetry in American literature is, as one would expect, in the pre-1776 period: in Anne Bradstreet and Philip Freneau and the Hartford Wits. We have many excellent counterparts to these, and to the tradition that runs through Emerson, but few if any good counterparts to Whitman, Sandburg, Lindsay, Jeffers or MacLeish. Early American poetry is traditional, but its tradition is a great one: and when the Americans gained maturity in government they lost some in poetry; for there is an assurance and subtlety in Bradstreet and Freneau that Longfellow and Whittier and many of those mentioned above do not possess. This is not to say that the best American poetry appeared before 1776, but as we seem to be stuck with at least some colonial characteristics, we may as well appreciate what virtues they have.

Nature in Canadian poetry, then, has little of the vagueness of great open spaces in it: that is very seldom material that the imagination can use. One finds rather an intent and closely focussed vision, often on something in itself quite unimportant: in Birney's slug, Finch's station platform, the clairvoyance of hatred in MacKay's "I Wish My Tongue Were a Quiver," Hambleton's sharply etched picture of salmon fishing. The first poet Mr. Smith includes, the Canadian Oliver Goldsmith, makes an accurate inventory of a country store, and he sets a tone which the rest of the book bears out. The vocabulary and diction correspond: the snap and crackle of frosty words, some stiff with learning and others bright with concreteness, is heard wherever there is the mental excitement of real creation, though of course most obviously where the subject suggests it: in, for instance, Charles Bruce's "Immediates":

> An ageless land and sea conspire
> To smooth the imperfect mould of birth;
> While freezing spray and drying fire
> Translate the inexplicit earth.

or in P. K. Page's "Stenographers":

> In the felt of the morning, the calico minded,
> sufficiently starched, insert papers, hit keys,
> efficient and sure as their adding machines.

But, according to Mr. Smith's book, the outstanding achievement of Canadian poetry is in the evocation of stark terror. Not a coward's terror, of course; but a controlled vision of the causes of cowardice. The immediate source of this is obviously the frightening loneliness of a huge and thinly-settled country. When all the intelligence, morality, reverence and simian cunning of man confronts a sphinx-like riddle of the indefinite like the Canadian winter the man seems as helpless as a trapped mink and as lonely as a loon. His thrifty little heaps of civilized values look pitiful beside nature's apparently meaningless power to waste and destroy on a superhuman scale, and such a nature suggests an equally ruthless and subconscious God, or else no God. In Wilfred Campbell, for instance, the Canadian winter expands into a kind of frozen hell of utter moral nihilism:

> Lands that loom like spectres, white regions
> of winter,
> > Wastes of desolate woods, deserts of water and
> > shore;
> A world of winter and death, within these regions
> who enter,
> > Lost to summer and life, go to return no more.

And the winter is only one symbol, though a very obvious one, of the central theme of Canadian poetry: the riddle of what a character in Mair's "Tecumseh" calls "inexplicable life." It is really a riddle of inexplicable death: the fact that life struggles and suffers in a nature which is blankly indifferent to it. Human beings set a high value on their own lives which is obviously not accepted in the world beyond their palisades. They may become hurt and whimper that nature is cruel to them: but the honest poet does not see cruelty: he sees only a stolid unconsciousness. The human demands that Patrick Anderson's Joe hurls at nature are answered by "a feast of no"; a negation with neither sympathy nor malice in it. In Birney's "David" a terrible tragedy of wasted life and blasted youth is enacted on a glacier, but there is no "pathetic fallacy" about the cruelty of the glacier or of whatever gods may be in charge of it. It is just a glacier. D. C. Scott's "Piper of Arll" is located in an elusive fairyland, but the riddle of inexplicable death is still at the heart of the poem. The same theme is of course clearer still in Pratt's sea narrative, especially the "Titanic".

Sometimes this theme modulates into a wry and sardonic humour. In the laughter of that rare spirit, Standish O'Grady, who in his picture of freezing Canadians huddling around "their simpering stove" has struck out one of the wittiest phrases in the book, something rather sharper sounds across the laughter:

> Here the rough Bear subsists his winter year,
> And licks his paw and finds no better fare.

In Drummond's finest poem, "The Wreck of the Julie Plante," the grim humour of the ballad expresses the same tragedy of life destroyed by unconsciousness that we find in Pratt and Birney:

> For de win she blow lak hurricane,
> Bimeby she blow some more.

Tim MacInnes has the same kind of humour, though the context is often fantastic, and his "Zalinka" is a parody of Poe which somehow manages to convey the same kind of disturbing eeriness. But whether humorous or not, even in our most decorous poets there are likely to be the most startling flashes of menace and fear. A placid poem of Charles G. D. Roberts about mowing is suddenly punctuated by the line "The crying knives glide on; the green swath lies." Archdeacon Scott writes a little poem on Easter Island statues which ends in a way that will lift your back hair.

But the poetic imagination cannot remain for long content with this faceless mask of unconsciousness. Nature is not all glacier and iceberg and hurricane; and while there is no conscious cruelty in it, there is certainly a suffering that we can interpret as cruelty. Hence the poet begins to animate nature with an evil or at least sinister power: night in Heavysege becomes a cacodemon, and spring in Dorothy Livesay a crouching monster. Mr. Smith's book is full of ghosts and unseen watchers and spiritual winds: a certain amount of this is faking, but not all: Lampman's "In November," with its ghastly dead mullens and the wonderful *danse macabre* in which it closes, is no fake. The "crying in the dark" in Lampman's "Midnight," the dead hunter in Eustace Ross's "The Death," the dead "lovely thing" in Neil Tracey's poem, the married corpses in Leo Kennedy's "Epithalamium": all these are visions, not only of a riddle of inexplicable death, but of a riddle of inexplicable evil. Sometimes, of course, this evil takes an easily recognized form: the Indians in Joseph Howe's spirited narrative and the drought wind in Anne Marriott have no spectral overtones. But it is obvious that man must be included in this aspect of the riddle, as it is merely fanciful to separate conscious malice from the human mind. Whatever sinister lurks in nature lurks also in us and Tom MacInnes's "tiger of desire" and the praying mantis of a remarkable poem by Anne Dalton have been transformed into mental demons.

The unconscious horror of nature and the subconscious horrors of the mind thus coincide: this amalgamation is the basis of symbolism on which nearly all Pratt's poetry is founded. The fumbling and clumsy monsters of his "Pliocene Armageddon" who are simply incarnate wills to mutual destruction, are the same monsters that beget Nazism and inspire "The Fable of the Goats"; and in the fine "Silences," which Mr. Smith includes, civilized life is seen geologically as merely one clock-tick in aeons of ferocity. The waste of life in the death of the Cachalot and the waste of courage and sanctity in the killing of the Jesuit missionaries are tragedies of a unique kind in modern poetry: like the tragedy of Job, they seem to move upward to a vision of a monstrous Leviathan, a power of chaotic nihilism which is "king over all the children of pride." I admit that "Tom the Cat from Zanzibar" in *The Witches' Brew* is good fun, but when Mr. Smith suggests that he is nothing more I disagree.

In the creepy ambiguity of the first line of Malzah's song in Heavysege, "There was a devil and his name was I," the same association of ideas recurs, and it recurs again in what is perhaps the most completely articulate poem in the book, Lampman's "City of the End of Things"; which, though of course it has no room for the slow accumulation of despair that "The City of Dreadful Night" piles up, is an equally terrifying vision of humanity's Iron Age. In the younger writers the satire on war and exploitation is more conventional and anonymous, but as soon as they begin to speak with more authority they will undoubtedly take their places in the same tradition—Patrick Anderson especially.

To sum up, Canadian poetry is at its best a poetry of incubus and *cauchemar*, the source of which is the unusually exposed contact of the poet with nature which Canada provides. Nature is seen by the poet, first as unconsciousness, then as a kind of existence which is cruel and meaningless, then as the source of the cruelty and subconscious stampedings within the human mind. As compared with American poets, there has been comparatively little, outside Carman, of the cult of the rugged outdoor life which idealizes nature and tries to accept it. Nature is consistently sinister and menacing in Canadian poetry. And here and there we find glints of a vision beyond nature, a refusal to be bullied by space and time, an affirmation of the supremacy of intelligence and humanity over stupid power. One finds this in Kenneth Leslie:

> Rather than moulds invisible in the air
> into which petals pour selective milk
> I seem to sense a partnered agony
> of creature and creator in the rose.

One finds it in Dorothy Livesay's apostrophe to the martyred Lorca:

> You dance. Explode
> Unchallenged through the door
> As bullets burst
> Long deaths ago, your breast.

One finds it in Margaret Avison's very lovely "Maria Minor" and her struggle to define "the meaning of the smashed moth" in a poem which makes an excellent finale to the book. And one begins thereby to understand the real meaning of the martyrdom of Brébeuf, the theme of what with all its faults is the greatest single Canadian poem. Superficially, the man with the vision beyond nature is tied to the stake and destroyed by savages who are in the state of nature, and who represent its mindless barbarity. But there is a far profounder irony to that scene: the black-coated figure at the stake is also a terrifying devil to the savages, *Echon*, the evil one. However, frantically they may try to beat him off, their way of savagery is doomed; it is doomed in their Nazi descendants; it is doomed even if it lasts to the end of time.

This is not, I hope, a pattern of thought I have arbitrarily forced upon Canadian poetry: judging from Mr. Smith's book and what other reading I have done this seems to be its underlying meaning, and the better the poem the more clearly it expresses it. Mr. Smith has brought out this inner unity quite unconsciously because it is really there: just as in his "Ode to Yeats" he has, again quite unconsciously, evoked a perfect image of the nature of poetic feeling in his own country:

> An old thorn tree in a stony place
> Where the mountain stream has run dry,
> Torn in the black wind under the race
> Of the icicle-sharp kaleidoscopic white sky,
> > Bursts into sudden flower.

Northrop Frye, "Canada and Its Poetry," *Canadian Forum*, December 1943.

F. R. SCOTT

A live movement in poetry will reflect and often foreshadow the creative movements in its social environment. Poets sensitive to the growing forces of their age will give symbolic expression to those forces and will become a potent instrument of social change. The more revolutionary their epoch the more markedly will their writing differ from that of their predecessors, for they will be obliged to experiment with new form and imagery in order to convey their new ideas. Their style will thus at first appear crude and unpolished, and will shock the established taste. They will be laughed at for their clumsiness and obscurity. So the poets of the Romantic Revival absorbed the revolutionary fervour of regicidal France, threw overboard the outmoded classicism of the eighteenth century, and faced misunderstanding and sharp criticism until time had carried their contemporaries forward to the new positions. So too the American poetry revival in the first quarter of this century, with its greater freedom, variety, and humanism, prepared the way for the new social thinking which emerged politically through the New Deal. Carl Sandburg's robust popular verse heralded the "forgotten man" of the new politics and broke ground for the CIO. The English revival of the 1930s showed at least a deep dissatisfaction with the pre-war English society.

A dead tradition of poetic writing, on the other hand, reflects nothing but the attitudes of the past, expressed in the clichés of the past. It will fear and oppose the new in literature because the new spells death to itself. In Canada, where so much tradition, deprived of content, has become mere habit, this influence produces the kind of poem with which we are all too painfully familiar—neat, accurate, unambiguous, earnest and ordinary. The surprising thing is how long such sterility can live and go on reproducing itself. Ultimately, however, the gap between itself and life grows so wide that collapse occurs. Usually the well-established tradition is sanctified by state approval in some form. At meetings of its devotees medals are given, the "moderns" are scorned, and tea is poured.

To read *Voices of Victory*, described as "Representative Poetry of Canada in Wartime" (Macmillan, 1941) is to find oneself buried in just this kind of tradition. In other days the inclination would have been to throw the book aside and waste no more time over it. In these days of critical choices for humanity, and for Canada as part of humanity, such a phenomenon as this anthology is perhaps worth a moment's analysis. We can all feel the uncertainty of the present world situation, poised as we are on a political watershed. Our doubt is not with regard to the peace, which can so easily be lost. There has clearly been little change since the war began in the social outlook of some of the principal Allied powers, and least of all in Canada. Perhaps in Canada more than anywhere else the old traditions are still with us, as dominant as before. Wherever we look—in politics, in the churches, in education, in business, in the press—the pre-war Canadian social order survives, slightly modified but basically un-reformed. Yet there are new forces stirring underneath the old crust, moving deeply in the hearts and minds of men, giving us common cause with other races and nations. Of these forces a vital poetic movement might be made. *Voices of Victory* does not seem to be aware that they exist. It is bad enough to have so little external sign of these new impulses in Canadian politics, but this is partly under-standable since the primacy of military effort over social reform appeals to many. What is more discouraging is the utter lack on the part of these Canadian writers of the sense of impending change, of the need for democratic advance, and of any new outlook on the contemporary world. Judging by this volume, nothing has altered in the realm of poetry or politics since 1914. Needless to say there is no new style or diction, no venture in original modes of expression.

These poems were selected from 766 entries to a contest organised by the Poetry Group of the Toronto Branch of the Canadian Authors' Association. The purpose of the contest, we are told, was two-fold: first, to contribute the proceeds of sales to the Canadian Red Cross British Bomb Victims Fund, and secondly, to "let poetic genius of Canada and the Canadian people sound a spiritual challenge to the brutality of enemy despots and tyrants." The frontispiece, a reproduction of a prize medal donated by the Athlones and containing their effigy, prepares the reader for this priority of ideas. Then comes Charles G. D. Roberts' "Canada Speaks to Britain":

> She calls. And we will answer to our
> last breath.

This sets the tone for what follows. Canada's essential colonialism stands out everywhere in this answer to England's call. One would gather that before the call came all was right with the world, and after the call ceases no doubt the poets will return to their non-American nightingales. The prize poem, "Recompense," leads us through the "faery foam/ of blackthorn blossoms breaking" to "England's dower/ of deathless loveliness." It has the lush glamour of a cricket match, all Gentlemen and no Players. The second prize goes to "Canadian Crusade," a poem which is at least free from nostalgia; its sentimentality is local rather than transatlantic. The third prize is given to a eulogy of Churchill.

There follow twenty poems receiving honourable mention, "in order of merit." After this the contributors are unranked. Most of the poems deal in traditional manner with the standard themes of sacrifice, suffering, death, with special reference to torpedoed children. Nowhere in the entire volume is there an echo, even faint, of a people's war or a people's peace, or of the war within the war represented by the great cry of exploited humanity for the promised four freedoms. Exception should be made for a poem by Kenneth Leslie (unranked) who has at least perceived the significance of Russia's part in the struggle. Nor is there any evidence that these writers perceive the profound drama of man's attempt to purge himself through suffering of his own making, or that they feel the profound tragedies of an age that threw away its last victory and hesitates now to make vital its war aims by an immediate application of their principles. All is apparently quiet on the philosophic front. So we get sentiment but no passion, loyalty but no dynamic assertion, Ministry of Information leaflets but very little poetry.

Of all the contributing factors that go to make up the state of mind reflected here the deepest and most dominant, in my opinion, is our Canadian colonialism. This has little (though some) relationship with outward governmental forms. It is more a cast of thought, a mental climate. The colonial is an incomplete person. He must look to others for his guidance, and far away for his criterion of value. He copies the parental style instead of incorporating what is best in something of his own. He undervalues his own contribution and overestimates what others can do for him. Old greatness is more to him than new truth. Above all he fears originality, which might cut him off from his secure base. The outside world of men seems foreign and hostile to him, and he will cling to ancient traditions long after they have been abandoned in his metropolis. No matter how great his sincerity or how devoted his attachment, he is incapable, while suffering from this political Oedipus complex, of rising above the ordinary. For the most perfect copy is second-rate, while the least originality is unique. How a country can shape itself out of this state of mind I do not know, but the duty of the poet is to help in the enfranchisement, not to decorate the ancient chariot.

When the Canadian Nationalists say that patriotism is a good thing, they are told to keep their wisdom for the copy-books; and the rebuke would be just if those who administer it would recognize the equally obvious truth that there can be no patriotism without nationality. In a dependency there is no love of the country, no pride in the country; if an appeal is made to the name of the country, no heart responds as the heart of an Englishman responds when an appeal is made in the name of England. In a dependency every bond is stronger than that of country, every interest prevails over that of the country. The province, the sect, Orangeism, Fenianism, Freemasonry, Odd-fellowship, are more to the ordinary Canadian than Canada. So it must be, while the only antidote to sectionalism in a population with strongly marked differences of race and creed is the sentiment of allegiance to a distant throne. The Young Canadian leaving his native country to seek his fortune in the States feels no greater wrench than a young Englishman would feel in leaving his country to seek his fortune in London. Want of nationality is attended, too, with a certain want of self-respect, not only political but social, as writers on colonial society and character have observed. Wealthy men in a dependency are inclined to look to the Imperial Country as the social centre and the mark of their social ambition, if not as their ultimate abode, and not only their patriotic munificence but their political and social services are withdrawn from the country of their birth.

Extract from Goldwyn Smith, *The Political Destiny of Canada*, 1878, p. 61.

F. R. Scott, "A Note On Canadian War Poetry," *Preview*, #9, November 1942.

NEUFVILLE SHAW

A. J. M. Smith's *The Book of Canadian Poetry* is the most complete survey of English Canadian verse we possess. Its completeness is not, in itself, a virtue for this has forced the inclusion of much trash whose only worth is historical and even this only in a special sense, for to understand any particular level of our poetry's history one must make tangential reference to English or American influence so that much of the work here reproduced is only confirmation of the lack of any national continuity in the growth of the country's literature. Further, its completeness is rather extenuated for the logic which includes Carman (a Canadian who spent most of his life in the U.S.A.) includes Anderson (an Englishman who has spent a few years in Canada). However this latter is of no importance to illustrate the fallaciousness of a national consideration of our verse.

With the exception of the Indian, which possesses the strength of unique and (for them) contemporary myth, the early verse is frankly derivative. Its eulogies of the "simpler virtues" are an inevitable result of a strenuous pioneering environment in which anything more subtle would have appeared unforgivable luxury and in which the demands on individual fortitude were so great that complex social analysis was entirely out of the question. The result is such verse as:

> They saw a strong-built mother boiling porridge,
> All in a chamber somewhat bare but neat
> (The goodman with his gun had gone to forage,
> While the goodwife kept home alive and feat),
> And, helping her, six barefoot little spartans,
> All clad in homespun grey instead of tartans.
>
> Duvar: "The Emigration of the Fairies"

Such hymning of ecstatic simplicity can be left to the sentimental curate. It is a rather tawdry example of a verse which, like propaganda, pays tribute to necessary action by gushing over it. A similar castration of a nature which must have been as awesome as it was terrible has occurred in such familiar Landseers as:

> And near yon bank of many-coloured flowers
> Browse two majestic deer, and at their side
> A spotted fawn all innocently cowers;
> In the rank brushwood it attempts to hide,
> While the strong-antlered stag steps forth
>   with lordly stride, . . .
>
> Sangster: "The St. Lawrence and the Saguenay"

The newer "Golden Age" poetry was written in an age which was determined to find the gold and little else. While expanding Canadian industry was merrily chasing the dollar across a thousand miles of prairies, the poet drearily painted golden sunsets or found Pan and Eurydice under every Maple Leaf. He had become civilized (at Oxford) and had reluctantly returned his soul carefully wrapped in a poultice compounded of Empire and Olympus. Out of the hodge-podge of nationalist and pre-Raphaelite verse arises only more derivative if somewhat sophisticated thought. As minor poets must, much reliance was placed on nature description. From the picturization of a sunrise one is supposed to derive the feeling of the rhythmic appearance of hope, of a lake (always solitary) the feeling of devast-ating solitude, et cetera. Instead of using nature as an illustration for a more important theme as a greater poet might, the phenomenon with the aid of the best imported larks and Grecian deities was left to impose itself with the superimposed addition of a cumbersome emotional directive dragged in by the heels along with the inevitable exclamation mark. This surrender to empty landscape is a curse which persists today in our painting but happily one which the next generation of writers was able to overcome.

The one exception to these generalizations is found in the work of Isabel Valancy Crawford which, while seeming heavy and shapeless beside the relative elegance of her contemporaries is not afraid to draw themes from its immediate environment. Her enthusiastic acceptance of industrialization, her realization of the role of the tool as the concrete of activity and the genuine suprise of her images set her far apart from her co-nationals. Lines like:

> The lean lank lion peals
> His midnight thunders over lone, red plains,
> Long ridg'd and crested on their dusty waves,
> With fires from moons red-hearted as the sun, . . .

remind one of the strangely incisive quality of a Rousseau night scene. If guilty of a heavy uneven technique, her statement embraces without seeming decorative and creates of sincerity rather than artificiality.

Proust has said somewhere that of each of the things we know we possess a double; that is, without recollection of it as facsimile there exists also the reality of its significance, a reality which exists far beyond the limits of its sensory definition. It is with this second element that modern poetry has concerned itself and pushed by its search for meaning has attained a range and a sense of evaluation which is far in excess of its predecessors. It is, perhaps, as A. J. M. Smith asserts, a bias for the contemporary that makes one appreciate modern Canadian writing far more than the rest of the work in this book; perhaps, also because it is more difficult to detect influence and thus estimate originality, but whatever the cause there can be little doubt that these people have placed an *a priori* art on the dust heap. We can no longer judge their work by its approximation to a model (this is good Tennyson, that is bad Swinburne, et cetera, et cetera) but rather by the success with which the poet has released his experience and the degree in which his form reveals his content. Their work is national in the best sense of the word—that is, an assertion of the value of their own attitude rather than one overshadowed by the awareness of the superiority of foreign cultural reaction.

I find that my estimation of them differs sharply from Smith's. Thus I can hardly agree that "Pratt is the greatest of contemporary Canadian poets for he is the only one who has created boldly and on a large scale," which is as true as saying that a poem about an elephant is greater than one about a flea. Pratt's "Dunkirk" comes unchanged from the propaganda mill, and his description of a whale at play or an eagle sadly considering the first aeroplane merits consideration for *National* (or rather *Canadian*) *Geographic Magazine*. Excitement sustained by exclamation points, expletive and tenuous extenuation do not constitute poetry despite the critics Smith so characteristically drags in to justify his judgment.

His work is in striking contrast to much of the last sections of this anthology where writers like Finch, Hambleton, Anderson, Page, or Smith himself have concentrated on economy of form and have, with a care (which is not the deliberateness of effeteness) elected images which spring from the trend of the theme without losing their relationship to it.

> In their eyes I have seen
> the pin-men of madness in marathon trim
> race round the track of the stadium pupil.

or

> on the shore the lion waves lay down on
> their paws

contain images which explode without our being aware of the frantic gasp of a creator who attempts by his exertion to hide his mediocrity.

A. M. Klein is a writer who, while being both "large" and "bold," has recognized the exigencies of form. His verse, dictated by a sense of tender indignation—reminding one of the work of one of the notable omissions from this anthology, Bruce Ruddick—is at its best in his "Autobiographical" in which the richness and warmth of Jewish custom are revealed to us in a vividly decorative manner which combines exoticism with strong social assertion.

Robert Finch's and A. J. M. Smith's glittering inconsequentials will impress anyone who has a place for that intellectually conditioned lyric which is, to a large extent, a focus on matters apart from the great issues of personality and which is disconcertingly attractive to all save those obsessed to the point of mania by a continual demand for political sloganing. Finch's "The Sisters" or Smith's "Shadows There Are" possess the cool tranquility of relatively unimportant phenomena which calmly assert themselves assured in their remoteness from fiercer problems.

It is the verse of Scott, Anderson, Page, and Wreford which makes us quite contentedly proclaim the death of the Maple Leaf for here we find a complete disregard for a dictated chauvinism and a didacticism which, while not constituting political directive, is a ruthless analysis of social falsehood. It is on this tide of affirmation that the future of Canadian verse rests for it is by a union with the great wave of social protest which is, at present, sweeping the country that a universalised statement can be made which carries within its scope all the proud and sweeping ramifications of mankind itself.

Neufville Shaw, "The Maple Leaf is Dying," *Preview*, No. 17, December 1943.

LOUIS DUDEK

It may occur after a while to anyone who reads Canadian poetry that a considerable part of our literature is being written in the universities, by professors and teachers. The list of Canadian poets who are in the academic profession includes a solid majority of the best Canadian writers, in proof of which a partial list can be given, gleaned from *The Book of Canadian Poetry* of A. J. M. Smith: E. J. Pratt, Earle Birney, F. R. Scott, Robert Finch, L. A. Mackay, A. J. M. Smith, Alfred G. Bailey, James Wreford, Patrick Anderson, Margaret Avison . . . . An amazing list, statistically, of writers who are pursuing an academic career of one sort or another as a profession.

Is this fact significant? It does not hold true for the major writers in English or American literature. The big names in America, from Walt Whitman and Bret Harte to Edgar Lee Masters, Sandburg, and Robert Frost, are characteristically removed from the colleges, although they may have been drawn into the orbit at times. They have come out of, and returned again to the cave of common men. In England, the group of writers who started off modern poetry, the imagists, were bohemian intellectuals—Pound, Aldington, Lawrence, and the rest. Theirs, again, was not an academic life of literature, although the writers had a background of learning and tradition.

It is significant, however, even outside of Canada, that during the so-called decline of the thirties, and in this war, there seems to be a preponderance of academic writing everywhere. A brief survey of *Poetry* (Chicago), or *Partisan Review*, will reveal that the poets appearing there are almost exclusively teachers and lecturers in the universities. By way of correlation, there is also a lack of liveliness in their poetry—except for the unnatural exploitation of the vivid image —an abundance of intellectual concentration, and a preference for word-patterns rather than poetry. Would it be a mistake to connect the two facts: the style of our latest poetry and the retreat into the ivy-wreathed tower, the university?

This arty literature—or, if you like, true culture—is finding the going hard, under the economic pressure of modern life. The artist is therefore running into the modern cloister, uncloistered as it is, the university, where he can find partial shelter. But neither blueblood artist nor the cloistered type of university seems to be destined to survive for long; in a last desperate effort, they are clinging together for comfort.

Now there are probably reasons why academic literature weighs so heavily in the balance in Canada. Some of these are described by E. K. Brown in his book *On Canadian Poetry* in the pages dealing with the difficulties of writing poetry in this country. Also, Canada is essentially commercial and dead to anything like literature; it is a conventional, narrow, and materialistic country; and in such a country, where there is no public, there can be no people's poets or artists. The lack must be found in both the people and the poets, and for the same sociological reasons: those conditions which produce readers of poetry produce poets also.

Then what are the effects of this state of affairs? A poet, more perhaps than any other man, is conditioned by his occupation, the habitual use which he makes of his mind and body. Poets in the academic profession are naturally influenced by their academic pursuits and environment. They are out of real everyday contact with the main currents of contemporary life, with the result that their poetry suffers. What they learn from libraries overbalances and spoils much of their poetry, enjoyable and competent as it often is. Without making any other comparison than this one (in fact, I admire the carvings of Smith, and the very clever verse of F. R. Scott), note the simple, direct lines of Raymond Knister, who worked for many years on a farm, beside the very different poetry of A. J. M. Smith who teaches at Michigan State College; or again, the rich, full-bloodedness of A. M. Klein, Montreal lawyer, beside the intellectual poems of F. R. Scott, who is on the faculty of McGill University. University writers may be good; but they are usually not much alive. There is usually a certain lack of liveliness, of the sense of reality, the human touch, a content of common sense. It is the difference between understanding through emotion and experience and through the book and the mind alone. Our sheltered poets may profit from experience "to the best of their ability," but the library logic gets the best of them in the long run.

In concluding this write-up, which should not be taken as a niggling criticism but merely as a suggestion about a common problem, I think that the trouble with "academic" poetry is related to a further and much broader issue. In Europe through the past centuries, learning, or the accumulated lore of Western civilization was developed by the priestly and later by the aristocratic or leisure classes of society, both of which were essentially parasitic on the economic life of the people. Our universities are an outgrowth of this civilization. And the tendency of our civilization in the past, for the reason just given, has often been to move away from its relation to the real currents of life; where by "real" I mean purposeful, related to the physical basis of life, work for sustenance, economic necessity, et cetera.

Our Western civilization, therefore, has largely been falsified throughout by its *idea*-lism, its unpragmatic values, its tendency to build spiritual castles in the air. No less than a complete revision, starting with a revolution in each individual's thinking, is what is now demanded. And the whole process may be the work of decades, requiring new forms of society.

Can we discover, in part at least, the art and poetry that this implies, on this new and gradually unfolding horizon of living and thinking?

Louis Dudek, "Academic Literature," *First Statement*, II, No. 8, August 1944.

JOHN SUTHERLAND

Reading through this volume by the 1946 winner of the Governor-General's Award, I felt that Mr. Finch was more concerned with the advantages of mental exercise in verse form than with the writing of poetry. There are, it is true, some fine effects of music and imagery in *Poems*; there are occasional poems which attain a higher level than the book as a whole. But in general the author is too much occupied with (a) versifying a moral truism and (b) playing a sort of verbal chess.

While we do not expect a poet to be intellectually profound, I know of no poet, except possibly W. H. Davies, whom we are satisfied to have intellectually bathetic. With sly, determined skill Davies contrives to assume the innocence of birds and flowers, and flowers and birds cannot help being trite because they cannot stop being themselves. But if Davies is sometimes nearly profound when he seems most simple, Mr. Finch is nearly always simple when he seems profound. He plays with rhyme and metre like a kitten with a ball of wool, and with an air of doing something mysterious and significant. Here are a few examples of his manner:

> Exacting nothing, one receives no less
> Than one exacts, possibly an excess.
>> ("Ask No Promise")

> They do not understand. For if they did
> There would be two instead of one adrift.
> To understand is to have shared the shrift,
> To have won or lost with someone, side by side.
>> ("The Formula")

> Bubble to bubble
> Is not more like
> Than trouble to trouble.
>> ("Alone")

> Your treason is my reason,
> Your poison is my raisin.
>> ("The Five")

From these quotations we can already deduce the principal theme of the poetry: life is never what it seems and we must school ourselves to accept its realities. The writer's bare statement of this platitude cannot substitute for poetry, and his attempt at irony does nothing to make it palatable. His irony is a facetiousness that springs out of an excessive self-consciousness. It can transform what is meant as a reserved statement into a coy and distressing confession. It forces us to listen for words left unsaid, and these words are naked and embarrassed because of it.

The would-be pedestrian moralist who dominates the latter part of *Poems* appears to be at odds with the dandified versifier of its opening pages. But in the decorative nature pieces, the poet is still at the mercy of the mental gymnast. Here is a characteristic sonnet, "The Smile":

> The lake has drawn a counterpane of glass
> On her rock limbs up to her island pillows
> And under netting woven by the swallows
> Sleeps in a dream and is a dream that has
>
> Strayed to sleep in the library of space
> Whose ceiling beams are purple over yellows
> And whose blue shelves behind a cloudy trellis
> Wait for tomorrow's volumes of new grace;
>
> Her restless hound at the Western fireplace
> Stretches a coaxing crimson claw to tell his
> Mistress the hunt is on, not over, zealous
> For a last smile before resuming chase:
>
> See the lake wake! You would take it for the dawn
> But for the flashlight of night's watchman moon.

Because the author refers to or forgets his principal metaphor just as he pleases, the conceits in this poem are illogical and silly. From the initial (and recurrent) comparison of the lake to a woman asleep in her bedroom, we pass on to a library hanging by no visible support from the ceiling of the bedroom, enter the great room of a manor to which the lady has been moved still sound asleep, and finally reach a factory setting where the moon is playing the role of night watchman. There are many ridiculous things in the course of all this. Not the least ridiculous is the notion that the "restless hound," who begs for fresh prey though his claws are already crimson, and who, on the evidence, should be literally climbing the walls and howling for blood, is less able to rouse his mistress than the wink of a flashlight! Such absurdities are possible because Mr. Finch is less concerned with poetry than with a game of similes. Given the general comparison of night and sleep, he changes the lake to a woman, the rocks to limbs, the islands to pillows, the swallows to weavers, the air to a library, et cetera, et cetera, and before he is through has managed to furnish several houses. His method is one of compilation rather than of composition. It merely suggests that a knack for making word-pictures has been gradually transformed into a hobby.

How, we may ask, did *Poems* receive the national award for poetry in a year which saw the publication of some unusually good books? I have made a list of some possible reasons:

1. Respectability. Finch is professor of French at the University of Toronto.

2. Precedent. The award has a habit of going to the sturdy Western farmer type or the etherialized academician. It has recently been granted to the following writers:

1942—Anne Marriott   1943—A. J. M. Smith
1944—Dorothy Livesay   1945—Earle Birney
1946—Robert Finch

3. Naïve wonder. Mr. Finch kept his first book up his sleeve for twenty years.

4. Fairness. Ryerson Press had won many times and Oxford never had.

5. Respect for age. Mr. Finch was old enough: the other candidates were not.

6. Sanctimoniousness. Mr. Finch was morally correct and sounded religious.

7. Hypocrisy. The politics of the younger writers was "out of place" in poetry.

8. Snobbery. Finch was billed as a talented musician and painter.

9. Credulity. The judges accepted Finch's verdict on his own work:

> His lines run wherever his pen goes,
> Mine grope the miles from heart to head;
> His will tire before he does;
> Mine will move when I am dead.

("Poet on Poet")

10. Ignorance. The judges knew of, but had not read, Louis Dudek, P. K. Page or Patrick Anderson.

11. Ignorance. The judges had not read Finch.

None of these reasons entirely satisfy me, but the thing is hard to explain.

John Sutherland, Review of *Poems* by Robert Finch (Toronto: Oxford, 1946), *Northern Review*, I, No. 6, August-September 1947.

EDITORIAL BOARD OF *NORTHERN REVIEW*

Certain changes have taken place in the editorial board of *Northern Review*, effective from the last issue. The following editors have resigned: Neufville Shaw, Patrick Anderson, A. M. Klein, F. R. Scott and A. J. M. Smith. Two regional editors, P. K. Page and Ralph Gustafson, have also resigned.

The reason for these changes was a difference of opinion about editorial policy, particularly concerning criticism and reviews. The immediate occasion for disagreement was a review of Robert Finch's poems by John Sutherland, which appeared in the last issue. The editors who resigned maintained that this review, and similar pieces of criticism, were too harsh and unjust for publication, while the present editorial board held that criticism of this kind was badly needed in Canada. Our readers can form their own opinions in the matter.

Elsewhere in this issue we have printed a short letter from P. K. Page, at her request, stating that she was ignorant of the review on Finch. Perhaps we should mention that our regional editors never saw contributions to the magazine before they were printed and were not entitled to vote on them.

The present editors are John Sutherland, R. G. Simpson, Mary Margaret Miller, John Harrison, Irving Layton and Audrey Aikman. We intend to carry on *Northern Review* in its present form. We hope that the concentration of responsibility in the hands of a smaller editorial board will result in greater efficiency and a more interesting magazine.

THE EDITORS

Editors of *Northern Review*, Notices of Resignation, *Northern Review*, II, No. 1, October-November 1947.

P. K. PAGE

The Editors:

To the readers of *Northern Review* who are not aware of the way the Editorial Board of *Northern Review* operates, I would like to say that I read the review of Mr. Finch's *Poems* for the first time when it appeared in print.

I very much regret the destructive level of the criticism and am sorry to see this article appear in a magazine devoted to encouraging creative writing.

I would be grateful if you would publish this letter.

Yours very sincerely,

P. K. Page.

P. K. Page, Letter to *Northern Review*, II, No. 1, October-November 1947.

IV

SIGNS OF REACTION, NEW AND OLD

Signs of Reaction, New and Old

From about 1948 modern Canadian poetry, as represented in the movement centered in Montreal, began to show distinct signs of self-doubt and reorientation. After the break-up of the joint editorship of *Preview* and *Northern Review*, the active members of both factions gradually dispersed and lost their unity as a group; the magazine *Northern Review* was left virtually in the hands of one editor, John Sutherland. For several reasons, some of which were wholly personal (Sutherland was suffering from a terminal illness, and became a convert to Roman Catholicism), the direction of John Sutherland's criticism had taken a conservative and even a reactionary line. This was clear to Raymond Souster who wrote to Dudek in a letter of June twenty-third, 1951:

I think you're probably as fed up with *Contemporary Verse* and *Northern Review* as I am, and I know there are plenty of others who feel the same way.

At about the same time (June seventh, 1951) Dudek wrote to Souster:

You've written me that NR [*Northern Review*] isn't what it was, that it's gone in for a conventional smoothness, lacks the old biff-bam of the war years. Why do you think that happened? My theory is that looking for "native quality" just shuts the eyes to what is new and different and alive.

In *Northern Review* itself the reaction and criticism appeared from about 1948, as John Sutherland gradually turned his interest toward the more traditional Canadian writers, and away from the larger experimental and militant themes of modern poetry. In the editorial for the October-November 1949 issue he expressed the new emphasis:

We need the kind of Canadianism, cosmopolitan in its breadth of outlook, that Lorne Pierce has expressed for us in "A Canadian People": "No nation can achieve its true destiny that adopts without profound and courageous reasoning and selection the thoughts and styles of another. . . ." It is in this spirit that our criticism should approach what is its most important problem: the relationship of the arts in Canada to the English tradition.

The quotation from Lorne Pierce, which so clearly turns its face against vigorous currents of influence from abroad, appeared on the back cover of this number of *Northern Review* and remained there regularly from then on.

In terms of book publication, also, a shift of interest and regional focus in Canada seemed to appear in these years. In 1947 several of the outstanding books of poetry were still expressions of the earlier poetry of the forties: Sutherland's anthology *Other Canadians*, Souster's *Go To Sleep, World*, Dorothy Livesay's *Poems for People*, Klein's *Seven Poems* (privately printed). In the following year, however, the list was dominated by writers of a new cast, no longer Montreal-centred (George Whalley, *No Man Is an Island*; Douglas Le Pan, *The Wounded Prince and Other Poems*; Robert Finch, *The Strength of the Hills*; Earle Birney, *The Strait of Anian*; and Roy Daniells, *Deeper Into the Forest*). The Montreal contingent produced two books, Layton's second, *Now Is the Place*, and A. M. Klein's *The Rocking Chair and Other Poems*. In 1949, the only two noteworthy books were Raymond Knister's *Collected Poems* (A posthumous volume from a writer of the 1920s), and James Reaney's *The Red Heart*. This change represents a wide extension and diversification of the modern poetry movement in Canada. It also implies, ultimately, a major shift in critical direction.

The Red Heart, James Reaney's first book, coincided closely with the first of Northrop Frye's annual reviews of Canadian poetry in the "Letters in Canada" survey of the *University of Toronto Quarterly*. This was also the period of *Here and Now*, an eclectic and handsome magazine, started in Toronto, and running through four numbers from December 1947 to June 1949. This magazine anticipated *Tamarack Review* (1956), which, also, is an eclectic, non-partisan periodical open to, and intended for a broader and more general readership. The poetry movement of the 1940s, therefore, shifted in this period from a highly concentrated and localized activity to a dispersed and varied literary scene, much of which now became centered on Toronto. There was, too, a new critical orientation which gathered momentum and adherents, and which expressed an attitude to poetry which is essentially antithetical to the old, aggressively realistic poetry of early modernism.

As the literary center of gravity was displaced, the Montreal movement experienced a temporary lull which characterized the late 1940s and the early fifties. The earlier poetry movement had lost its impetus, and the tough-fisted confidence of the war years which had spawned it seemed to be shaken. In the midst of this interlude several voices of a distinctly conservative cast and reactionary intent made themselves heard, among these, ironically, that of John Sutherland, editor of *Northern Review.*

Sutherland, by this time, had turned explicitly and vigorously against what he chose to call "the modern literary decadence." His most explicit rejection of the modern movement occurred in the opening paragraph of an essay on four British writers, three of them Catholic and the fourth a visionary extra-religious critic of modern man. The entire paragraph is worth quoting:

There is not the slightest doubt that modern literary decadence is now on its death-bed. All that was fathered by Joyce and Pound is obviously on the verge of complete extinction. As Edward Dahlberg phrased it in a recent issue of *Poetry Chicago,* [sic] "By now James, Pound, Eliot, Joyce are dowds, jades and trulls of Parnassus, and we are weary of them. It may be that they will be curios again in some other time, but now they do not provide the spectacle of remoteness so significant in literature." What is to follow this debacle of the moderns? There are increasing signs that the younger generation, weary as it is of a rabid experimentalism, is turning back to the School of the Great Equestrians. The Equestrians have provided one of the few oases in the wasteland of our times. While the rest of the literary world has been standing on its head, they alone have been seated firmly in the saddle. They have been virtually the one healthy vein in a diseased and corrupt body. As the twilight of the "moderns" deepens into darkness, we can anticipate the moment when these apostles of Equestrianism will come riding towards us over the sunny, dew-besprinkled meadows of the dawn. It will be a glorious dawn— perhaps one of the most glorious in the whole of literary history.

And who are the Great Equestrians? Their names are all familiar to you. The chief members of the School are G. K. Chesterton, D. H. Lawrence, Roy Campbell and C. S. Lewis: respectively the White Horse of Wessex, the Laughing Horse, the Talking Bronco, and the Lizard-Horse, in the order of their chosen equine rank.*

In the essay "The Past Decade in Canadian Poetry" presented in this section, Sutherland gave a brief historical sketch and interpretation of Canadian poetry in the 1930s and 40s. He argued that soon after 1946 "the whole purpose and driving spirit of the 'new movement' were in a state of decay." This he attributed to disillusionment with the political aims of the forties poetry and to a return to traditionalism and to religious concerns. His essay ended with a rather ambiguous prophecy, and with typical Sutherland irony: "I believe the present religious trend may become more marked; if not, I believe there will be a reaction against it."

The other essays in this section are taken from an anthology of

*John Sutherland, "The Great Equestrians," *Northern Review,* October-November 1953, p. 21.

Canadian poetry published by the Ryerson Press in 1954. This anthology was based on a book, *Our Canadian Literature*, edited by Albert Durrant Watson and Lorne Pierce in 1922 (revised edition, 1923). The book was therefore in the most conservative Canadian tradition. A. D. Watson was a Canadian poet of the 1860s generation; on his death in 1926, Bliss Carman, veteran of the Sixties Group, and poet of the Romantic twilight in Canada, was invited to enlarge and revise the anthology. This work was left unfinished on Carman's death in 1929: as explained somewhat obscurely by Lorne Pierce in the foreword reproduced here, the Carman-Pierce revision of the book appeared in 1935. This was again revised and enlarged by a conservative senior Canadian critic, V. B. Rhodenizer of Acadia University in 1954. Both the Introduction of Professor Rhodenizer and the Foreword by Dr. Lorne Pierce are interesting documents of conservative retrenchment at this point in modern Canadian poetry.

The debate between the Moderns and the Traditionalists is a perennial one. It reappears in British and American literature as a "return to traditional forms" and "respect for traditional themes" at various points in twentieth-century literature. In Canada, the temporary retreat from modernist positions to a greater traditionalism, whether in the writing of John Sutherland or in that of Lorne Pierce and V. B. Rhodenizer, is not perhaps important in itself; it is significant of a general and recurrent pull toward traditional positions. Both Sutherland and Pierce had served as valuable editors to the new poetry after 1942; the retreat of both champions from the front lines provides an interesting counterpoint to the forward movement of this poetry.

JOHN SUTHERLAND

The present is an appropriate time to conduct a survey of recent Canadian poetry, since the end of 1950 also marks the conclusion of a distinct and important decade of poetic development in Canada. I date the beginning of this decade from the first publication of *Contemporary Verse* in 1941—I believe in the first months of 1941 —for many of the poets who appeared during the forties were introduced in the early issues of that magazine. Shortly afterwards, some of the same writers came together in Montreal and began producing publications of their own—*Preview* and *First Statement*, the two magazines which combined to form *Northern Review*—but *Contemporary Verse* had already stolen part of their thunder, and it deserves the first credit.

I would like to give a brief account both of the beginnings of this movement in Canadian poetry and of the changes that have taken place in it. I would gladly dispense with any mention of the beginnings, since they are now of ancient date, if anyone else had bothered to define them or recognize them *as* beginnings. People have begun to realize that the forties were a very active period in Canadian poetry, and have even said so in print: they have not explained that 1941 marks the beginning of a distinct period, but have simply lumped the thirties and forties indiscriminately together. It is time to correct this oversight. Critics who cannot see beyond the ends of their own categories, are lowly creatures, but the categories are necessary for the regular intake and discharge of facts.

It is true that the gap between the two periods has narrowed considerably in the past four years or so—a fact I will try to explain later. It is also true that the work produced by the younger poets, in the first few years of the forties, was in part a development of a tendency already quite apparent in the thirties. Apart from E. J. Pratt, and one or two others, Canadian poetry in the thirties was largely the product of three main groups: the so-called group of "Montreal Poets"—A. M. Klein, A. J. M. Smith, Leo Kennedy and F. R. Scott—whose work first began appearing in the *McGill Fortnightly Review*, and who dealt with religious problems to a large extent and showed the influence of T. S. Eliot; the group of Raymond Knister, W. W. E. Ross and other poets who were influenced by the imagists; and the Western group of Earle Birney, Dorothy Livesay, Anne Marriott and others, whose early work was imagist with affinities with Ross and Knister, but whose main interest lay in the West rather than in rural Ontario and who broke completely with imagism as they developed. In the latter part of the thirties, under the impact of the depression and the prairie drought, and of the English Marxist school of Auden and Spender, the poets in these three groups either fell by the wayside (Ross was apparently an early casualty) or turned to political problems and identified themselves with the interest of a class. For some, this reformation was itself a swan-song. Leo Kennedy, a poet of very considerable promise, wrote a poem entitled "Calling Eagles," summoning the intellectual eagles down from the "glacial crags" to the lowlands where the vital issues were being decided: he came down; and he has scarcely been heard from since— not at all in the past ten years. A. J. M. Smith had a poem in the first issue of *Contemporary Verse*, in which he said "Replace the slave state face/ With a face of bread": he has published virtually nothing else in ten years. Although his first volume, *News of the Phoenix*, appeared belatedly in 1943, little or none of it was recent work. Anne Marriott has remained productive, but has never lived up to the promise of *The Wind Our Enemy* (1935).* On the other hand, F. R. Scott, who was concerned with the issues of class from the very beginning, and A. M. Klein, who was comparatively unaffected by them, have continued to produce and to develop—notably Klein; and Earle Birney and Dorothy Livesay reached maturity under the stress of social problems and produced some of their best work.

The political theme had been announced, in some cases calamitously, and with no concerted voice: its full expression had to wait until the forties. The large group of new poets who appeared then— James Wreford, P. K. Page, Louis Dudek, Raymond Souster, Patrick Anderson, Miriam Waddington, Ronald Hambleton and several others—were all concerned, to a greater or less extent in individual cases, with the problems which they believed then arose from class divisions in society. Nor was the difference between the thirties and the early forties simply a quantitative one: there were also important differences in technique and in the approach to the political theme. The most clear-cut political group of the thirties—Birney, Livesay and Marriott—was mainly concerned with the land and with the fate of an agricultural class: the new poets of the forties—nearly all of them residents of the East—saw the class issue in urban and industrial terms. The political poets of the thirties were essentially pragmatic in their outlook, prepared to adopt a cause and to devote their talents directly to its realization: the poets of the forties saw the contemporary world in psychological as well as political terms, and relied as much on Freud as Marx. The older poets had felt the impact of the English Marxist poetry of the thirties, but were relatively little influenced by the technical experiments of Auden and Spender or by those of Dylan Thomas and George Barker—while endeavouring to preserve the burden of the political theme. These main differences, and others that might be enumerated, make it clear that a new kind of Canadian poetry was being written in the early forties.

Perhaps there was never a time in Canada when so many poets of promise appeared simultaneously or when, within the general pattern of the movement, there was so much creative variety, as in the early years of the forties. I suppose it is sacrilege to speak of it as a *Canadian* movement when the majority of its members professed a

The Wind Our Enemy was published in 1939, not 1935.

cosmopolitan faith and were opposed to the national idea in any form: yet Canadian in part it obviously was. The phenomenal development of Canada during the last war, relatively greater than that of any country in the same period, gave a marked impetus to poetry as it did to the arts generally. There was an excitement in the air to which no one—least of all the poet—could fail to respond. Even that political point of view, which generally left the national question out of account, was very much influenced in an indirect way by national factors. It is significant that the high point of this movement in Canadian poetry corresponded with the peak of leftist sentiment among Canadians generally.

How suddenly it all changed! The First Statement Press had no sooner published *Other Canadians*, "An Anthology of the New Poetry in Canada, 1940-1946," which I furnished with a bristling, defiant introduction, than the whole purpose and driving spirit of the "new movement" were in a state of decay. We had barely rushed to the side of this challenger of tradition, holding up his right—or rather his left—hand in the stance of victory, when the challenger laid his head upon the block and willingly submitted to having it removed. What were the causes? Not *Other Canadians*, or my introduction to it: it went deeper than that. With the end of the war, there came a realization that, in the world at large, Russia and the United States were not in a state of undeclared brotherly love, and that, at home, the Canadian socialist movement had very shallow roots. It would be foolish to base a literary judgment of this movement on the value of its political ideas: but there is no doubt that one of the driving forces behind it was politics, and that one of the reasons it lost part of its momentum was because it lost its political faith. There were, of course, other factors involved in its marked if temporary decline: for example, the slowing down of the tempo everywhere by the return from war to a partial peace; the tapering off of the Canadian movement of expansion; and, last but not least, the poor durability of the poetic talents.

Apparently some of the poets I included in *Other Canadians* are no longer writing. Well, since they have ruled themselves out, it is better to forget about them and to concentrate on the remainder of the "new movement" and its prospects for the future. These prospects are less bleak than they were even a short while ago. It is evident that some of the younger poets are beginning to recover from their inertia of the late forties and that they are acquiring a new sense of purpose.

They are acquiring a new idea—or a variation of an old idea. In the introduction to *Other Canadians*, I wrote that the younger poets were resisting the dominant religious element of Canadian poetry, uniting and throwing off their chains. That was only half-true then and it is not at all true now. I criticized Mr. Smith, the editor of the *Book of Canadian Poetry*, for his religious emphasis, and I protested that his effort to force a religious interpretation on the new poets was not abiding by the rules and prophesied that it would prove futile. Well, I take it back. I still think Mr. Smith was forcing matters at that time, but the event has shown that he was substantially right. For the new poets have come back, if not always to religion, at least to a soul-searching which has strong religious implications, and to an attitude of mind more in harmony with that of earlier Canadian poets. In their writing they no longer attribute the present state of the world to class oppression, but to a guilt which makes no class distinctions and which involves every individual, including the poet. They speak now in a more personal way, exhibit a willingness to bear their share of the universal guilt, and seem to imply that the puritanical fury with which they once attacked the "middle class" was really a blustering way of hiding their own feeling of guilt. They look back to the poetic traditions, strive for a greater simplicity, and try to sing rather than to bluster forth protests.

A positive religious note is most apparent in the work of Kay Smith and James Wreford—two poets who have increasingly emphasized the religious element which was inherent even in their "socialist" poems. There is witness to Mr. Wreford's development in his new book, *Of Time and the Lover*, and to Miss Smith's in her powerful poem, the "Footnote to the Lord's Prayer," published in the previous issue of *Northern Review*. We will find the same general tendency in the recent work of Patrick Anderson, in the preoccupation with auto-biographical themes, in the absorption in the idea of guilt, and in the effort to associate the ideal of love with the vision of the artist who orders but does not judge. We will find it in recent poems by Miriam Waddington, in their exploration of the recesses of the self with the aid of recent psychological investigators, and in their use of a quasi-mystical language. We will also find it in the work of P. K. Page, who expressed the changing attitude of the younger poets in this poem published in 1947:

> Forgive us, who have not
> Been whole or rich as fruit;
> Who, through the eyes' lock enter
> A point beyond the centre
> To find our balance shot . . .
> Our blueprint was at fault.

> The edifice we build
> Disintegrates and falls:
> Haunting its ruined halls
> The spectre of our guilt . . .

Perhaps there is not one of the socialist poets who appeared in *Other Canadians* who would not say today that the "blueprint was at fault." There are few who have not been profoundly affected by what Miss Page calls "the spectre of our guilt." It would be misleading to conclude from this that we have harvested a new crop of "religious poets," but there is certainly a marked religious tendency in most recent work.

I hope no one is assuming that all this has occurred in an isolated vacuum, or only in the minds of Canadian poets (that is not meant as it sounds). The state of the world has given added emphasis to a religious tendency which has been present in contemporary poetry generally since the mid-thirties. Our own Canadian temper, which is strongly religious, and the example of T. S. Eliot, Edith Sitwell and other poets writing in England, incline poets in Canada to be receptive to poetic ideas of this kind. As a common religious interest has led to a rapprochement between the older and younger generations in England so for the same reason the poets of the thirties and the poets of the forties have drawn closer together in Canada. We will find some, or all of the same tendencies that I have been describing, in Earle Birney, Dorothy Livesay and Anne Marriott, in Robert Finch and A. J. M. Smith, and in F. R. Scott who, while he continues to express a political point of view in his verse, has seemed to stress more and more the religious metaphors and symbols which have always played a rather ambiguous role in his work.

This, then, is a general picture of how the movement of the forties developed and of its present condition. What, you may ask, is the value of the recent poetry, as compared with that produced in the early forties, and what is its development likely to be? I will answer the second part of the question first: I believe the present religious trend may become more marked; if not, I believe there will be a reaction against it. In explanation of this answer, I may say it is based on my experience in making prophecies in *Other Canadians*. I cannot think of a better basis.* As for the first part of the question, it seems obvious to me that the recent work of the younger poets is inferior to their work in the early forties, but that, nevertheless, the

*There are, of course, the possibilities that neither, or both, of the developments I prophesy will occur. In England at present there seems to be strong criticism of the resigned attitude of the religious poets, coupled with a demand that poetry embody a principle of action. For the editors of *Nine* at least, this seems to mean action based on traditional religious principles.

principles behind this recent work are potentially better principles for poetry. It is generally better for the poet to accept than oppose the values inherent in his society; it is better for him to be honestly himself than to disguise himself in a big abstraction—political *or* religious; it is better for him to aim at simplicity, than to perpetuate the obscurity which is gradually killing off the respect for poetry in the minds of intelligent readers; and it is better for him to use and not oppose the traditions of poetry—and for the Canadian poet not to completely ignore his relation to the tradition of poetry in Canada. These are all admirable tendencies in present-day Canadian poetry: so far they have not been realized fully enough to produce very striking or at least very extensive results. The question is whether the poet can find a new point of stability, rediscover the basic moral and religious values of our society, and by so doing achieve these results. But I already answered this when I answered the other part of my question.

John Sutherland, "The Past Decade in Canadian Poetry," *Northern Review*, IV, No. 2, December-January 1950/51.

LORNE PIERCE

Bliss Carman desired to compile a comprehensive anthology, covering the field of Canadian poetry from the earliest times to the present, and interpreting both east and west. Moreover, he aimed at a reasonably critical collection. While verses were included which time has endeared to a host of readers, he sifted from the body of Canadian poetry those poems which are significant, both for their content and their technical merit. He was friendly to poems reflecting the genius of the Dominion, as well as those cast in traditional moulds. Still, he was willing to welcome others representing days of change and experiment, provided there was substance in them, and music.

Much of his time, during the last three years of his life, was occupied with this anthology. While the selections reflected his personal tastes, Bliss Carman felt that they also represented the progress of poetry in Canada. It was my duty, as his literary executor, to put the manuscript in shape for the press. We had often discussed the anthology together, and I adhered as closely as possible to his known wishes. Some abridgment was necessary, chiefly owing to copyright restrictions. On the other hand I included poems which appeared after his death, feeling that they represented what he was pleased to call, "the valiant and joyous spirit which we find in the verse of our own times."

Within a few months of his death the world plunged into the abyss of the great Depression, and then came another and more wicked World War. Suffering and despair overwhelmed us on a world scale. Bitterness, fear, and disillusionment profoundly affected the arts and letters for an entire generation. A new era had begun.

There have been numerous anthologies of Canadian verse published since 1935, the year in which the latest revision of this anthology appeared. With one or two exceptions they have been concerned with the work of our new poets, and have performed a useful service. There has been a remarkable flowering of Canadian verse during the past quarter of a century, and I am happy that the publishing house of which I have been editor has been an unfailing ally of these new voices. Certainly it seemed our duty to assist these young poets, full, though they were, of the attitudes and techniques of their mentors abroad, for we knew that time would ripen them, that personal experience of a more mature kind would refine away their second-hand notions and tricks of style. A birthright Canadian poetry was in the making.

In completing the anthologies, known as *Our Canadian Literature Series*, which contains the most representative of our short stories, humour, essays and speeches, we decided to revise Carman's anthology as a part of the series. We hoped to make the revision in the spirit of the first edition, believing that his point of view was sound. It would be historical and representative, and it would present no thesis nor favour any school. With that in mind, as well as a general intention to avoid duplicating the left-of-centre collections, we invited Professor V. B. Rhodenizer, Ph.D., Litt.D., Head of the Department of English at Acadia University, to assume the principal responsibility of revision. We are grateful to him for the care with which he has completed his task.

Bliss Carman was most anxious, when the first edition appeared, that both poets and publishers should be thanked. This I do gladly once again, both for him, and for Dr. Rhodenizer and myself.

Lorne Pierce, Foreword to *Canadian Poetry in English* (Toronto: Ryerson, 1954).

V. B. RHODENIZER

By Way of Background

The history of Canadian poetry is so short, compared with that of Old-World nations, that the general reader requires little in the way of historical background in order to enjoy it. He naturally expects to find that our earliest poetry in English was written by men and women who came to what is now Canada from England, Scotland, and Ireland (the absence of a Welsh strain is conspicuous), either directly or by way of what is now the United States. Some poets of Irish extraction, unless they had come under the influence of the contemporaneous English tradition before coming to Canada, may show delightful traces of Irish folklore and, if they did not leave Ireland too early, of the romanticism of Tom Moore, who himself visited Canada in 1804, making the occasion memorable by giving us one of our two highly prized Canadian boat songs. Similarly, and more definitely, early poets from Scotland wrote in the manner of Burns. The early poets who came from England brought with them the classic tradition of the eighteenth century, and they and their successors were considerably slower than poets who remained in England in accepting, but ultimately did accept, the Romantic mode of writing poetry.

Two migrations from the United States, a minor and a major, affected the development of Canadian poetry. The minor, that of New Englanders to the lands from which the Acadians had been removed, could result, because of the predominance of Puritanism among the settlers, in religious literature only, which reached its lyric best in Henry Alline's *Hymns* (1786). The major migration, that of the Loyalists, not only contributed largely to the development of Canadian poetry but reinforced for a time the prevailing conservative adherence to the eighteenth-century classical tradition.

In the poetry of those who came to Canada after reaching maturity in the land of their birth, whether across the Atlantic or in what is now the United States, there is bound to be some expression of homesickness. What is significant from the Canadian point of view is the change by which the country of their adoption comes to be loved as home.

Patriotism in any land rests on two fundamental bases, love of the country itself and admiration for the achievements of its great men. Canada is still a young country, and in the days of the early settlers and for a considerable period thereafter, its history was very much in the making, so that patriotism rested almost wholly on the first basis, and even that, up to the time of Confederation, was regional. Till then, patriotism in what is now Canada could not be based on a unit larger than a province, and sometimes the patriotic unit was even smaller than that.

This makes it easier to understand the tremendous impetus that Confederation gave to poetry by Canadian-born poets, especially those who were entering the most impressionable period of their lives in 1867. All of the major poets of the "Confederation School"— Roberts, Carman, Campbell, Pauline Johnson, and the Scotts—were born in the short period 1860 to 1862. Even the youngest of them could probably remember the accomplished fact of Confederation, and all received the full impact of its early effect on the new nation. They established a poetic tradition that is still the true Canadian variant of the great poetic tradition of the English-speaking nations, itself only a variant of the fundamental and indispensable poetic tradition of all time.

Of this tradition, no requirement is more fundamental than one that poetry shares with all literature and all of the other arts; namely, that the art process is not complete until the experience of the artist is communicated, through the appropriate medium of the art, to those aesthetically capable of sharing the experience. Failure so to communicate can be due only to incompetence of the would-be artist in the use of his medium.

This and other basic aspects of poetic tradition Canadian poets on the whole, with characteristically sane conservatism, followed until after the First World War. Very few of them, major or minor, attempted even free verse, which, however it may have appealed to certain types of French and American temperaments and however much it may be justified *in theory* as an artistic rhythmic intermediary between the rhythm of prose and the meter of verse, seems to have had little appeal to Canadian poets and to have elicited little response from Canadian readers. Even MacInnes and Service, who stand strikingly apart from the main current of Canadian verse, do so almost wholly because of the content of their work, not because of their attitude to traditional poetic form. In general it may be said that the difference between major and minor poets is not in the kind of subject matter chosen or the artistic mould into which it is cast but in the degree of excellence attained in the use of similar subject matter expressed in traditional forms.

Also, the best Canadian poetry since the First World War has been written by poets who have remained true to the basic fundamentals of the authentic Canadian poetic tradition, modifying the merely conventional aspects, as is always permissible, to suit their individual artistic temperaments. Without in any way sacrificing the clarity and power of their work they have expressed themselves, to a large extent in genuine free verse, by means of imagery as startlingly original as that of the neometaphysicals at their most obscure. In this worthy succession, outstanding new names are Kenneth Leslie, Arthur S. Bourinot, Robert Finch, Earle Birney, Audrey Alexandra Brown, Laurence Dakin, Charles Bruce, Anne Marriott, James Wreford (Watson), and Raymond Souster. Others who have made a commendable contribution will be noted at the appropriate places in the anthology.

In comparison with lyric poetry, narrative poetry, especially when based on actual occurrences, has little opportunity to depart from indispensable tradition, so that Pratt, because of his almost exclusive devotion to narrative poetry based on fact, stands apart in solitary grandeur, an isolated mountain peak on one of the tablelands of the Canadian Olympus. In his critical discussion of the attitude of the poet to the permanent core of tradition (University of Toronto Quarterly, October, 1938, pp. 1-10), he is solidly on the side of the angels.

Had all of Canada's potential poets who have begun to publish since the First World War adopted the same sane attitude toward what is unchangeable in poetic tradition, it would have been much better for Canadian poetry. And such would probably have been the case had Canadian poetry been left to continue its natural course of development without the introduction of new or revived poetic techniques from abroad. As the co-editor of this anthology has sagely remarked, "No nation can achieve its true destiny that adopts without profound and courageous reasoning and selection the thoughts and styles of another." Left to themselves or aided by sound constructive criticism, most or all of the younger Canadian poets interested in experimentation with new content and modification of established forms, as well as those who were unduly imitative of the work of the "Confederation Group," would probably have worked out their own salvation, as others before them had done, and as some of both groups did despite the fact that they were not left to themselves.

Three of our professorial critics were unduly impressed by the value of the poetry they studied while doing research abroad. In their criticism of Canadian poetry, though still talking about the old "colonial" criticism, which seemed to regard Canadian literature as necessarily inferior to English and American literature but which had disappeared evidently without their being aware of the fact, they introduced, ironically enough, a new and more harmful colonial attitude to Canadian poetry; namely, that its development would be faster and greater by grafting certain foreign techniques on the native tradition. Most of all they favoured the method of one poem, "The Waste Land" (1922), by T. S. Eliot, who himself had said, at least two years before that poem was published, that youth is everywhere prone "to form itself on one or two private admirations." (*The Sacred Wood: Essays on Poetry and Criticism* [1920].) Moreover, many of Eliot's admirers do not yet seem to realize that, soon after writing "The Waste Land," Eliot himself turned wholeheartedly to the English classic tradition.

What is the method employed by Eliot, an American expatriate who became a resident of England in 1914 and a naturalized subject in 1927, in writing "The Waste Land"? In content it shows, as C. Day Lewis (*A Hope for Poetry,* Eighth Edition, p. 23) aptly phrases it, "symptoms of the psychic disease that ravaged Europe as mercilessly as the Spanish influenza." The method is a blend of that of the seventeenth-century English metaphysical poets with that of the French symbolists, by now influenced for the worse by inheritance or accretion of undesirable aspects of the practice of the French decadents and Parnassians, by dadaism, dating from 1916 and in purpose utterly destructive of all accepted values in art and elsewhere, and by a development within itself, surrealism, which by 1924 was strong enough to become a separate cult. Symbolism at its best, that is, when it has both clarity and imaginative power, is only one means of poetic expression; at its worst it results in obscurity, sometimes to the degree of incomprehensibility. The latter result is almost certain with the method of the metaphysical poets, for their imagery is characteristically far-fetched.

To give the ideas of his poem imaginative expression by this synthetic method Eliot turned for image and symbol to *From Ritual to Romance* (1920), by Jessie Laidlay Weston (? -1928), a book on the Grail legend that shows its relation to pre-Christian fertility cults and that gave Eliot his title, plan and much of his symbolism, and to Frazer's *The Golden Bough,* in particular to the material on the Phrygian deity Attis, the Greek Adonis and the Egyptian Osiris, all three associated in one way or another with death and revival. These main sources of image and symbol are supplemented by quotations from and allusions to various literary and religious works, with most of which the general reader would be as little acquainted as with the main sources.

With regard to the influence of "The Waste Land" on Canadian poetry, W. E. Collin, who studied at the University of Toulouse, tells us in *The White Savannahs* (1936) that one of its effects was "to convert *The Golden Bough* into a manual for young Canadian poets," giving them a body of "myth and ritual and symbolism" through which to express their emotions, thereby increasing "the interest and Strength" of their poetry (p. 194). Few persons acquainted with Frazer's monumental achievement would question the judgment of a recent panel of competent critics placing the one-volume edition among the first five of the ten greatest books, but to attempt to make its content the basis of imaginative appeal in poetry before that content has become generally known is to take poetry away from the people, especially in a country like Canada, where the population as shown by the 1951 census is still only slightly less than half rural and where a large part of the statistically urban population was rurally reared.

By having access to the manuscripts of the "new poets" who were to appear in *New Provinces: Poems of Several Authors* (1936) Collin was able to write of their work and yet synchronize the publication of his book with that of theirs. Of the six poets in *New Provinces,* Pratt and Finch, as we have already seen, are in the great tradition. The other four are F. R. Scott, largely responsible for the publication of the volume, A. J. M. Smith, Leo Kennedy, and A. M. Klein. With the finest of scholarship but with amazing critical inconsistency, Collin proceeds to minimize the achievement of two of Canada's great poets, Marjorie Pickthall and Archibald Lampman, by showing the influences that had shaped their poetry, and then to magnify the achievement of the Waste-Landish poets by exactly the same method, showing what influences had shaped their poetry. The "new poets" discussed by Collin, as well as others that may be similarly classified, will receive individual consideration at the appropriate places in this volume.

The late E. K. Brown (1905-1951) studied at the Sorbonne. His criticism of Canadian poetry in the annual *Letters in Canada* from 1935 to 1949 and in the Governor-General's-Award-winning *On Canadian Poetry* (1943, 1944) tends to underrate the work of conservative Canadian poets and to overrate that of those who follow the Waste-Land formula. Answering complaints of admirers of the poetry of Roberts to the effect that the critic had been "grudging" in his comments on the work of the poet, Brown says that if there is any ground for such complaint, "it lies in the fear I had lest his great age, the strong loyalties he evoked and the immense influence he had come to wield should prejudice the reception throughout the country of some kinds of poetry that he did not fully appreciate." (*Letters in Canada,* 1943, p. 314.) In his book he says, "The poetry of the Montreal group and their disciples and associates is the core of

Canadian verse during the past twenty years" (p. 70, 1944 ed.). He gives them space in proportion to this opinion.

The attitude of A. J. M. Smith to the established Canadian poetic tradition seems to be almost wholly the result of a bias in favour of the seventeenth-century English metaphysical poets acquired while doing graduate work at Edinburgh under Professor Grierson, authority on John Donne; although before he left McGill he had come into close contact with symbolism by way of study of the later and more obscure Yeats, who, like Eliot, was influenced by French symbolism. In any case, Smith, in his introductions to the different editions of *The Book of Canadian Poetry* (1943, 1948), is fair to the poets who established the Canadian tradition, though his criticism of the "new poets" of Canada is unduly slanted in their favour.

As might be expected, the new poets and their sponsoring critics tended to blame the difficulty that Canadian readers experienced with the new poetry, because of its obscurity, on the inability of those readers to appreciate ideas in poetry. This attitude is clearly implied as late as 1952, when the journalistic critic B. K. Sandwell, an ardent admirer of the new poets and critics, intimates in a review of Earle Birney's *Trial of a City and Other Verse* that Canadians are not so surprised as they used to be at finding ideas in poetry. Canadians have never been surprised at finding ideas in poetry. They have been surprised and mystified at finding ideas presented in the form of virtual cryptograms instead of in the form of genuine poems, but not in the works of Earle Birney.

This obscurity of much of the new poetry, the almost inevitable result of the methods of the new poets, whether the cocktail method of "The Waste Land" or the revived pure method of the seventeenth-century metaphysical poets of England, is particularly unfortunate, for it did its greatest harm in the field in which Canadian poetry most needed development, the field of the poetry of ideas, of reflective lyric.

New Provinces was followed by *Unit of Five* (1944), edited by Ronald Hambleton, who had visited England and there met some of the new poets. Besides examples of his own work, he included poems by James Wreford (Watson), who has so far rid himself of metaphysical tendencies as to win the Governor-General's Award, P. K. Page, Louis Dudek, and Raymond Souster, who does not belong here, still less among the unit of three—Irving Layton, Louis Dudek, and himself—represented in *Cerberus* (1952), the title of which we hope is not indicative of future titles by the Contact Press, in which the same three are interested.

Poets of *Unit of Five,* along with Kay Smith, Irving Layton, and Patrick Anderson, appear in *Other Canadians,* "An Anthology of New Poetry in Canada, 1940-1946" (1947), edited by John Sutherland, of Montreal, Managing Editor of *Northern Review,* who has been associated with a number of new but sometimes shortlived magazines and who seems hospitable to poetry of social amelioration, but, whether or not in the pure metaphysical tradition, certainly not in the Eliotic manner.

To the inherent weakness of at least the pure metaphysical theory and practice was added the utterly mistaken idea, particularly emphasized by Smith, that poetry speaks the language of the intellect. Ideas, the legitimate basic content of reflective lyric, can never *in themselves* be poetry, for the simple reason that they *are* expressed in the language of the intellect. They become poetry only when expressed in language that *communicates* them to the reader with clarity approaching the best of which the language of the intellect is capable and also with the power that all readers have the right to expect from poetry; that is, in the language of the imagination, which always has been, still is, and always will be (unless the leftists should succeed in destroying poetry altogether) the language of poetry.

Even the language of imagination will not produce poetry of ideas (or any other kind) unless the imagery, symbolism, and other means of appeal to the imagination fall within the range of the reader's experience. He will not get the ideas because he cannot comprehend their intended expression. Hence the absurdity of trying to write Canadian poetry of ideas for the imaginative appeal of which *The Golden Bough* is a manual or the far-fetched imagery of the metaphysicals the only means. In the latter case, the "new poets" fail to realize that originality is not enough. The imagery of the lunatic is the most original possible to man but the least sharable. Some of the imagery of our neometaphysicals is dangerously near the "lunatic fringe." The newest idea cannot become poetry unless it is *communicated* with clarity and power through the language of the imagination. The oldest significant idea will make a good new poem whenever a good new poet expresses it in imaginative language that is startlingly fresh and yet so sharable that some readers may even wonder why they themselves had not thought of putting it that way.

Where were the supporters of our Canadian variant of world poetic tradition while leftist critics were encouraging "new poets" to write in the manner of foreign poets? By the time *New Provinces* was published, the older university professors interested in Canadian literature and the journalistic critics had for several years been working so harmoniously together that the former were no longer regarded as "academic" but rather were looked upon as guides, philosophers (in critical theory), and friends. Indeed, some of the professors had been conducting weekly book columns in the newspapers, notably A. M. MacMechan (1862-1933) as "The Dean" in the Montreal *Standard* and W. T. Allison as literary editor of the Winnipeg *Tribune*. The professorial critics who had a sound attitude to tradition either did not fully realize or did not take seriously what the leftists were trying to do or were so busy with their worthy intellectual pursuits that, except for the article by Pratt referred to earlier, virtually nothing was published to correct the errors in the theory of poetry advanced by their leftist fellow professors. This theory either bewildered the journalistic critics (who had come to trust professors) or gave them an inferiority complex as regards their ability as critics.

The harmful effect that this state of affairs has had on the Canadian reflective lyric may be partly indicated by a brief general consideration of the work of poets who consciously followed the "new" theory of poetry and of those who, without realizing the nature of the theory, simply wrote in the manner of the former. (To a leftist critic it is highly commendable for one leftist to write in the manner of another but reprehensible for one traditionalist to write like another.) If we symbolize by sunlight the clarity of expression that characterizes every good reflective lyric, then the various degrees of obscurity found in the works of the "new poets," whether from poet to poet or from poem to poem by the same poet, may be symbolized by haze, smoke, fog, mist, and "smog." At times, even the most obscure achieve clarity by letting genuine poetic gift triumph over mistaken theory, as shown by the poems by which they are represented in this volume. But a preponderance of obscure poems in an anthology or a book by an individual poet made it decidedly detrimental to the cause of true poetry, never more so than when it was a book that had been awarded a Governor-General's Medal by a panel of leftist judges. Such an award might ensure the sale of the book but would not ensure its being read. Readers confronted with such a book naturally said, if this be poetry, I'll none of it, which means that they turned away not only from the "new poetry" but also from that written in the authentic tradition. Canadian poetry was relatively the least read of literary types in Canada from 1936 to the end of the first half of Canada's century. The "new poets" took poetry away from the people, and, as one college president wittily remarked, they did not give it to anybody else. A good omen is that Charles Bruce and E. J. Pratt won the latest two Governor-General's Awards. It is the hope of the editors of this anthology to give poetry back to the people by presenting them with poetry they can understand and to heighten their enjoyment of it by giving them a few suggestions for its appreciation.

In Aid of Appreciation

The reader of Canadian poetry will enjoy its distinctive characteristics more intelligently if he appreciates them against the background of the characteristics common to all poetry. Like the other forms of literature and also like the fine arts other than literature, poetry depends for its effects on the communication, through an artistic medium, to persons of taste, of a sharable aesthetic experience. The medium of poetry, as of all literature, is language, and the poet's command of this medium depends on his imaginative ability to make his language as specific and concrete as possible, by the use of examples, illustrations, incidents, comparisons, figures of speech, symbols and literal images, the last of which it is the primary function of imagination to create. Imagination in its basic aspect is the power of calling to mind absent objects that we have formerly experienced by one or more of the five senses. Since most people recall most readily objects experienced by the sense of sight, the word *image,* which originally meant a mental picture only, has been extended in meaning to include a mental impression of any kind of sense experience. Thus we have, according to the five senses, visual, auditory, gustatory (or palatal), olfactory and tactile images. A special kind, the motor image, is experienced when the reader or hearer performs in imagination movements suggested by words or phrases.

The language of poetry is rhythmical as well as imaginative, and so we consider briefly the nature of rhythm as it occurs in the English language in general and in Canadian poetry in particular. The inadequate conventional explanation that it depends merely on a succession of accented and unaccented syllables and has nothing to do with time (as have the classical metres made up of a succession of long and short syllables) may cause most readers to miss the major part of its appeal. Rhythm depends not merely on accents but also on their recurrence at *approximately* equal time intervals. (Mechanical regularity is the negation of art.) When approximately the same time interval between accents is continuously maintained and the number of unaccented syllables to each accent kept down to one or two, the resulting rhythm is regular verse, or metre, which every normal person can appreciate, because, once the pattern is established in the mind, it is easy to follow. When approximately the same time interval between accents is maintained for only a few beats in succession and then changed and when more than two syllables occur between some of the accents, the result is the rhythm of prose or of free verse, as the case may be. Readers unable to appreciate these constantly changing rhythms need not be disturbed by the fact, for they are in a position analogous to that of a dancer who, accustomed to dancing to orchestras that play one kind of dance through to the end before beginning another kind, is suddenly confronted by an orchestra that plays three bars of a polka, five bars of a waltz, four bars of a foxtrot, similarly small portions of a rumba, a samba, a conga and so on. Not many can make the constant readjustment essential to an appreciation of rhythms other than metrical.

The tendency to write in free verse instead of meter has decidedly increased among modern Canadian poets. Even those who have succeeded have handicapped their readers as indicated above, and those who do not know what free verse is have achieved nothing better than shredded prose, or, as Sydney J. Harris, of the Ottawa *Evening Citizen*, phrases it, "hysterical prose."

Canadian poetry employs all of the four primary modes of literary writing that communicate sharable aesthetic experience through the medium of imaginative and rhythmical language—the descriptive, the lyric, the narrative, and the dramatic. Of these, the simplest (not necessarily the easiest to appreciate) is the descriptive. Of literary description there are two pure types, the pictorial and the atmospheric. The poet writes pictorial description primarily or wholly to communicate to the reader a mental picture of some object, scene, or person, observed as he writes, or remembered, or imagined. He has in mind a definite physical point of view, which may be implied or definitely stated. The reader of a pictorial description may enjoy it to the maximum by noticing what visual images give the outline of the picture, fill in the colour and suggest light and shade; what images of other kinds make the description more vivid; whether there is also a trace of atmospheric description; to what extent the total effect is heightened by appropriateness of form.

In atmospheric description the poet communicates to the reader the mood evoked by what is observed, remembered, or imagined. He never ceases to describe, but he chooses only or mainly such images and uses only or mainly . . . such other imaginative devices as will cumulatively suggest in the course of the description the mood to be communicated. The less trace there is of word picture, the more impressive the atmospheric effect will be. The appreciation of atmospheric description thus depends on perceiving the predominating mood, recognizing the skill with which it is more and more powerfully communicated, and noticing, even more than in pictorial description, the added effectiveness of harmonizing content and form.

The Canadian scene lends itself admirably to descriptive writing, and Canadian poetry is consequently rich in both pictorial and atmospheric description, not only as pure types, but also as incidental material in lyric, narrative and dramatic poetry, in the last of which it is restricted to the description of characters and stage setting.

Next to the descriptive mode of writing in simplicity (though not necessarily the easiest or even second easiest to appreciate) is the lyric mode, of the production of which the most obvious example is of course the lyric, originally a poem suited to being sung to the accompaniment of a lyre and therefore naturally emotional in content and musical in expression. As a result of its origin, most conventional comment on the lyric has made and still makes it always emotional in content. This theory, if it ever did correspond wholly with the facts, does so no longer. Of the great body of modern lyrics, more are reflective in content than are emotional; that is, they are written primarily to express *thought* rather than emotion. Thus there are two simple or pure types of lyric, the emotional and the reflective, according to whether the purpose is to express the emotion or the thought of the poet.

In either kind, the stimulus may or may not be recorded. If the emotion or the thought cannot be effectively communicated to the reader without his sharing in imagination the experience that gave rise to it, the good poet records the stimulus. This is frequently the case when the contemplation of some aspect of nature gives rise to the emotion or thought, and then the stimulus is likely to be recorded by pictorial description or atmospheric description or both, kinds of writing that the reader has already learned how to appreciate. If the stimulus is not recorded, the reader immediately proceeds to determine the emotion or the thought that constitutes the basic subject matter of a lyric. After that comes the culminating phase of appreciation, the discovery of the ways in which the emotion or the thought is given concrete expression through appeal to the imagination. In the case of a reflective lyric, the imaginative expression of the thought creates a *by-product* of emotion, without which the finished poem would not be poetry at all but merely expository verse. Failure of conventional criticism to realize that the emotional appeal of reflective lyric is in the *expression* and not in the *matter expressed* may be another reason why such criticism makes the lyric always emotional in content.

The progressive and desirable change to more reflective content in the lyric has during the second quarter of the twentieth century been accompanied by an undesirable and largely unnecessary departure from the other primal characteristic of the lyric, musical language. Even in Canada where, as we have seen, the attitude to literary tradition has formerly tended to a sound conservatism, some of the "new poets" previously discussed have endeavoured to dissolve the felicitous union, mythologically approved of Apollo, of "music married to immortal verse." What Apollo has joined together let not the metaphysicals put asunder.

The more complex lyric types are simple or pure lyrics with modifications or additions in content or in form or in both. The content of the simple or pure lyric is always the poet's own emotion or thought. If he expresses instead the emotion or thought of another with whom he imaginatively identifies himself, the result is the dramatic lyric in its simplest form. If he expresses his own emotion or thought to an audience (of one or more) indicated but not identified, the result is a dramatic lyric of a slightly different but still simple kind. If he expresses the emotion or thought of another who speaks for himself to an audience as in the immediately preceding type, the result is a dramatic lyric of the subtlest kind. Again, pure lyric content may be expressed in one of the most exacting of forms, the sonnet. Even so elaborate a type as the formal elegy consists of an artistic sequence of three lyric responses to a stimulus (the death of an individual): the grief (emotional), the questioning (reflective) and the consolation (reflective).

As in the case of the simple or pure types of description, the Canadian scene lends itself admirably to the writing of nature lyrics of the two simple or pure types. In fact, the reader who knows how to appreciate simple or pure lyrics, emotional and reflective, written in ordinary metrical and stanzaic patterns, and lyrical content expressed in one or the other of the two types of sonnet, knows how to appreciate almost the entire body of Canadian lyric poetry.

The fundamental content of the third mode of writing, the narrative, is action. The nature of action may most easily be understood by considering it against the background of our discussion of the method of pictorial description, which depends very largely on visual imagery. Action may be regarded as a specialized form of visual imagery. To make this clear, let us use an ant hill as an example. We might come upon it when all of the ants were at rest. A word picture of it in that state would be a "still-life" description. We might then disturb the ants and cause a scene of disorderly movement. A word picture of this scene would still be description, but the movement depicted would cause it to differ from and become more interesting than the "still-life" description. After a few moments of disorder, we might discover on the part of one or more ants a purposive movement in the face of obstacles; for example, the struggle to carry a pupa to a place of safety. This purposive movement, communicated to the reader by a special use of visual imagery, becomes action. That is, we have passed from description to narration. In this case, as in many narratives, the struggle that gives rise to the outward and physical action is itself outward and physical. A more subtle kind of outward and physical action is that which proceeds from an inner conflict, mental, or moral or both.

Whatever the origin of the struggle or conflict, the simplest kind of narrative requires purposive movement or action made by characters within appropriate limits of space and time. Hence the three essential elements of narration are action, character and setting. To these may be added either or both of two other elements: atmosphere, to which all three of the essential elements may contribute and the nature of which is already clear from our discussion of atmosphere in description; an idea which is expressed indirectly by means of the narrative, not directly as in the reflective lyric.

The simplest kind of narration follows the course of a single line of action resulting from a struggle or conflict between two opposing forces and ending, after a period of suspense during which it seems at times as if the character or characters are winning and at other times quite the reverse, in final success (happy ending) or final failure (unhappy ending which, if made to seem inevitable and to end in catastrophe, becomes tragic). The various turns in favour of or against the central character or characters in the course of the action that precedes the decisive turn (major crisis) may be called minor crises, and their artistic purpose is to hold and increase interest. Since even so simple a plot can have a high degree of interest, it is obvious that the interest intensifies as further conflicts are added.

Canadian narrative poetry has thus far been largely concerned with the heroic struggles of actual persons—discoverers, explorers, pioneer settlers, missionaries and railroad builders—in actual settings, and so has a strong historical as well as literary appeal.

The preceding discussion of narrative technique leads easily and naturally to a consideration of the last of the four modes of writing, the dramatic. To make successful acted drama, in which the story is not narrated but presented in dialogue and action on the stage by actors who impersonate the characters, the plot must be such that it can be presented in no other way so well as on the stage, and it must fall within the time limits set by the stage. Drama is at once the most vivid and the most difficult of all forms of literary art. The one-act play makes even more exacting demands on the skill of the dramatist than does the full-length play, for the former, if true to type, has perfect unity of time (unbroken action) and perfect unity of place (a single scene).

In addition to plays written primarily for the stage, there are also "closet dramas," which, though having every aspect of dramatic form, are better suited to reading than to stage representation. This is a fortunate state of affairs for the writers of poetic drama in Canada, for while some of the verse plays by Canadians may be "good theatre," most of them are intended to be read. Canadian readers may enjoy them in printed form as readily as they enjoy descriptive, lyric and narrative poetry. Complete verse plays are beyond the scope of an anthology of poetry, but skilful choosing of extracts can suggest their poetic power.

V. B. Rhodenizer, Introduction to *Canadian Poetry in English* (Toronto: Ryerson, 1954).

V

RESURGENCE

Resurgence

Every bit of so-called reaction is useful, mainly, to stir up the fires of revolt. No sooner had the Pierce-Rhodenizer anthology been published than a sharp review in the Montreal magazine *CIV/n* took a swipe at the conservative position of these older critics. Robert Currie, a satirical writer and poet (he turned later to novel writing) then connected with the little magazine *CIV/n,* dissected the Canadian sentimental syndrome in his witty review piece.

The sentimental syndrome was, and still is, deeply entrenched in the *Canadian Poetry Magazine,* official publication of the Canadian Authors' Association, established in 1921 and dominated in the twenties by Bliss Carman and Charles G. D. Roberts. Curiously enough, Earle Birney, a leading figure in the modernist movement since the appearance of *David and Other Poems* (1942), attempted to win over this magazine on behalf of modern poetry by taking its editorship in 1946. The experiment failed, and Birney's resignation in June of 1948 marked a return to the old order within this organ of the Canadian Authors' Association. His letter resigning the editorship is reprinted from the magazine *Here and Now* where it survives as an interesting record indicating the lines drawn by this divorce, and suggests a militant return to forthright experiment and genuine modern creativity.

In the same period, a more central reintegration of the poetry movement occurred among poets in Toronto and Montreal. Here, we must recall that the Montreal group had dispersed in 1944 (an actual agreement of dissolution of the partnership of Layton, Dudek and Sutherland in *First Statement* was signed on September first, 1944) and that late in 1947 a gradual weakening of Sutherland's sense of modernism had created a lull in the literary scene. Raymond Souster, becoming increasingly restive in the face of this literary reaction, pushed for the launching of a new little magazine which would challenge the hegemony of Sutherland's *Northern Review.* *Contact* magazine was founded (after much soul-searching on the part of Dudek and Souster) in January of 1952, and the mood of revived activism in Canadian poetry which it generated led to the founding of Contact Press and the publication of its first title: the embattled book *Cerberus* containing individual prefaces and poetry by Dudek, Layton and Souster.

Both *Contact* magazine and the press which stemmed from it, were events of major significance for the Canadian scene. Not only was the poetry of a tough and uncompromising realism making itself heard once more, but the connections which Souster was able to establish with a new middle generation of American poets (Creeley, Corman, Olson and others) through the agency of his magazine (*Contact*) produced an infusion of newly-developed American tendencies in poetry, and would be related to the success, ten years later, of the influence which this school of writing would have on Canadian poets on the West Coast.

LOUIS DUDEK

Poetry in Canada needs a new start. To the young, the field is wide open. Our younger poets are getting grey about the temples. The work of the forties is by now old and yellow: it was a good beginning, but not yet the real thing. There is now a ready audience for any young writer with something fresh and bouncing to say, someone with a new technique, a vision, or a gift for making art out of matters of fact. But where are the young? Where is the "new" generation?

Possibly they don't know where to begin! Lack of "contact," of information, is the principal gap in our education; that is, the sort of education which is active in life and enriches experience. There can be no continuity in our culture if we do not understand what has happened and what is happening. It is good to see a new magazine, *Contact*, proposing to attack the vacuum of ignorance.

Here is the situation. Canada needs poets now who will have learned from the experimental and realistic writing of the last ten years and who will go on from there. Let them learn at least what to avoid: certainly not to repeat.

Examples. Imagination, the raw stuff? Yes, we are capable of it; exuberantly. Social realism, ditto. Free verse, we can do. Seven types of ambiguity? We have surpassed. Why go on; we are capable of writing modern poetry of a rudimentary kind in various forms and schools.

But in Canada we have not written the perfectly original thing, nor even the perfectly finished imitation in any one kind. The poet we are waiting for is one who will not be an amateur but a professional (in craftsmanship, not cash), one who will not be merely interested in poetry, but will be dedicated to the art. This is not a matter of economics, but of the direction of will. Can the "new generation" carry it this far? Probably not. We cannot expect too much. But that is the direction.

Specifically, one could suggest a few immediate aims. Let the young poet keep away from abstractions, the prime ailing of Canadian amateur verse. Let there be concrete images: let them grow into symbols, drama, physical experiments, nightmares or apocalyptic fantasies; but let the poem be made of pigs and perambulators, not ————————ness, ————————tion, ————————uth!

Let there be energy. The tone of a poem need not be limited to grey *nature morte*, melancholy and meditation. There are other emotions, states of mind! Activities! Let's take poetry out of its present boundaries. Carry the gods to a new Latium.

And thought. Let the poem contain thought, or the results of thought. Poetry is communication of something worth saying. One must think through to a meaning others will find it worth their time to consider. The death of poetry is its reduction to a purely ornamental, or "cultural" function; we must scrap the ornament and come back to meaning.

Poetry today aims at making the major integration of life.

But the poem must be worked on. Again and again. It has been said that poetry is a craft, like music or painting, or carpentry. The tools are free to anyone who will use them: they are in all the great poems that have been written; their present handling may be studied in the work of contemporary poets. We learn, not by rule, but by example.

The young poet must read the books and mags. The knowledge of what has been thought and said since 1910 is hard to come by in Canadian libraries and book stores. The books have not been given to our young people. They know nothing of the living literature of our time, Canadian or any other. College students graduate in ignorance of the one kind of knowledge that might save them from advertisers, publicity men, propagandists. So the young in Canada must lift themselves by their own bootstraps; spend every possible cent on books, on the living poets, on criticism, on the knowledge that alone can bring this country forty years forward into the present.

There is no time to waste. It's beginning to rain bombs. Let us at least receive them in the present tense when they fall on us; or the poetry will be in the pity. The poet has more to say and understand today than he has ever had at any other time in history. Why are the young poets at a loss for words?

Louis Dudek, "Où sont les jeunes?", *Contact*, I, No. 1, January 1952.

LOUIS DUDEK

People have always known, before the age of machines and mechanistic science, that it is imagination—as poetry, faith, ethics—which gives order and beauty to life. Modern man, become a tool of industrial, commercial, and political machinery, believes that this work of the imagination is false, trivial, or irrelevant: a belief which makes him the petty monster that he is. The failure of imagination, bad poetry, makes him a Prufrock, a Babbitt, a Boob.

The way to freedom and order in the future will lie through art and poetry. Only imagination, discovering man's self and his relation to the world and to other men, can save him from complete enslavement to the state, to machinery, the base dehumanized life which is already spreading around us.

Language is the great, saving first poem, always being written; all others are made of it. We must prize it, protect it against the destroyers and perverters of our time. Journalists and advertisers, all who use words to "sell," whether goods or ideas, destroy the reverence and life-giving power of good speech; they are enemies of mankind whom all must learn to fear and repel.

Anyone who understands this is capable of assuming a responsibility, of becoming a citizen of the world. Anyone who reads a good poem with understanding—a poem that bites into the evil, or that retrieves a truth—creates an order in himself. Every person who does this, who opposes the life-destroying forces of modern life with the assertion of full humanity as one finds it in the best poetry of our time and of past times, is helping to make men free, true to their greatest capability of work and happiness.

We three in this book share the same affirmations and therefore the same negations in the face of the present. For all three of us the external horrors of the world today, as well as its scattered beauty, are much the same. If our affirmations are not filled with more hallelujahs, it is only because all affirmations are pushed aside by the threatening destructiveness that faces us all. Our theme is love. But who can sing of love at the walls of Hiroshima, Belsen, Korea?

Poetry cannot change the world in a day, the world of wars, oppressions and mob-suicide which men have prepared for themselves. But in the end, only poetry, imagination, can do so. Actuality itself is a metaphor made of iron, the diseased poem which man has erected out of mass frustration, out of centuries of evil. Poetry, therefore, opposed to this, has power, immense power for good, because it is the true poem, the epic all men would live if they were free. And that is, after all, what we want.

Louis Dudek, Preface to Louis Dudek's Poems, *Cerberus* (Toronto: Contact Press, 1952).

IRVING LAYTON

Dudek, Souster and I hold different opinions on a number of subjects, ranging from the war in Korea to the optimum size of women's bathing suits. What brings us together in *Cerberus* is the belief that to write poetry is to say a loud nix to the forces high-pressuring us into conformity or atomic dispersion. Also, that the best part of any man today is the hell he carries inside him; and that only poetry can transmute that into freedom, love, intelligence.

The Canadian poet, however, is an exile condemned to live in his own country. He has no public, commands no following, stirs up less interest than last year's licence plate. It is worthwhile to speculate on the reasons that make this the most philistine country in the world, not excepting the United States. Is it professionalized sports? The ape intelligence of a vicious, profit-seeking press? An educational system bevelled to the needs of business and technology? These, of course, are partly to blame. More important, I think, is the drag of middle-class morality, suspicious of all enjoyment and neurotically hostile to the release of art and sex; and gentility, the gilded and gelded pseudo-culture of flourishing bankers and brewers.

Gentility, propriety, respectability—give the thing any name you will—is responsible for nine-tenths of the miserable, devitalized stuff that passes for poetry in this country; and for the infantile pruriency that is the stock response of the great majority of Canadians to the appeal of art. So powerful is the grip of gentility that even those poets who are in rebellion against it write a kind of well-dressed, empty, pseudo-mystical nature verse, or leftist poetry with a Methodist flavour. Unless we fold up this genteel tradition, a tradition called into existence by a graceless leisure class but preserved by clergymen, underdeveloped schoolmarms, university graduates, and right-thinking social workers, very little vigorous and original artistic work will ever be seen in Canada. Whitman's "barbaric yawp" is wanted to send them finger-plugging their ears and scurrying for cover under their tea-tables.

We have one other reason for publishing *Cerberus* at the present time. Some editorial jackass—the name is superfluous—started a rumour flying that the poetic ferment which had begun with so much promise in the middle forties had petered out scandalously before the end of the decade. After that, several other Missouri canaries lumbered forward to announce the same heart-breaking discovery. How touching it was to see them shaking their well-proportioned asinine heads and to hear their woebegone cries. Since a good deal of that poetry was a protest against war and social inequality, the genteel at once took heart at the news and began to crawl out of their kennels. By the clever whachamacallit of returning manuscript after manuscript our editorial burro was able to pretend that the bright rebellious talents which had appeared during and after the war years had stopped writing and—final touch of the macabre—even to drop tears at the mysterious disease which had carried them off unfulfilled to an early literary grave.

It is, in part, to help revise this mendacious account of an exciting period in the literary history of this country that we are publishing the present collection of poems. We intend, moreover, to drive the point home by publishing shortly the volumes of other "dead" but now happily resurrected poets.

Irving Layton, Preface to Irving Layton's Poems, *Cerberus* (Toronto: Contact Press, 1952).

RAYMOND SOUSTER

Souster (hereafter S.) never went past high school, and has learned everything about poetry the hard way. Much the way Louis the Dudek tells it in his article "Où Sont Les Jeunes?" in *Contact One*. Shouldn't say "learned," for he's still learning, hopes he'll go on learning; when he stops doing that, the poetry will probably stop with it.

S. has always believed (and still believes) that the primary function of poetry is to communicate something to somebody else. Not too important what that something is, the big thing is to get it across, "make contact." If you fail here all that follows, everything else you throw in, is wasted, and you might as well start all over again. Ninety percent of modern poetry fails here. And will go on failing until it learns this and puts the remedy into practice.

S. has been dissatisfied for a long time with existing forms, feeling bound within them, mummified. But up until a year ago didn't have a clue. Now he's been shown the signs of an opening, a possible right road for the future. It starts somewhere in the *Cantos* of Ezra Pound and goes on to Charles Olson. You've heard of Ez: never mind too much about Olson, he'll come to the top soon enough; you can't keep talent like he has down. His basic idea, *Composition by Field*, as opposed to inherited line, may well start a revolution in English poetry. Worth studying; worth taking a personal crack at.

S. wishes that all critics would get off the backs of the poets; encourage them, have patience, don't label them and then try to keep the same labels pasted on even after they've moved on into another direction, advanced or fallen by the wayside. Above all, be positive— show them the way or the way you'd like to see them go. Only find out where your direction leads to first.

S. in closing wishes the universities might wake up and produce something besides gutless scholars and chemical engineers. How about a few poets? Or have they already killed off the potential crop for the next fifty years?

Raymond Souster, Preface to Raymond Souster's Poems, *Cerberus* (Toronto: Contact Press, 1952).

EARLE BIRNEY

> *Extracts from a letter to Mr. Philip Child, Bursar of the Canadian Authors' Association, in resigning from the Association, 15 November, 1948.*

. . . I joined the CAA in 1946 after considerable hesitation had arisen from several years of reading the official organs and hearing the official speeches of leading members of the Association, which had led me to feel that the CAA was primarily concerned with boosting the literary products of its members, whether they be good or bad, and not infrequently also in leading the attack on the healthy attempts at experimentation among younger writers. Nevertheless I felt that I could not in fairness judge the Association without becoming one of its members and working within it for a more liberal approach to literary art. Since that time until I resigned from the editorship of the *Canadian Poetry Magazine* in June of this year

I have worked to the best of my ability, and often to the detriment of my own writing, to promote the point of view that I held, both by participation in the work of local branches and by editing the *Canadian Poetry Magazine*. I have now come to realize that the attitude of the majority of the Association, or at least of the members who control its public statements, makes further participation on my part both a waste of time and a compromise of my artistic principles.

. . . In the CAA a writer's success is judged by his sales, his ability to win local prizes or to say kind things about his own wares and the wares of the leading figures in the Association. The standards of judgment are those of the Victorian age only . . . . As the months went by in my editing of CPM I found that while the slightest effort to secure subscriptions would greatly increase the circulation outside the CAA, there was a steady drop within the CAA from members who had submitted, to my mind, thoroughly worthless verses which I had rejected. Throughout the two years I found that most of my volunteer support, and my encouragement through letters, subscriptions and publicity, came from outside the CAA, while within it there was a steady whispering campaign, especially in the Toronto branch, against the magazine, and, in some cases, actual sabotage of my efforts. . . . The CAA, to my mind, is predominantly a body of aging hacks and reactionaries who maintain a dubious prestige simply by persuading a number of genuine writers such as yourself to represent them in the public eye. It is for this reason particularly that I have come to feel the CAA is actually a hindrance to the growth of a mature literary culture in this country. It compromises the serious artist by associating him with its attacks on the younger writer's experimentalism and with its general Puritanical and venal approach to the problem of writing. I think the time has come for the serious writer in this country to break with the CAA and form a guild of craftsmen who stand for the principles of artistic freedom and integrity and sound standards of craftsmanship. I can only hope that you yourself will come to agree with me. For to age is common, but not as the CAA ages, for by its hostility to the work of the young it fails to renew itself with the blood of youth.

Sincerely yours,

Earle Birney

Earle Birney, Letter of Resignation from the Editorship of *Canadian Poetry Magazine*, in *Here and Now*, I, No. 3, January 1949.

ROBERT A. CURRIE*

Every Canadian knows Bliss Carman, or at least *of* him. For generations earnest schoolmarms have chucked him at captive schoolchildren and made them memorize huge chunks of his more mellifluous verses. In spite of that kind of introduction to him, some of us remember him as a good poet. He has fallen into bad company.

Dr. Lorne Pierce and Dr. V. B. Rhodenizer are prime examples of the evil companions an unsuspecting poet can pick up through the years. Neither of them poets, each postures as a critic of Canadian poetry, and each attempts to shape and foster what is unabashedly referred to as "the great Canadian tradition."

The first piece of low comedy was begun in 1922 and fully enacted in 1934. Carman had intended bringing out a comprehensive anthology of Canadian poetry, had worked on it for a number of years, was working on it at the time of his death. And he can be forgiven the spiritless stuff he collected; a definitive anthology of Canadian verse at that time could perform a real function as a commentary on the dreary state of Canadian poetry. It was left for Dr. Pierce to bring the thing out in 1934 under the title *Our Canadian Literature* (Ryerson, 361 pp.).

This was in many ways a book of arresting charm, a wonderful little piece of grotesquerie. It contained the work of 80-odd English-speaking poets as well as the verses of some 30 French-Canadian talents, each in a separate section, with the likenesses of the various poets scattered profusely throughout the book in woodcut. The female poets, writers for the most part of what can best be described as newspaper verse, usually have three names and one poem (about God, apple blossoms or the Indians), and in a stroke of gallantry Dr. Pierce made them timeless by avoiding publication of their dates of birth. Dr. Pierce had to reach far into the barrel (over the shoulders of Carman) to fatten the book with rhymesters that were better left forgotten. But even at that he complained, like a zealous stamp-collector, that the anthology was incomplete. "Copyright restrictions," he said, "have prevented the inclusion of anything by William Chapman (1850-1917)" as one might say, "if only we had the 1850 tupenny magenta on blue paper."

No one would want to criticize Dr. Pierce for this period piece. The wretched thing is tasteless enough by present standards, but it does have the aroma of an old Victorian leather Morris chair and if you were a sentimentalist (as I secretly suspect Dr. Pierce must

*Robert Currie died as this anthology was being prepared; his novel remains unpublished.

be), you could probably even churn up a perverted kind of affection for the book and the forgotten people and events it records.

But then Dr. Rhodenizer came out of the wolds of Wolfville, Nova Scotia, joined forces with Dr. Pierce, and the result is a remarkable work called *Canadian Poetry in English Chosen by Bliss Carman, Lorne Pierce and V. B. Rhodenizer* (Ryerson, 1954, 4 bucks).

The two anthologies have much in common. Virtually every English-speaking poet that appeared in the first finds his way into the second, together with 120 additional versifiers, many of whom were dead and buried, literally and figuratively, before the turn of the century. The Kathryn Munro Tuppers and the Frances Beatrice Taylors are back and you wonder perhaps what justification Dr. Rhodenizer could summon for perpetuating something like this thing by Beatrice Redpath:

THE STAR

I think God sang when He had made
A bough of apple bloom,
And placed it close against the sky
To whiten in the gloom.
But, oh, when He had hung a star
Above a blue, blue hill,
I think God in His ecstasy
Was startled . . . and was still.

It needs no comment. Nor does this 20th-century addition to the great tradition by Marjorie Freeman Campbell:

ONLY THE HEART

Teach me, life,
To take my friend as he is:
Confident that only he,
And God who shapes him on the potter's wheel,
Can estimate what strains and stresses,
What conditioning of circumstance
Have moulded him.
Man's eye may judge
Alone the finished form
Only the heart knows its own despair!

A very lovely sentiment, I dare say. And this, in 1954, is being offered as representative Canadian poetry.

Dr. Rhodenizer's views as expressed in the introduction are, from a supposedly literate man, even more surrealistic than the mass of quaint doggerel he has accumulated. The following are some of his observations taken at random:

Also the best Canadian poetry since the First World War has been written by poets who have remained true to the basic fundamentals of the authentic Canadian poetic tradition, modifying the merely conventional aspects, as is always permissible, to suit their individual artistic temperaments.

The professorial critics who had a sound attitude to tradition either did not fully realize or did not take seriously what the leftists were trying to do or were so busy with their worthy intellectual pursuits that . . . virtually nothing was done to correct the theory of poetry advanced by their leftist fellow professors. It is the hope of the editors of this anthology to give poetry back to the people by presenting them with poetry they can understand . . .

Apart from the literary fascism implicit in the foregoing quotations, there are comic elements in the piece. For some curious reason Dr. Rhodenizer has felt obliged to include the work of poets who are patently anathema to him, and his running commentaries on them are delightful. Of P. K. Page he remarks that "her imagery is sometimes daring beyond the point of clarity"; he enjoins Souster to "Come out from among them, (Dudek and Layton) and be ye separate"; and he calls Layton "the Ishmael of Canadian poets." But comic as all this may be, our antique and scholarly friend has a lot to answer for. Wounded nostalgia leads him to misrepresent the state of poetry in Canada today by cluttering the scene with the work of duds whose Mss should have been sealed with them in their coffins, and at the same time leads him to give inadequate space to the so-called "new poets" who represent the beginnings of the only real poetry that has appeared in Canada. But even the venerable Dr. Rhodenizer, for all his mischief, can't hurt serious Canadian poetry. His book, after all, is only a publisher's hoax.

Robert A. Currie, "Don't Blame This On Bliss," *CIV/n*, No. 7, *ca* April 1954.

VI

POINTS OF VIEW

Points Of View

The growth of any new literature presupposes a corresponding body of criticism and literary theory. As we have seen earlier, in A. J. M. Smith's essay on Canadian criticism, Canada has been slow in developing critical theory pertaining to its literature. However, a number of significant developments in this direction are worth noting.

Both Bliss Carman and Archibald Lampman wrote some literary criticism. Carman's high-minded theory of art as literature—*The Friendship of Art* (1904), *The Kinship of Nature* (1904), *The Poetry of Life* (1905), and *Talks on Poetry and Life* (1926)—is derived from some of the thinking of the Late Romantics and the Symbolists. Lampman's essay "Two Canadian Poets"—a lecture delivered in 1891, deals with Canadian poetry as a literature in its beginnings, and sees it in terms of "excellence as judged from the purest standpoint," an outlook common in the ambience of the genteel culture of the England of the time.

There is almost no developed literary theory from E. J. Pratt and the poets of the transition. The first consistent modern critical thought appears with A. J. M. Smith, in his essays "Wanted—Canadian Criticism" (1926) and "Contemporary Poetry" (1928). Modern poetry begins to have its supporting criticism. F. R. Scott's occasional critical writing is practical and unpretentious, and expresses his radical political views rather than a literary doctrine. The poets of the 1930s foreshadow a coming theoretical reconstruction, but the main lines of the position remain to be defined.

In the 1940s we see several substantial attempts to define the modern critical position in Canada. There is John Sutherland whose essays appear in earlier sections of this book; A. J. M. Smith is prominent again with his Introduction to *The Book of Canadian Poetry* (1943) and other writings; Irving Layton in various prefaces and fugitive articles reveals a vigorous, aggressive literary position directly related to the literature of social realism and anti-Victorian protest. Louis Dudek moves from a didactic theory of literary realism to larger intellectual perspectives which provide the motive for his philosophically-oriented poetry. Even Raymond Souster who rarely speaks as a critic appears in various prefaces and occasional statements as a convinced proponent of a North American realist poetry.

The didacticism of the forties poets is relieved by the other critical writings of the period. Desmond Pacey, our foremost chronicler of literary history, leans towards a socio-historical interpretation but holds to an essentially neutral and descriptive approach. Earle Birney reveals a generous humanism in which literature serves as an intellectual delight and higher entertainment. His short Preface to the anthology *20th Century Canadian Poetry* (1953), which is included here, contains ideas very similar to those treated more extensively in his *The Creative Writer* (seven talks for the CBC which were published by the Corporation in 1966).

The next branch of Canadian criticism, antithetical to the school of social realism, has taken its impetus from the writings of Northrop Frye. His two lectures on "The Educated Imagination" reproduced here emphasize the importance of myth or dream as distinct from so-called reality, and show the historical unity of mythopoeic conceptions in the Bible and in classical mythology. The essays of James Reaney and Eli Mandel are closely related to these ideas. The antiscientific orientation of mythopoeic poetry and its derivation from the work of William Blake are distinctly revealed. The Preface of Eli Mandel foresees a realigning of Canadian poetry in the light of these principles.

The most recent school of critical writing, the Tish school in Vancouver, has returned to a naturalistic theory of poetry and poetic form. It is directly derived from William Carlos Williams who stands in the American realist tradition (examples of this criticism appear in Section VIII of this collection). Other trends in recent Canadian poetry seem to follow the same pattern of development in Alden Nowlan, Al Purdy, Milton Acorn and the urban realist poets in magazines like *Yes, Cataract* and *Delta*. Like American literature in general, Canadian poetry divides into two branches: one related through British writing to European literary culture, formal and rooted in traditional sources of the imagination; the other, spontaneous and original in its sources, and relying on the direct report of local experience.

EARLE BIRNEY

This is a selection of verse written by Canadians between the years 1900 and 1950. Since the anthology confines itself to our century, it must omit a few well-known nineteenth-century poets, such as Lampman and Crawford, who died before 1900; but it has also been free to avoid a quantity of dull and faded "Victorian" versifying which historical collections feel bound to include. Moreover, the total span of Canadian writing is so short that the present book, without moving out of its period, has been able to present some of the last and best work of our chief poets in the nineteenth century tradition, Bliss Carman and Sir Charles G. D. Roberts.

The poetry has been divided into twelve sections, roughly according to subject matter. These sections are so arranged that the reader may begin with a view of Canada as a whole, as a nation, and then move across its changing face from Newfoundland to British Columbia, considering the world of non-human life, and then human beings in town and city, as children and teen-agers, as individuals and as members of groups or categories. There follow poems about the real or imagined past of Canada, the never-never land of the imagination, and the country of ideas. The eleventh section has to do with Canadian experience and reaction to twentieth-century war. The selection ends with poems on the basic theme of life and death. The editor hopes that this pattern will help the general reader to appreciate the range of our Canadian poetry, and the teacher to select groups of poems for comparative study.

This is, then, an anthology designed equally for the general reader and for the teacher and student of Canadian literature, particularly at the matriculation and university level. If some of the poems seem, at first sight, to be more "advanced" than high school students are accustomed to, it is because the editor believes that far too thin fare has, in the past, been served up to them as Canadian poetry, out of a false notion that they would be "put off" by anything involving subtleties of interpretation. The maturing student wants more challenging literature than he gets, and until he gets it he will not enter into a real enjoyment of poetry.

On the other hand this collection has sought to avoid fashionably obscure or highly experimental work which, however "great" it may eventually turn out to be, can offer at the moment little of the food of the imagination except to the very sophisticated palate.

Other considerations have inevitably entered into the selection. Long works, such as the narratives of E. J. Pratt, could be represented only through extracts. A few writers do not appear at all because of copyright difficulties. This anthology in no way pretends, therefore, to present all the Canadian verse of this century worth reading; but its seventy poets and one hundred and twenty-five poems offer, I think, a more varied fare than can be found elsewhere.

No book, however carefully made, can succeed without the co-operation of its readers. A poem, like any other work of art, is created to be enjoyed, and the ability to enjoy it is to some extent an acquired one. We are not born with a mature appreciation of Beethoven or Shakespeare; and we can fail even to acquire it if we limit our listening to the tunes of Tin Pan Alley and our reading to nursery jingles. And yet, if we recall the joys we once got from Hickory-Dickory-Dock, we have a guide to the adult pleasure of poetry-reading. When we were young we did not need to be urged to let our imaginations work; we *saw* the cow jump over the moon, and we laughed, with the little dog, seeing it happen; we tasted the sounds of Humpty-Dumpty and we beat our hands to the fun of its rhythm. Much adult poetry is still inviting us to do the same, to take a holiday from our grown-up world of sober reason, making-a-living, worry, routine, mechanized entertainment and spectator-sports, and to let the colour and rhythm and cadence of words, those most magical of all human inventions, unloose our imaginations to run where they will.

Good poetry asks, and gives, still more. It expects to be read many times, for full enjoyment; and it expects to be absorbed with the ear open, to be read aloud, or at least to be sounded in the inner ear. For in a good poem every word has been chosen not only to make a meaning (and as much meaning as possible) but to make an audible excitement and pleasure out of that meaning. A poem is a poet speaking to you out of the depth of himself, out of his own unique experience of life and in a tone of voice and habit of phrasing which is peculiarly his own. That is why a poem can be profoundly "true" even when it is making nonsense out of sober reasoning or respected truisms; a good poem is the most genuine expression of the whole personality of the man or woman who made it, and for that reason alone it can bring extraordinary insights into a human mind and heart. Also, since the poet is generally speaking about those things most difficult to talk about, the complex emotions and feelings that well out of our subconsciousness, he is speaking not only about himself but about the essential human things in all of us.

The reader who approaches poetry in this way will not be disappointed, because he will not be expecting poetry to do what it is not trying to do. He will not expect to be able to "paraphrase" a poem entirely into prose, for example; poetry deliberately concentrates its phrases and constructs ambiguities in order to say the most in the least words. If the poet could have said it in prose, or in any other way, he would not have written a poem. Nor will the understanding reader impose limits on the poet's method of creating his poem. Poetry exists in a free world; no rule ever made by critics has been proved not breakable. The poet has the total vocabulary of his language to choose from, as a painter has all colours; and he has all the ideas and notions and sensations and emotions of the human species, so far as he has experienced them, or imagined them, to draw on. We may criticize him for his narrowness of subject, or thinness of language, in relation to what was open to him; but we should be wary of judging him because he uses a word or embraces a subject strange or harsh to us. If he *communicates* an experience and, through the excitement of verbal shape and sound and rhythm, stirs our imagination and widens our understanding, he has succeeded in doing what he set out to do.

Each generation, of course, is different from the past, and its artists, when they are genuine, find ways of expressing this difference. The poets of our time, like its painters and musicians, have shown preference for certain techniques. You will find, in many of the younger poets in this book a tendency toward toughness of mind, in reaction to Victorian sentimentality; toward a higher concentration in style, in preference to nineteenth century lyrical clarity; a preference for images and themes drawn from the urban machine-age world; a serious or "poetic" use of the pun, to emphasize the strange doubleness of things, and to create ironies of tone. Such techniques seem strange only at first; they are part of what makes the poetry authentic, a communication of the imaginations of Canadians to their fellow-men in this twentieth century.

At the end of this book there are comments on the individual poems. These are designed to help the student understand why the poems are written the way they are. Occasionally "translations" of more complex passages are offered, but the fervent hope of the editor is that they will be used not as instruments for dissecting (and perhaps in consequence extinguishing) the poems, but as aids in the enjoyment of them.

Earle Birney, Introduction to *Twentieth Century Canadian Poetry* (Toronto: Ryerson, 1953).

DESMOND PACEY

The past decade has been a period of considerable but often confusing activity in English-Canadian poetry. It is probably impossible, at this close range, to perceive the really significant directions and achievements, but the attempt is worth making: at best, one may succeed in marshalling the facts in some sort of provisional order; and at least one may provoke discussion and debate.

1944 was a good year, perhaps the most productive single year in our poetic history. It saw the publication of E. J. Pratt's long awaited *Collected Poems,* two books of verse by A. M. Klein, Dorothy Livesay's *Day and Night,* Ralph Gustafson's *Flight into Darkness,* Arthur S. Bourinot's *Nine Poems*, Dick Diespecker's *Between Two Furious Oceans,* and Joseph Schull's *I, Jones, Soldier.* In addition, there appeared a small anthology, *Unit of Five,* which gave the public its first substantial sampling of the work of five most promising new poets: P. K. Page, Louis Dudek, Raymond Souster, James Wreford, and Ronald Hambleton.

The four years that followed were each almost equally productive. One became accustomed to expecting, instead of the one or two annual volumes of good verse of the twenties and thirties, five or six books worthy of serious attention.

1949, however, brought a sudden ominous pause in this triumphant progress. Only one really striking book of verse was published that year—James Reaney's weird but fascinating *The Red Heart.* Much the same was true of 1950, which produced only James Wreford's *Of Time and the Lover,* Norman Levine's tiny *The Tight-Rope Walker,* and a couple of slim chapbooks by Livesay and Bourinot.

How are we to explain the surge of activity from 1944 to 1948, and the sudden slackening of 1949 and 1950? The last years of the war and the first years of the peace were the high water marks of economic prosperity and of the sense of national well-being in Canada. The country was prosperous, prices were still controlled, and more people had money for relative luxuries such as books of verse; and at the same time the sense of national excitement and pride created by the war made more people interested in Canadian books. Even those who opposed the war, or had doubts about the nature of the peace to follow it, were stirred up by it, and were anxious to learn of other people's reactions to it. This interest was heightened by the appearance of several anthologies and critical studies of Canadian poetry: Ralph Gustafson's *Canadian Poetry* (1942), A. J. M. Smith's *Book of Canadian Poetry* (1943), Ronald

Hambleton's *Unit of Five,* and John Sutherland's *Other Canadians* (c. 1947).

Magazines were founded which at once catered to the interest and augmented it. *Contemporary Verse* began its distinguished twelve-year career under the editorship of Alan Crawley in 1941, *Preview* and *First Statement* appeared in 1942, John Sutherland's influential *Northern Review* was launched in 1945, and the lavishly produced *Here and Now* was born in 1947.

Underlying all these developments, and affecting both the poets and their audience, was a community of values such as Canada had not known for many years. In foreign relations, there was general agreement that victory and a stable peace were the most urgent objectives, that the Nazis must be stopped and the Russians supported. Domestically, the Canadian mood was almost unanimously leftist. Price controls, family allowances, subsidized housing, all the elements of the planned economy and the Welfare State, were fundamental shared convictions.

And then, in a period extending from 1947 to the present, all this brave atmosphere began to evaporate. The Russian spy scare, inflation, the Cold War, the Truman Doctrine, the Korean War, the war in Indo-China—these developments in their various but connected ways, smashed the unity of Canadian thinking. We were left relatively embittered, bewildered, cynical, or frustrated. In this new atmosphere of indecision and confusion both the writing and publishing of poetry became much more difficult. Poets, not quite sure of the direction of their thinking, wrote less, or wrote with less conviction; publishers, uncertain of the future and aware that their potential customers were distracted, cut back their lists. *Here and Now,* which had offered Canadian poets the most handsome magazine outlet they had ever had, expired in 1949 after a lifespan of only eighteen months.

The profound nature of the crisis can perhaps best be realized by reference to the other leading literary magazine of the period, John Sutherland's *Northern Review.* Sutherland has been an important figure in Canadian poetry for a dozen years, even since in 1942 he began to edit *First Statement.* At that time Mr. Sutherland was quite clearly, to paraphrase Mr. T. S. Eliot's famous pronouncement, a socialist in politics, a nationalist in literature, and a sceptic in religion. He remained such for the next five years. In 1945 he began to publish *Northern Review,* with the avowed purpose of creating "a national magazine." Not content with that contribution, he began to issue from his press books of verse by other young writers with socialist and/or nationalist convictions—books such as Irving Layton's angry *Here and Now* (1945, this should not be confused with the magazine of the same name), Patrick Anderson's impassioned *A Tent for April* (1945) and Miriam Waddington's pity-filled *Green World* (1945). In 1946 or 1947 (the book is not dated) he followed these with his lively and radical anthology, *Other Canadians*.

In the introduction to this anthology, with a bravado which can now be seen to have resulted from his own uncertainty, he nailed his rather lurid colours to the mast. A. J. M. Smith was condemned as a conservative, pious, spiritual old fuddy-duddy, and the Canadian poetic future was charted according to Karl Marx: "If God still talks to these poets in private, he carries less weight than Karl Marx or Sigmund Freud . . . Mr. Smith's oxygen tent with its tap to the spirit will keep a few remnants breathing for a while, but can hardly impede the growth of socialism in Canada, or prevent the radical consequences which must follow for the Canadian writer."

Shortly after the appearance of these words, Mr. Sutherland began to undergo a great mental transformation. His series of books of verse ceased for several years, and when it was resumed in 1951 it brought us non-political volumes such as Kay Smith's liturgical *Footnote to the Lord's Prayer* and Anne Wilkinson's neo-pastoral *Counterpoint to Sleep*. The verse of left-wing poets such as Dudek, Layton, and Souster ceased to appear in *Northern Review,* and instead the contents of that magazine, including Mr. Sutherland's own contributions, took on a preponderantly religious tone. Lately he has sponsored lecture tours, and published work by, politically conservative and religiously orthodox writers such as Roy Campbell and Peter Viereck.

All this is not to be construed as an attack upon Mr. Sutherland. He is entitled to his own beliefs and in outspokenly expressing them he has proved that he has the courage of his convictions. But his fundamental change of direction is indicative of the spiritual crisis which overtook Canadian intellectuals at the end of the nineteen-forties.

The period when this crisis was in its most acute phase—roughly 1948 to 1950—was a kind of interregnum in the history of Canadian poetry. By 1951 the left-wing school had given Sutherland up and had established its own press and magazine—*Contact*.* Augmented by their contributions, but fed largely by writers who had made their reputations before or during the War, the stream of verse began to flow again. Several new poets of promise have joined the stream—

*Contact Press and *Contact*, the magazine, were both launched in 1952.

Philip Child, Elizabeth Brewster, Alfred G. Bailey, Eli Mandel—but no startling change of speed or direction has occurred.

For all its interruptions and uncertainties, the stream of Canadian poetry in the past ten years has brought us many good things.

E. J. Pratt's *Collected Poems* is probably the most important single volume to appear in the decade, if not in the half century. In range, in power, in diversity he easily outstrips all Canadian rivals. His work has originality of texture and bears the imprint of a distinctive personality. Although his name is chiefly associated with vigorous narrative poems like *The Cachalot* and *Brébeuf and His Brethren,* he is almost equally at home with the lyric, satire, and the verse-portrait. For a few years after the publication of his *Collected Poems* he seemed to be in decline—*They Are Returning* (1945) and *Behind The Log* (1947) are only superior verse journalism—but his *Towards the Last Spike* (1952) has done much to restore his reputation. Here, in the story of the building of the CPR, Pratt found a theme in which his talents could display themselves at or near their best. The poem is rich in humour, in characters of legendary proportions, in suggestive symbols, and in that sense of struggle between vast forces which is Pratt's special note.

The combination of strength and tenderness, of force and subtlety, which we find in E. J. Pratt may be found also in his chief rival for the position of English-Canada's greatest living poet, A. M. Klein. Klein's poetry, however, because of his Hebrew religious origin and his Montreal residence, has a very different substance. His Jewishness was a very prominent quality in *Poems* (1944) and the source of the intense bitterness of the satire in *The Hitleriad* (1944). In his most recent volume, *The Rocking Chair* (1948), his knowledge of Montreal has enabled him to treat, with a piquant mixture of sympathy and satire, the life of French Canada. He has been keenly conscious of social injustice and personal malice, and has deliberately made his verse a weapon against them. At the same time he has been aware of the love, pity and splendour lurking in ordinary people and places. This combination of anger and delight, together with the audacity of his images, the strength and richness of his diction, and the variety of his rhythms, has made his poetry fresh and distinctive. Occasionally he goes too far—his pathos at times degenerates into bathos, his satire into invective—but he never becomes dull by lack of daring.

Another poet whose energy occasionally betrays her into shrillness is Dorothy Livesay. The poems in *Day and Night* are bold and passionate in their denunciation of capitalism, but they sometimes sound forced, as if their author were trying to convince herself. In *Poems for People* (1947), however, her aggressive radicalism has been replaced by a more tolerant humanism, and in the process her technique has become firmer. The subjects of her later poems are more specifically feminine—love, children, the family—and in treating these traditional subjects in a modern vocabulary, contemporary metaphors and experimental forms, she has often seemed excitingly creative.

Earle Birney, whose *David* was the sensation of Canadian poetry in 1942, has been a more consistent poet than either Klein or Livesay: he has produced poetry more steadily, and he has changed remarkably little in either subject-matter or style. Although he has written movingly of war, love, and mountain climbing, his chief concern has always been with the interpretation and evaluation of the Canadian social scene. This concern is uppermost in all the best poems in the three volumes he has published in the past decade: *Now Is Time* (1945), *The Strait of Anian* (1948), and *Trial of a City* (1952). No other poet is more successful than he in capturing the feel of contemporary Canada: he sees the ugliness of its slums, the shallowness of its values, the adolescence of its culture; but he also sees and appreciates its attempts at self-understanding, its naïve optimism, its basic goodwill, and its real promise. These themes he treats in our own idiom, and in a style which owes singularly little to outside influences. His long, loose, loping lines, his casualness of tone and diction, his indigenous images—all seem genuinely of our own stuff.

These four—Pratt, Klein, Livesay, and Birney—have been the major figures of the decade; the remaining poets must be considered more briefly and arranged, for convenience's sake, in groups.

The main tradition of Canadian poetry until at least 1925 was that of romantic nature verse, associated chiefly with the names of Carman, Roberts, Lampman, and D. C. Scott. This tradition was largely displaced in the thirties and forties by two others: the metaphysical tradition stemming directly from T. S. Eliot, Ezra Pound, and the later Yeats, and indirectly from English poets of the seventeenth century; and the tradition of social protest stemming from Auden, Spender and Day-Lewis. In the forties two new but closely related influences made themselves felt—Gerard Manley Hopkins and Dylan Thomas—but the effect of these poets was to enrich and modify existing traditions rather than initiate a new one. American influences, strangely enough, have had little effect, although in recent years there have been some indications that Robert Frost is making a belated impact.

The old and honourable tradition of romantic nature verse has not been altogether abandoned. It has survived in the work of Arthur S. Bourinot, Audrey Alexandra Brown, and a host of minor versifiers. Mr. Bourinot and Miss Brown achieve their best effects in the expression of deep personal feeling and in the creation of glowing effects of colour.

The metaphysical tradition in Canada was first espoused by the so-called Montreal Group of the twenties—A. J. M. Smith, F. R. Scott, A. M. Klein, and Leo Kennedy. These poets, with the exception of Klein, have been relatively quiet in the last decade, though I understand that Scott, Smith, and Kennedy have volumes ready for early publication. Generally speaking, they have not yet fulfilled the high hopes that were expressed for them by E. K. Brown in his *On Canadian Poetry*. Smith has been increasingly engrossed in his pursuits as an anthologist and critic, Scott in politics and constitutional law, and Kennedy in advertising and public relations work in the United States.

But the type of poetry which the Montreal Group introduced in Canada—erudite, intellectual, complex, impassioned, ironic, and anxiously contemporary—has been widely practised in the last decade. Ronald Hambleton (*Object and Event,* 1953), Ralph Gustafson (*Flight into Darkness,* 1944), Roy Daniells (*Deeper Into the Forest,* 1948), James Wreford (*Of Time and the Lover,* 1950), Alfred G. Bailey (*Border River,* 1952) and Douglas Le Pan (*The Wounded Prince,* 1950; *The Net and the Sword,* 1953)—all these men have produced poetry to which the above adjectives apply. They are not indistinguishable, but they have a great deal in common. Most of them are professors, all of them are highly educated, and they draw upon their special knowledge to set the present time in perspective. Daniells, for example, achieves distinctive effects by drawing upon his knowledge of myth and symbol, Bailey by introducing material and images from his knowledge of anthropology and history, Wreford by employing images from his geological and geographical learning. All of them are conscious and conscientious poetic draftsmen, aware of the English tradition and of contemporary masters such as Eliot and Thomas. All of them are repelled by the vulgarity, cruelty, and violence of the modern world, and all seek to redress the balance by appealing to the traditional values of Christian humanism. Their collective influence in the country, both as poets and teachers, is far greater than in their moments of despondency they believe; in the young they keep alive all that is best in the Western heritage.

Many of these poets protest against various conditions in our society, but a more direct and blunt type of social protest is associated with the left-wing school of Louis Dudek, Irving Layton, and Raymond Souster. In the early forties these three were colleagues of John Sutherland in the production of *First Statement;* more recently they have collaborated in the publication of the magazine *Contact,* the collection *Cerberus* (1952), and the anthology *Canadian Poems, 1850-1950* (1953).* They have, then, been extremely active, and deserve our thanks for helping to keep poetry alive in a difficult age.

The energy they have exhibited in their publishing enterprises they have also displayed in their poetry. With an unsparing hand they have flayed our complacency, our conservatism, our prudery, and all the other sins to which we bourgeois Canadians are prone. The picture they paint is not a pretty one, nor altogether fair, but it is always lively if sometimes too lurid. They have at least had shock value, and they have dared to say many thing that needed saying.

The most blunt and powerful of the trio has been Irving Layton: he has often scattered his ammunition, but he has scored some fine hits. His poems are sometimes rough and ready in technique, but his frequent revision of them is proof that he has an artistic conscience. Dudek is a more deliberate craftsman, more ready to perceive fragments of beauty amid the rubble of now, more diverse in subject and style. Souster is a quieter, simpler poet than either of them. His special and often very appealing quality is a kind of naïve wistfulness and sincere pity which only rarely bursts into anger.

Because they have been impatient of criticism and quick to scent condescension, these three young poets have not received their full due from our preponderantly academic critics. Theirs are fresh and genuine voices without which the present Canadian choir would be much less interesting.

Standing midway between what we have loosely labelled the metaphysical and social protest schools is a group of poets who combine many of the features of both—P. K. Page, Patrick Anderson, Miriam Waddington, and Anne Marriott are more complex and sophisticated than the Dudek-Layton-Souster group, but they have been usually more directly concerned with immediate social and political objectives and problems than the mataphysical school.

Patrick Anderson arrived in Canada in 1940 with his head full

*Canadian Poems, 1850-1952 had its first edition in 1952.

of the social philosophy of Karl Marx and the verse rhythms of Dylan Thomas. He proceeded to establish the magazine *Preview* and to urge Canadian poets to dedicate themselves wholeheartedly to the world struggle against Fascism. His own books—*A Tent for April* (1945), *The White Centre* (1946), and *The Colour as Naked* (1953)—are full of light and fire. His words leap and tumble, his images proliferate with exciting rapidity and range. There is an irresistible swing to his verse and a power to move us now to anger, now to love. It is only after the initial excitement has worn off that we begin to wonder where we were being led, and for what precise purpose. Sober second thought reveals much rhetoric and not a little sentimentality, but still plenty that is genuine and powerful. In his latest volume especially there is more discipline and artistic conning, and a greater maturity of outlook.

P. K. Page seemed likely, about 1945, to become the leading poetess of Canada. The poems she contributed to *Unit of Five*, and her own volume *As Ten, As Twenty* (1946), were obviously influenced by Auden and Anderson, and yet they were sufficiently personal in both technique and substance. They expressed, in unusual but effective imagery, a sensitive woman's response to the world of war, want, and fascism. Such poems as "The Stenographers" seemed to hold out the promise, if not quite the reality, of greatness. Unfortunately, Miss Page has published very little during the last five years: it will be a great pity if her very subtle talent is lost to our poetry.

Anne Marriott is another woman poet who has not yet lived up to the expectations her early work aroused. Her first book—*The Wind Our Enemy* (1939)—is already established as a minor Canadian classic. It records, in colloquial language and consistently domestic imagery, the plight of the Western farmer during the dust storms of the thirties. Since that time she has published a number of reputable poems in the magazines, and one small chapbook (*Sandstone,* 1945), but nothing to rival her first success.

The emotion of pity, dominant in *The Wind Our Enemy,* is also dominant in Miriam Waddington's *Green World* (1945). A social worker by profession, Miss Waddington has seen much of the seamy side of Canadian city life, and has become aware of "The slow surge of cold hatred/Flowing through secret passages/Under our tunneled cities." Against this hatred, she sets the positive values of love and tenderness. Her technique is less complex than that of Page and Anderson, and reminds us rather of Souster. Her diction is simple and colloquial, her images are drawn from familiar sources, and there is almost no obscurity in her verse. She is one of the most immediately attractive of our poets.

These, then, have been the major trends, but some new directions have lately been apparent. For one thing, there has been a revival of the regionalism which was a strong element in the poetry of Roberts and Lampman in the late nineteenth century. Charles Bruce, especially in *The Flowing Summer* (1947) and *The Mulgrave Road* (1951), had dealt sincerely, lovingly and unpretentiously with his memories of youth amid the fishermen and farmers of Nova Scotia; Philip Child, in *The Victorian House* (1951), has recorded his own early years in Hamilton, Ontario in a poem that is grave, straightforward, and patently honest; Thomas Saunders in *Scrub Oak* (1949) and *Horizontal World* (1951), has recreated in simple but often convincing fashion the places and people of Manitoba; and Elizabeth Brewster, in *East Coast* (1951) and *Lillooet* (1954), has etched clear if slightly satirical pictures of her native New Brunswick landscape and society. These poets are exceptional too in that they have been influenced as much by American as by English examples. Thomas Saunders, for instance, is an obvious disciple of Robert Frost, and Elizabeth Brewster more subtly blends the influences of Emily Dickinson, E. A. Robinson, and Edgar Lee Masters. The regionalist vein these four poets have struck has still much poetic ore to yield, and it is to be hoped that they will attract other workers.

But perhaps the most distinctive poet to emerge in the past decade has been James Reaney. He has as yet published only one volume— *The Red Heart*—but his poems have continued to appear in the magazines and we may expect a second volume in the near future. His originality consists not so much in technique as in the revelation of a unique sensibility. He makes his poems of seemingly familiar subjects—plum trees, farm kitchens, car-crowding highways—but he makes these things new by describing them from an unexpected and exciting angle. He has Wordworth's gift of investing the familiar with strangeness, of making that which we had seen many times seem suddenly exciting and exotic. He is almost certainly the most promising of the younger poets.

In the last year or two there have been signs of a revival of interest and energy in Canadian poetry. New anthologies have been edited by Earle Birney and (jointly) by Louis Dudek and Irving Layton; new magazines (*Contact, CIV/n*) have been established and older ones (notably *The Fiddlehead*) expanded in scope. Best of all, new poets such as Fred Cogswell, Phyllis Webb, Robert Gibbs, Eli Mandel, Gael Turnbull, and Collene Thibaudeau have begun to publish regularly in the magazines, and their work may soon be expected to appear in book form.

Progress in the arts is slow, and we need not feel discouraged that no single poet or school of poetry of world significance has yet appeared in English-speaking Canada. There has been an advance, more than we often recognize. We have left behind us many obstacles that once deterred us. We no longer debate the futile question of the distinctiveness of our poetry: the Canadian poet worthy of the title cannot avoid introducing his environment into his poetry—it is simply there, in the idioms, the images, the rhythms if not in more obvious form. We no longer argue the merits of cosmopolitanism as against nationalism: we recognize that the poet must we aware of both his place and his time. We no longer feud over the respective claims of free verse and regular metres: the poet is free to choose the medium which suits him best. We need no longer defend the poet's right to treat any subject that pleases him, for this right is now almost universally conceded. And if our poets at the moment are somewhat confused and uncertain, if they write chiefly, as Patrick Anderson has lately put it, poems "where anxiety trembles upon the rim of faith," they are only accurately recording the temper of our time. After all, it is not the function of the poet to re-make the world, but to make us more intensely aware of it.

Desmond Pacey, "English-Canadian Poetry, 1944-1954," *Culture*, XV, No. 2, June 1954.

LOUIS DUDEK

Poetry today is not a popular art; Canadian poetry is even less known than English poetry in general; but as art, it is poetry, not prose, which will in the end prove to be the successful literary medium of this century. We should by now begin to realize—what our newspaper reviewers don't even suspect—that the vast majority of books, novels mainly, that reach the public nowadays, have no real pretension and can never have any place as literature, as permanent art. Poetry, though ignored, is at least made to last. For this reason, a close look at the almost secret activity (so far as the public is concerned) of Canadian poets just now might bring the general reader a little closer to what is more real, even more immediate, than the long-winded entertainments of fiction.

The first thing to observe is that in this country we have in the last decade and a half seen an amazing wave of creative work in poetry breaking into print. The period is analogous to, and superior to, the first outburst of poetry in Canada during the eighties and nineties of the last century. The following is a partial list of our poets who have come out with their first books within the last fifteen years: A. J. M. Smith, F. R. Scott, Robert Finch, Earle Birney, A. M. Klein, Anne Marriott, P. K. Page, Patrick Anderson, Irving Layton, Ronald Hambleton, Kay Smith, Raymond Souster, James Wreford, Douglas Le Pan, Anne Wilkinson, James Reaney—and an additional half-dozen recognized poets in the younger age group.

To anyone who has even a bare anthology acquaintance with these names and the work they stand for it is hardly necessary to interpret what this means. Canada has just produced a literature of its own in poetry in this century. Taking this with the late-romantic verse of the eighties and nineties — Carman, Roberts, Lampman, D. C. Scott, Wilfred Campbell, Isabella Crawford—and the work of Drummond, Service and Pratt in between, Canadian poetry can now stand without a blush, though still a junior, beside English and American poetry of the last seventy-five years. What we need is a critic who will take a survey of our present stature.

Even before the present poetry movement had declared itself, two critics appeared ready to do service to Canadian poetry: W. E. Collin (*The White Savannahs,* 1936) and E. K. Brown (*On Canadian Poetry,* 1943). They wrote their intelligent analytic criticism of the modern movement in Canadian poetry before most of the poets listed above had appeared in book form. (Collin, in fact, worked from the manuscript of *New Provinces.*) Today, when twentieth-century poetry native to Canada has been put on record through books, anthologies, readings, radio broadcasts, and even TV, we do not have a single critic with the necessary equipment who has been willing to undertake the task of interpreting this poetry seriously, analytically. The chapters on poetry in Desmond Pacey's *Creative Writing in Canada* are the best work to date in that direction, but Pacey's is a very simplified treatment.

Our newspaper and magazine critics are ignorant of the poetry they try to write about when they do try. High school and university teachers, for the most part, are too far behind the spirit of our poetry, too timid and conservative altogether, to dare make an honest statement about literature or its relation to life today. Students in most colleges never get the chance to find out: the libraries don't even have the necessary books. And do the professors of English in our provincial colleges (both senses) read or understand the poetry of this century? Or are they still "anti-Eliot," "anti-modern"? Is the literature they recognize as the best of our time Rupert Brooke, Edna St. Vincent Millay, John Masefield, and now at last—Edwin Muir? Don't blush, gentlemen!

(Those who don't believe this may read Professor Rhodenizer's crackerjack article—against the moderns—in the *Dalhousie Review* for autumn, 1953.)

Canada needs a few bright young critics who will roll up their sleeves and make criticism in this country their job. Some of those now plugging for academic credits with ambitious essays on John Donne or T. S. Eliot's concept of "time past" and "time future" might do well to turn their eyes on "time present" and read *News of the Phoenix*, or *The Red Heart*, or the two recent books by Layton, *Love the Conqueror Worm* and *In the Midst of My Fever*.

There are critical finds to be made: berries where no one has picked before. One of the things about which our critics—the few tired voices one hears—are wrong, is the notion that the activity in recent poetry started suddenly in 1940 and finished suddenly in 1945. A bit of reflection on the probable historical position of the new poetry should make it apparent that the activity of 1940 was only a beginning. Modern rhythm, forms, diction, ideas and imagination, the characteristic attack of contemporary poetry on life, was bound to come to Canada; the thirties were preparing for it in the work of Klein, Scott, and Smith; the forties produced the printed books. This and the next few decades will show the expansion of this poetry in all directions; the process is now going on.

To test the issue, I would offer the reader books recently out, or just coming off the press: *Trio*, containing the first poems of Gael Turnbull, Phyllis Webb, and F. W. Mandel (Contact Press, 28 Mayfield Ave., Toronto); Reaney's *The Red Heart* (McClelland & Stewart Ltd., Toronto); Anne Wilkinson's *Counterpoint to Sleep* (First Statement Press, 2475 Van Horne Ave., Montreal); my own long poem *Europe* (recently published by Contact Press); or Layton's *In the Midst of My Fever* (Divers Press, Mallorca, Spain). Among other things, the reader will find that Canadian poets at this moment, in the midst of world chaos, do "have something to say." And in this respect they are unlike recent British and American poets.

E. J. Pratt, for example, has something to say, however unprepossessing and stereotyped the message at the core may seem to some: *Towards the Last Spike* comes on the heels of a long list of whacking solid books, reminding us of a reputation that will not easily be questioned. Earle Birney's *Trial of a City* places modern life on trial before a court which includes William Langland, an old-time sailor, and an Indian Chief—pretty good "tests to go by" as Robert Frost would say. A. M. Klein published *The Second Scroll* in 1941, a novel and poetry about world Jewry and the Jewish faith. Books have recently come off the press from the pens of Ronald Hambleton, Patrick Anderson, Douglas Le Pan, and the three heads of *Cerberus* —Souster, Layton and myself—all of these as angry and concerned about life values and the realities as ever, and no longer to be shelved away easily as "socialistic," or "imitative" of English trends. Others, moreover, F. R. Scott, P. K. Page and Anne Wilkinson, have new books ready for publication. The generation of poets who started out fifteen years ago are still producing, and most of them have shown some development in ideas and forms. Also, a dozen new poets have appeared on the scene in the magazines: these deserve a brief examination.

The new poets are little known because they have mainly appeared in obscure places. In the last few years *Northern Review* has provided less and less outlet to enterprising work of the kind I would call modern, i.e. continuing the lines opened up by poets as varied as Cummings, Williams, Pound, Marianne Moore, Eliot, Auden, et cetera. (The editor of that magazine has recently declared in print that he favors such writers as C. S. Lewis, G. K. Chesterton, and Roy Campbell, rather than Joyce, Eliot or Pound!) The new Canadian poets have therefore looked elsewhere, and have gone unobserved even by the small audience which exists for poetry in Canada. *Contemporary Verse* has ceased publication. To make up for the losses in magazines, however, *The Fiddlehead* (Fredericton, N.B.) appeared in print last year: *CIV/n*, edited by Aileen Collins, was started in Montreal; and *Contact* was started by Souster in Toronto, a mimeographed magazine with a printed cover—as *Preview* and *First Statement* were in their day. Souster's *Contact* has brought to a handful of young poets in Canada the work of *Origin* magazine in the United States, and the poetry of Charles Olson, Cid Corman, Robert Creeley and other poets of an interesting group now working in the States. Our underlying position in *Contact* (as well as in *CIV/n*, the Montreal magazine) is one of sharp social criticism, but not a criticism based on political or economic grounds alone: it is a cultural attack, a criticism of contemporary life in the name of the whole range of liberal values; and the poetry that we make on this basis is as varied as the personalities of poets can be.

The poets who have appeared in these little magazines have, some of them, true talent and serious artistic purpose. Phyllis Webb (from Victoria, B.C.) is a young writer with a nervous, original style all her own; D. G. Jones (now to Kingston) is developing a skill in a formal style which is just the example we need; F. Fyfe (now in Hamilton) is a young poet with abundant energy and freedom, somewhat like James Reaney in this respect; Gael Turnbull (in Iroquois Falls, Ont.) writes whimsically and almost too wisely, but with an underlying moral earnestness and social concern which produce a unique combination; E. W. Mandel (St. John, Que.) handles Greek myths and legends as if they were contemporary facts, and uses them to interpret modern life realistically, almost violently, in their light; Leonard N. Cohen (Montreal), the most recent arrival, has a sensitive and imaginative mind, and a ballad-maker's imagination and voice. All this new poetry may be described as highly individualistic and imaginative, ranging into high fantasy rather than stooping to prosaic fact. It is a kind of poetry that began in Canada with James Reaney's *The Red Heart*. It is extravagant at times; but it is no less objective in its implied antagonisms to existing culture than was the poetry of F. R. Scott or Earle Birney.

Of the older poets in *Contact* and *CIV/n* Patrick Anderson has contributed some prose; Ralph Gustafson has given examples of his usual skill; Souster has matured in emotional tone, but retained all the vivid intensity of his first books. Irving Layton, most important, has in the last few years shown a grasp of poetic complexity and a sense of human tragedy which puts him in the very first rank of Canadian poets. This must be seen in his recent books.

But in addition to all the recent and current books and the new poetry in magazines, anthologies can be taken as a barometer of activity. A. J. M. Smith's anthology is to be reprinted in a new edition; and a re-editing of the Ryerson anthology of Bliss Carman and Lorne Pierce as *Canadian Poetry in English* (Ryerson) has recently been published. Contact Press has put on record a new reading, or cross-section, of the literature in *Canadian Poems: 1850-1952*; and Earle Birney, through Ryerson, has edited *Twentieth Century Canadian Poetry*, which for all its lack of balance in selection is a vital exhibition of our contemporary poetry. These books are creating a new audience for poetry in the universities and schools: at McGill alone, some 700 entering students every year are introduced to the principal Canadian writers through lectures and textbooks—a work started by Professor Arthur L. Phelps. If colleges across Canada undertook to introduce Canadian novels and poetry in combination with the regular English survey, we might be getting somewhere.

Finally, as one hates to leave an article on poetry without a few lines of quotation, I offer each of the following as picked stones for the reader to dwell on for some time; they may begin to glow and reveal to him something of what I have been saying.

First, from Layton's *Love the Conqueror Worm*.

> "Imagination
> Makes nothing happen, being
> The shadow of a beggar's plate
> On snow."

This from Anne Wilkinson:

> "I am so tired I do not think
> Sleep in death can rest me.
> So line my two eternal yards
> With softest moss,
> Then lengths of bone won't splinter
> As they toss,
> Or pierce their wooden box
> To winter . . ."

From Dorothy Livesay, in *Fiddlehead*, Nov. 1953.

> "What moved me, was the way your hand
> Lay cool in mine, not withering;
> As bird still breathes, and stream runs clear—
> So your hand; your dead hand, my dear."

And from my poem *Europe*, because it seems to fit here:

> "The past speaks in the remaining monuments
>   and a few pages
>   of the dead poets,
>   judging the Esso empire
>   and the new Milanese
>   without mercy.
> What should we say, we few,
> who know what we know,
>   but for these records?
> Where would we get words
>   for our recriminations?"

So this is the scene in 1954, or one view of it. I don't suppose that the present list of names and these comments are sufficient information about the whole range of our poetry now. Each must see it from his own position. The poetry must be read to be valued properly. The presentation given here may sound too optimistic but, who knows, if the reader will go through the books and magazines for himself, he may decide I have not boasted enough for the poets. They rise in power in proportion as you have the power to see them—being spiritual genii.

Louis Dudek, "The State of Canadian Poetry: 1954," *Canadian Forum*, October 1954.

IRVING LAYTON

This volume contains all the poems I wrote between 1942 and 1958 that I wish to preserve. They are taken from twelve collections I have published during this period; except for retouching lightly two or three poems I have let them stand as they were. To these I have added the following poems: "The Warm Afterdark," which I wrote in the summer of 1957, and "Divinity," "A Bonnet for Bessie," "Love Is an Irrefutable Fire," "Young Girls Dancing at Camp Lajoie," "For Mao Tse-Tung: A Meditation on Flies and Kings," and "My Flesh Comfortless," which I wrote the summer following, after the publication of my last volume, *A Laughter in the Mind*. Looking back upon this period—how to say this tongue-in-cheek yet mean it; how to make love with a hot potato in one's mouth—I see my work as an effort to achieve a definition of independence. Not, though, of disaffiliation. Aristotle was surely wrong: it isn't reason but cruelty distinguishes our species. Man is not a rational animal, he's a dull-witted animal who loves to torture. However, I have my share in the common disgrace; project along with others the fearful rigidities, crippling and comforting, of family, state, and religion. The free individual—independent and gay—is farther from realization than he ever was. Still, in a world where corruption is the norm and enslavement universal, all art celebrates him, prepares the way for his coming. Poetry, by giving dignity and utterance to our distress, enables us to hope, makes compassion reasonable.

Why are people destructive and joy-hating? Is it perception of the unimportance of their lives finally penetrating the bark of their complacency and egotism? The slow martyrdom of sexual frustration? The feeling they're objects of use and not of love? The knowledge they're marked out for death, their resentment hardening with their arteries? Whichever is the reason, they can't for long endure the sight of a happy man. You might as wisely light a match in a room filled with cyclopropane as go among them with a pleased expression. Tear if off your face they must, let their fingers be crushed in the attempt. Because many poets have averted their eyes from this radical evil, they strike me as insufferable blabbermouths. They did not retch enough; were too patient, courteous, civilized. A little brutality would have made them almost men.

My extraction has made me suspicious of both literature and reality. Let me explain. My father was an ineffectual visionary; he saw God's footprint in a cloud and lived only for his books and meditations. A small bedroom in a slum tenement, which in the torrid days steamed and blistered and sweated, he converted into a tabernacle for the Lord of Israel; and here, like the patriarch Abraham, he received his messengers. Since there was nothing angelic about me or his other children, he no more noticed us than if we had been flies on a wall. Had my mother been as otherworldly as he was, we should have starved. Luckily for us, she was not; she was tougher than nails, shrewd and indomitable. Moreover, she had a gift for cadenced vituperation; to which, doubtless, I owe my impeccable ear for rhythm. With parents so poorly matched and dissimilar, small wonder my entelechy was given a terrible squint from the outset. I am not at ease in the world (what poet ever is?); but neither am I fully at ease in the world of the imagination. I require some third realm, as yet undiscovered, in which to live. My disease has spurred me on to bridge the two with the stilts of poetry, or to create inside me an ironic balance of tensions. Unlike Keats, I have not wished to escape into the unreal domain of the nightingale nor to flee, as the more cowardly do, from imagination to fact. Mercifully all poetry, in the final analysis, is about poetry itself; creating through its myriad forms a world in which the elements of reality are sundered; are, as it were, preserved for a time in suspension.

Yet this rift reflects something actual and objective, is as tensing and generative as that of the Hebrew and pagan in Occidental civilization. A real division exists in the human world where at certain points art and life, like thought and instinct, are hostile to each other. It's a truism to say normal people do not write poetry. Philistinism is the permanent basis of human existence: a world in which everyone was an artist or a philosopher would perish in a week. The Canadian philistine, of course, enjoys advantages—his Anglo-Saxon connection, numbers, natural resources, prosperity— philistines of other countries may perhaps envy. But human life anywhere on this planet very wisely preserves itself by spawning more stenographers, trade-union bosses, military leaders, hashslingers, and second-rate presidents than it does poets. The aesthete, nursing incurable ego-wounds, has the relationship down pat—life is the raw material for art! I can't persuade myself this is so. In my very bones I feel it isn't. Art also finally crumbles into the pondscum that surrounds it. Though art transcends pain and tragedy, it does not negate them, does not make them disappear. Whatever its more perfervid devotees may think and write, poetry does not exorcise historical dynamism, macabre cruelty, guilt, perversity, and the pain of consciousness.

Each poem that thumbs its nose at death is a fusion of accident and destiny. As such it is a structure in which the bronzed, athletic philistine is not interested. In any event, he can live without it. For accidents he has insurance policies; for destiny, his image of Napoleon, should he be a profound intellectual suburbanite; the assurances of dialectical materialism, if he is a Marxist proletarian. Before these, the poet unwilling to act as choirboy or morale-builder must appear ailing, furtive, hysterical; one who bumps his forehead against a wall, then exclaims: "Look at the lovely bump I have! Isn't the shape of it glorious? Aren't the colours extraordinarily beautiful?" That's the sort of poetry the genteel and "cultured" especially like. (The poet, of course, *should* strike his head against the wall of men's ferocity and senselessness, but let him yell and curse; not whimper, not bleat.) At this point Byron's contempt and Nietzsche's for the poet becomes understandable; my mother's commonsensical expletives begin ringing in my ears. And so rapturously, too, does he sing of his griefs, this poet, while the dull muttonheads pick their teeth or mount their females. Miserable clown! Can one think of anything more ludicrous? ironic? zany? Squeaking and throbbing, chittering and twittering; demon-driven or driven by their peacock vanity—so the poets, or so I sometimes see them, even the best of them. "What have these jigging fools to do with wars?" Shakespeare understood. Patricians or mob, what have they to do with the joy and wonder that is poetry: they are far happier killing or intriguing to kill. Too long have poets sung with blocked noses, their suffocating complaints and sudden euphoric sneezes filling the indifferent air. They deceive themselves—would they might deceive the hard-faced and heartless. Nevertheless the world remembers them, needs them. They alone are authentic. Bypassing the philistine suburbs of purgatory, they alone have the imagination to commute between heaven and hell.

So what I've written—besides my joy in being alive to write about them—has been about this singular business of human evil; the tension between Hebrew and pagan, between the ideal and real. The disorder and glory of passion. The modern tragedy of the depersonalization of men and women. About a hideously commercial civilization spawning hideously deformed monstrosities. Modern women I see cast in the role of furies striving to castrate the male; their efforts aided by all the malignant forces of a technological civilization that has rendered the male's creative role of revelation superfluous—if not an industrial hazard and a nuisance. We're being feminized and proletarianized at one and the same time. This is the inglorious age of the mass-woman. Her tastes are dominant everywhere—in theatres, stores, art, fiction, houses, furniture—and these tastes are dainty and trivial. Dionysus is dead: his corpse seethes white-maggotty with social workers and analysts. Not who is winning the Cold War is the big issue confronting mankind, but this: Will the Poet, as a type, join the Priest, the Warrior, the Hero, and the Saint as melancholy museum pieces for the titillation of a universal babbitry? It could happen.

The poems in this collection are all leaves from the same tree. A certain man living between 1942 and 1958 wrote them. That man is now dead, and even if he could be resurrected wouldn't be able to write them in the way they were written. Nor would he want to. They belong to a period of my life that is now behind me: a period of testing, confusion, ecstasy. Now there is only the ecstasy of an angry middle-aged man growing into courage and truth. Unlike the scholar or literary historian who writes about life, the poet enjoys it, *lives* it. Lives it with such intensity that he is often unable to say coherently or in plain words what the experience was like. I have in these paragraphs tried to set down those things that have most violently engaged my feelings and entered into the composition of my poems. For me, a poet is one who explores new areas of sensibility. If he has the true vocation he will take risks; for him there can be no "dogmatic slumbers." It will not do to repeat oneself, life is fluid and complex, and become with Housman or Jeffers a one-note Johnny. Or having grown respectable, to trot out a sterile moralism or religiosity, that favourite straw of poets with declining powers. I too have seen the footprint in the cloud, though somewhat gorier than my father saw it. When all is said, I have no choice but to walk after it.

Irving Layton, Foreword to *A Red Carpet For the Sun* (Toronto: McClelland & Stewart, 1959).

NORTHROP FRYE

I've been trying to explain literature by putting you in a primitive situation on an uninhabited island, where you could see the imagination working in the most direct and simple way. Now let's start with our own society, and see where literature belongs in that, if it does. Suppose you're walking down the street of a Canadian city, Bloor or Granville or St. Catherine or Portage Avenue. All around you is a highly artificial society, but you don't think of it as artificial: you're so accustomed to it that you think of it as natural. But suppose your imagination plays a little trick on you of a kind that it often does play, and you suddenly feel like a complete outsider, someone who's just blown in from Mars on a flying saucer. Instantly you see how conventionalized everything is: the clothes, the shopwindows, the movement of the cars in traffic, the cropped hair and shaved faces of the men, the red lips and blue eyelids that women put on because they want to conventionalize their faces, or "look nice," as they say, which means the same thing. All this convention is pressing towards uniformity or likeness. To be outside the convention makes a person look queer, or, if he's driving a car, a menace to life and limb. The only exceptions are people who have decided to conform to different conventions, like nuns or beatniks. There's clearly a strong force making toward conformity in society, so strong that it seems to have something to do with the stability of society itself. In ordinary life even the most splendid things we can think of, like goodness and truth and beauty, all mean essentially what we're accustomed to. As I hinted just now in speaking of female makeup, most of our ideas of beauty are pure convention, and even truth has been defined as whatever doesn't disturb the pattern of what we already know.

When we move on to literature, we again find conventions, but this time we notice that they are conventions, because we're not so used to them. These conventions seem to have something to do with making literature as unlike life as possible. Chaucer represents people as making up stories in ten-syllable couplets. Shakespeare uses dramatic conventions, which means, for instance, that Iago has to smash Othello's marriage and dreams of future happiness and get him ready to murder his wife in a few minutes. Milton has two nudes in a garden haranguing each other in set speeches beginning with such lines as 'Daughter of God and Man, immortal Eve'—Eve being Adam's daughter because she's just been extracted from his ribcase. Almost every story we read demands that we accept as fact something that we know to be nonsense: that good people always win, especially in love: that murders are complicated and ingenious puzzles to be solved by logic, and so on. It isn't only popular literature that demands this: more highbrow stories are apt to be more ironic, but irony has its conventions too. If we go further back into literature, we run into such conventions as the king's rash promise, the enraged cuckold, the cruel mistress of love poetry—never anything that we or any other time would recognize as the normal behaviour of adult people, only the maddened ethics of fairyland.

Even the details of literature are equally perverse. Literature is a world where phoenixes and unicorns are quite as important as horses and dogs—and in literature some of the horses talk, like the ones in

Gulliver's Travels. A random example is calling Shakespeare the 'swan of Avon'—he was called that by Ben Jonson. The town of Stratford, Ontario, keeps swans in its river partly as a literary allusion. Poets of Shakespeare's day hated to admit that they were writing words on a page: they always insisted that they were producing music. In pastoral poetry they might be playing a flute (or more accurately an oboe), but every other kind of poetic effort was called song, with a harp, a lyre or a lute in the background, depending on how highbrow the song was. Singing suggests birds, and so for their typical songbird and emblem of themselves, the poets chose the swan, a bird that can't sing. Because it can't sing, they made up a legend that it sang once before death, when nobody was listening. But Shakespeare didn't burst into song before his death: he wrote two plays a year until he'd made enough money to retire, and spent the last five years of his life counting his take.

So however useful literature may be in improving one's imagination or vocabulary, it would be the wildest kind of pedantry to use it directly as a guide to life. Perhaps here we see one reason why the poet is not only very seldom a person one would turn to for insight into the state of the world, but often seems even more gullible and simple-minded than the rest of us. For the poet, the particular literary conventions he adopts are likely to become, for him, facts of life. If he finds that the kind of writing he's best at has a good deal to do with fairies, like Yeats, or a white goddess, like Graves, or a life-force, like Bernard Shaw, or episcopal sermons, like T. S. Eliot, or bullfights, like Hemingway, or exasperation at social hypocrisies, as with the so-called angry school, these things are apt to take on a reality for him that seems badly out of proportion to his contemporaries. His life may imitate literature in a way that may warp or even destroy his social personality, as Byron wore himself out at thirty-four with the strain of being Byronic. Life and literature, then, are both conventionalized, and of the conventions of literature about all we can say is that they don't much resemble the conditions of life. It's when the two sets of conventions collide that we realize how different they are.

In fact, whenever literature gets too probable, too much like life, some self-defeating process, some mysterious law of diminishing returns, seems to set in. There's a vivid and expertly written novel by H. G. Wells called *Kipps*, about a lower-middle-class, inarticulate, very likeable Cockney, the kind of character we often find in Dickens. Kipps is carefully studied: he never says anything that a man like Kipps wouldn't say; he never sounds the 'h' in home or head; nothing he does is out of line with what we expect such a person to be like.

It's an admirable novel, well worth reading, and yet I have a nagging feeling that there's some inner secret in bringing him completely to life that Dickens would have and that Wells doesn't have. All right, then, what would Dickens have done? Well, one of the things that Dickens often does do is write *badly*. He might have given Kipps sentimental speeches and false heroics and all sorts of inappropriate verbiage to say; and some readers would have clucked and tuttutted over these passages and explained to each other how bad Dickens's taste was and how uncertain his hold on character could be. Perhaps they'd be right too. But we'd have had Kipps a few times the way he'd look to himself or the way he'd sometimes wish he could be: that's part of his reality, and the effect would remain with us however much we disapproved of it. Whether I'm right about this book or not, and I'm not at all sure I am, I think my general principle is right. What we'd never see except in a book is often what we go to books to find. Whatever is completely lifelike in literature is a bit of a laboratory specimen there. To bring anything really to life in literature we can't be lifelike: we have to be literature-like.

The same thing is true even of the use of language. We're often taught that prose is the language of ordinary speech, which is usually true in literature. But in ordinary life prose is no more the language of ordinary speech than one's Sunday suit is a bathing suit. The people who actually speak prose are highly cultivated and articulate people who've read a good many books, and even they can speak prose only to each other. If you read the beautiful sentences of Elizabeth Bennett's conversation in *Pride and Prejudice* you can see how in that book they give a powerfully convincing impression of a sensible and intelligent girl. But any girl who talked as coherently as that on a street car would be stared at as though she had green hair. It isn't only the difference between 1813 and 1962 that's involved either, as you'll see if you compare her speech with her mother's. The poet Emily Dickinson complained that everybody said 'What?' to her, until finally she practically gave up trying to talk altogether, and confined herself to writing notes.

All this is involved with the principle I've touched on before: the difference between literary and other kinds of writing. If we're writing to convey information, or for any practical reason our writing is an act of will and intention: we mean what we say, and the words we use represent that meaning directly. It's different in literature, not because the poet doesn't mean what he says too, but because his real effort is one of putting words together. What's important is not what he may have meant to say, but what the words themselves say when they get fitted together. With a novelist it's rather the incidents in the story he tells that get fitted together—as D. H. Lawrence says, don't trust the novelist; trust his story. That's why so much of a writer's best writing is or seems to be involuntary. It's involuntary because the forms of literature itself are taking control of it, and these forms are what are embodied in the conventions of literature. Conventions, we see, have the same role in literature that they have in life: they impose certain patterns of order and stability on the writer. Only, if they're such different conventions, it seems clear that the order of words, or the structure of literature, is different from the social order.

The absence of any clear line of connexion between literature and life comes out in the issues involved in censorship. Because of the large involuntary element in writing, works of literature can't be treated as embodiments of conscious will or intention, like people, and so no laws can be framed to control their behaviour which assume a tendency to do this or an intention of doing that. Works of literature get into legal trouble because they offend some powerful religious or political interest, and this interest in its turn usually acquires or exploits the kind of social hysteria that's always revolving around sex. But it's impossible to give legal definitions of such terms as obscenity in relation to works of literature. What happens to the book depends mainly on the intelligence of the judge. If he's a sensible man we get a sensible decision; if he's an ass we get that sort of decision, but what we don't get is a legal decision, because the basis for one doesn't exist. The best we get is a precedent tending to discourage cranks and pressure groups from attacking serious books. If you read the casebook on the trial of *Lady Chatterley's Lover,* you may remember how bewildered the critics were when they were asked what the moral effect of the book would be. They weren't putting on an act: they didn't know. Novels can only be good or bad in their own categories. There's no such thing as a morally bad novel: its moral effect depends entirely on the moral quality of its reader, and nobody can predict what that will be. And if literature isn't morally bad it isn't morally good either. I suppose one reason why *Lady Chatterley's Lover* dramatized this question so vividly was that it's a rather preachy and self-conscious book: like the Sunday-school novels of my childhood, it bores me a little because it tries so hard to be good.

So literature has no consistent connexion with ordinary life, positive or negative. Here we touch on another important difference between structures of the imagination and structures of practical sense, which include the applied sciences. Imagination is certainly essential to science, applied or pure. Without a constructive power in the mind to make models of experience, get hunches and follow them out, play freely around with hypotheses, and so forth, no scientist could get anywhere. But all imaginative effort in practical fields has to meet the test of practicability, otherwise it's discarded. The imagination in literature has no such test to meet. You don't relate it directly to life or reality: you relate works of literature, as we've said earlier, to each other. Whatever value there is in studying literature, cultural or practical, comes from the total body of our reading, the castle of words we've built, and keep adding new wings to all the time.

So it's natural to swing to the opposite extreme and say that literature is really a refuge or escape from life, a self-contained world like the world of the dream, a world of play or make-believe to balance the world of work. Some literature is like that, and many people tell us that they only read to get away from reality for a bit. And I've suggested myself that the sense of escape, or at least detachment, does come into everybody's literary experience. But the real point of literature can hardly be that. Think of such writers as William Faulkner or François Mauriac, their great moral dignity, the intensity and compassion that they've studied the life around them with. Or think of James Joyce, spending seven years on one book and seventeen on another, and having them ridiculed or abused or banned by the customs when they did get published. Or of the poets Rilke and Valéry, waiting patiently for years in silence until what they had to say was ready to be said. There's a deadly seriousness in all this that even the most refined theories of fantasy or make-believe won't quite cover. Still, let's go along with the idea for a bit, because we're not getting on very fast with the relation of literature to life, or what we could call the horizontal perspective of literature. That seems to block us off on all sides.

The world of literature is a world where there is no reality except that of the human imagination. We see a great deal in it that reminds us vividly of the life we know. But in that very vividness there's something unreal. We can understand this more clearly with pictures, perhaps. There are trick-pictures—*trompe l'oeil,* the French call them—where the resemblance to life is very strong. An American painter of this school played a joke on his bitchy wife by painting one of her best napkins so expertly that she grabbed at the canvas trying to pull it off. But a painting as realistic as that isn't a reality but an illusion: it has the glittering unnatural clarity of a hallucination. The real realities, so to speak, are things that don't remind us directly of our own experience, but are such things as the wrath of

Achilles or the jealousy of Othello, which are bigger and more intense experiences than anything we can reach—except in our imagination, which is what we're reaching with. Sometimes, as in the happy endings of comedies, or in the ideal world of romance, we seem to be looking at a pleasanter world than we ordinarily know. Sometimes, as in tragedy and satire, we seem to be looking at a world more devoted to suffering or absurdity than we ordinarily know. In literature we always seem to be looking either up or down. It's the vertical perspective that's important, not the horizontal one that looks out to life. Of course, in the greatest works of literature we get both the up and down views, often at the same time as different aspects of one event.

There are two halves to literary experience, then. Imagination gives us both a better and a worse world than the one we usually live with, and demands that we keep looking steadily at them both. I said in my first talk that the arts follow the path of the emotions, and of the tendency of the emotions to separate the world into a half that we like and a half that we don't like. Literature is not a world of dreams, but it would be if we had only one half without the other. If we had nothing but romances and comedies with happy endings, literature would express only a wish-fulfilment dream. Some people ask why poets want to write tragedies when the world's so full of them anyway, and suggest that enjoying such things has something morbid or gloating about it. It doesn't, but it might if there were nothing else in literature.

This point is worth spending another minute on. You recall that terrible scene in *King Lear* where Gloucester's eyes are put out on the stage. That's part of a play, and a play is supposed to be entertaining. Now in what sense can a scene like that be entertaining? The fact that it's not really happening is certainly important. It would be degrading to watch a real blinding scene, and far more so to get any pleasure out of watching it. Consequently, the entertainment doesn't consist in its reminding us of a real blinding scene. If it did, one of the great scenes of drama would turn into a piece of repulsive pornography. We couldn't stop anyone from reacting in this way, and it certainly wouldn't cure him, much less help the public, to start blaming or censoring Shakespeare for putting sadistic ideas in his head. But a reaction of that kind has nothing to do with drama. In a dramatic scene of cruelty and hatred we're seeing cruelty and hatred, which we know are permanently real things in human life, from the point of view of the imagination. What the imagination suggests is horror, not the paralyzing sickening horror of a real blinding scene, but on exuberant horror, full of the energy of repudiation. This is as powerful a rendering as we can ever get of life as we don't want it.

So we see that there are moral standards in literature after all, even though they have nothing to do with calling the police when we see a word in a book that's more familiar in sound than in print. One of the things Gloucester says in that scene is: 'I am tied to the stake, and I must stand the course.' In Shakespeare's day it was a favourite sport to tie a bear to a stake and set dogs on it until they killed it. The Puritans suppressed this sport, according to Macaulay, not because it gave pain to the bear but because it gave pleasure to the spectators. Macaulay may have intended his remark to be a sneer at the Puritans, but surely if the Puritans did feel this way they were one hundred per cent right. What other reason is there for abolishing public hangings? Whatever their motives, the Puritans and Shakespeare were operating in the same direction. Literature keeps presenting the most vicious things to us as entertainment, but what it appeals to is not any pleasure in these things, but the exhilaration of standing apart from them and being able to see them for what they are because they aren't really happening. The more exposed we are to this, the less likely we are to find an unthinking pleasure in cruel or evil things. As the eighteenth century said in a fine mouth-filling phrase, literature refines our sensibilities.

The top half of literature is the world expressed by such words as sublime, inspiring, and the like, where what we feel is not detachment but absorption. This is the world of heroes and gods and titans and Rabelaisian giants, a world of powers and passions and moments of ecstasy far greater than anything we meet outside the imagination. Such forces would not only absorb but annihilate us if they entered ordinary life, but luckily the protecting wall of the imagination is here too. As the German poet Rilke says, we adore them because they disdain to destroy us. We seem to have got quite a long way from our emotions with their division of things into "I like this" and "I don't like this." Literature gives us an experience that stretches us vertically to the heights and depths of what the human mind can conceive, to what corresponds to the conceptions of heaven and hell in religion. In this perspective what I like or don't like disappears, because there's nothing left of me as a separate person: as a reader of literature I exist only as a representative of humanity as a whole. We'll see how important this is in the last talk.

No matter how much experience we may gather in life, we can never in life get the dimension of experience that the imagination gives us. Only the arts and sciences can do that, and of these, only literature gives us the whole sweep and range of human imagination as it sees itself. It seems to be very difficult for many people to understand the reality and intensity of literary experience. To give an example that you may think a bit irrelevant: why have so many people managed to convince themselves that Shakespeare did not write Shakespeare's plays, when there is not an atom of evidence that anybody else did? Apparently because they feel that poetry must be written out of personal experience, and that Shakespeare didn't have enough experience of the right kind. But Shakespeare's plays weren't produced by his experience: they were produced by his imagination, and the way to develop the imagination is to read a good book or two. As for us, we can't speak or think or comprehend even our own experience except within the limits of our own power over words, and those limits have been established for us by our great writers.

Literature, then, is not a dream-world: it's two dreams, a wish-fulfilment dream and an anxiety dream, that are focused together, like a pair of glasses, and become a fully conscious vision. Art, according to Plato, is a dream for awakened minds, a work of imagination withdrawn from ordinary life, dominated by the same forces that dominate the dream, and yet giving us a perspective and dimension on reality that we don't get from any other approach to reality. So the poet and the dreamer are distinct, as Keats says. Ordinary life forms a community, and literature is among other things an art of communication, so it forms a community too. In ordinary life we fall into a private and separate subsconscious every night, where we reshape the world according to a private and separate imagination. Underneath literature there's another kind of subconscious, which is social and not private, a need for forming a community around certain symbols, like the Queen and the flag, or around certain gods that represent order and stability, or becoming and change, or death and rebirth to a new life. This is the myth-making power of the human mind, which throws up and dissolves one civilization after another.

I've taken my title for this talk, "The Keys to Dreamland," from what is possibly the greatest single effort of the literary imagination in the twentieth century, Joyce's *Finnegans Wake*. In this book a man goes to sleep and falls, not into the Freudian separate or private subsconscious, but into the deeper dream of man that creates and destroys his own societies. The entire book is written in the language of this dream. It's a subsconscious language, mainly English, but connected by associations and puns with the eighteen or so other languages that Joyce knew. *Finnegans Wake* is not a book to read, but a book to decipher: as Joyce says, it's about a dreamer, but it's addressed to an ideal reader suffering from an ideal insomnia. The reader or critic, then, has a role complementing the poet's role. We need two powers in literature, a power to create and a power to understand.

In all our literary experience there are two kinds of response. There is the direct experience of the work itself, while we're reading a book or seeing a play, especially for the first time. This experience is uncritical, or rather pre-critical, so it's not infallible. If our experience is limited, we can be roused to enthusiasm or carried away by something that we can later see to have been second-rate or even phoney. Then there is the conscious, critical response we make after we've finished reading or left the theatre, where we compare what we've experienced with other things of the same kind, and form a judgment of value and proportion on it. This critical response, with practice, gradually makes our pre-critical responses more sensitive and accurate, or improves our taste, as we say. But behind our responses to individual works, there's a bigger response to our literary experience as a whole, as a total possession.

The critic has always been called a judge of literature, which means, not that he's in a superior position to the poet, but that he ought to know something about literature, just as a judge's right to be on a bench depends on his knowledge of law. If he's up against something the size of Shakespeare, he's the one being judged. The critic's function is to interpret every work of literature in the light of all the literature he knows, to keep constantly struggling to understand what literature as a whole is about. Literature as a whole is not an aggregate of exhibits with red and blue ribbons attached to them, like a cat-show, but the range of articulate human imagination as it extends from the height of imaginative heaven to the depth of imaginative hell. Literature is a human apocalypse, man's revelation to man, and criticism is not a body of adjudications, but the awareness of that revelation, the last judgment of mankind.

Northrop Frye, "The Keys to Dreamland," *The Educated Imagination* (Toronto: CBC Publications, 1963).

NORTHROP FRYE

In my first four talks I've been building up a theory of literature. Now I'm ready to put this theory to a practical test. If it's any good, it should give us some guidance on the question of how to teach literature, especially to children. It should tell us what the simple and fundamental conceptions are that we should start with, and what more advanced studies can later be built on them. It seems clear that the teaching of literature needs a bit more theory of this kind, and suffers in comparison with science and mathematics from not having it.

My general principle, developed in my first four talks, is that in the history of civilization literature follows after a mythology. A myth is a simple and primitive effort of the imagination to identify the human with the non-human world, and its most typical result is a story about a god. Later on, mythology begins to merge into literature, and myth then becomes a structural principle of story-telling. I've tried to explain how myths stick together to form a mythology, and how the containing framework of the mythology takes the shape of a feeling of lost identity which we had once and may have again.

The most complete form of this myth is given in the Christian Bible, and so the Bible forms the lowest stratum in the teaching of literature. It should be taught so early and so thoroughly that it sinks straight to the bottom of the mind, where everything that comes along later can settle on it. That, I am aware, is a highly controversial statement, and can be misunderstood in all kinds of ways, so please remember that I'm speaking as a literary critic about the teaching of literature. There are all sorts of secondary reasons for teaching the Bible as literature: the fact that it's so endlessly quoted from and alluded to, the fact that the cadences and phrases of the King James translation are built into our minds and way of thought, the fact that it's full of the greatest and best known stories we have, and so on. There are also the moral and religious reasons for its importance, which are different reasons. But in the particular context in which I'm speaking now, it's the total shape and structure of the Bible which is most important: the fact that it's a continuous narrative beginning with the creation and ending with the Last Judgment, and surveying the whole history of mankind, under the symbolic names of Adam and Israel, in between. In other words, it's the *myth* of the Bible that should be the basis of literary training, its imaginative survey of the human situation which is so broad and comprehensive that everything else finds its place inside it. Remember too that to me the word myth, like the words fable and fiction, is a technical term in criticism, and the popular sense in which it means something untrue I regard as a debasing of language. Further, the Bible may be more things than a work of literature, but it certainly is a work of literature too: no book can have had its influence on literature without itself having literary qualities. For the purpose I have in mind, however, the Bible could only be taught in school by someone with a well-developed sense of literary structure.

The first thing to be laid on top of a Biblical training, in my opinion, is Classical mythology, which gives us the same kind of imaginative framework, of a more fragmentary kind. Here again there are all sorts of incidental or secondary reasons for the study: the literatures of all modern Western languages are so full of Classical myths that one hardly knows what's going on without some training in them. But again, the primary reason is the shape of the mythology. The Classical myths give us, much more clearly than the Bible, the main episodes of the central myth of the hero whose mysterious birth, triumph and marriage, death and betrayal and eventual rebirth follow the rhythm of the sun and the seasons. Hercules and his twelve labours, Theseus emerging from his labyrinth, Perseus with the head of Medusa: these are story-themes that ought to get into the mind as early as possible. Resemblances between Biblical and Classical legend should not be treated as purely coincidental: on the contrary, it's essential to show how the same literary patterns turn up within different cultures and religions. A poet living in the days of Shakespeare or Milton got this kind of training in elementary school, and we can't read far in *Paradise Lost*, for example, without realizing not simply that we need to know both the Bible and the Classical myths to follow it, but that we also have to see the relation of the two mythologies to each other. Modern poets don't get the same kind of education, as a rule: they have to educate themselves, and some of the difficulty that people complain about in modern poets goes back to what I think is a deficiency in the earliest stages of literary teaching, for both poet and reader. I've taken the title for this talk, "Verticals of Adam," from a series of sonnets by Dylan Thomas, "Altarwise by owl-light," which tells the story of a "gentleman," as Thomas calls him, who is both Adam and Apollo, and moves across the sky going through the stages of life and death and rebirth. These sonnets make very tough reading, and I think one reason why they're so obscure is that the shape of the central myth of literature broke in on Thomas suddenly at a certain stage of his development, and that it broke with such force that he could hardly get all his symbols and metaphors down fast enough. His later poems, difficult as some of them are, are still much simpler, because by that time he'd digested his mythology.

The Greeks and Romans, like the authors of the Old Testament, arranged their myths in a sequence, starting with stories of creation and fall and flood and gradually moving into historical reminiscence, and finally into actual history. And as they move into history they also move into more recognizable and fully developed forms of literature. The Classical myths produced Homer and the Greek dramatists; the ancient traditions of the Old Testament developed into the Psalms and the Book of Job. The next step in literary teaching is to understand the structure of the great literary forms. Two of these forms are the pair familiar to us from drama, tragedy and comedy. There's also another pair of opposites, which I should call romance and irony. In romance we have a simplified and idealized world, of brave heroes, pure and beautiful heroines, and very bad villains. All forms of irony, including satire, stress the complexity of human life in opposition to this simple world. Of these four forms, comedy and romance are the primary ones; they can be taught to the youngest students. When adults read for relaxation they almost always return to either comedy or romance. Tragedy and irony are more difficult, and ought to be reserved, I think, for the secondary-school level.

Romance develops out of the story of the hero's adventures which the student has already met in myth, and comedy out of the episode of the hero's triumph or marriage. It's important to get the habit of standing back and looking at the total structure of every literary work studied. A student who acquires this habit will see how the comedy of Shakespeare he's studying has the same general structure as the battered old movie he saw on television the night before. When I was at school we had to real *Lorna Doone*, and a girl beside me used to fish a love-story magazine out of her desk and read it on her knee when the teacher wasn't looking. She obviously regarded these stories as much hotter stuff than *Lorna Doone*, and perhaps they were, but I'd be willing to bet something that they told exactly the same kind of story. To see these resemblances in structure will not, by itself, give any sense of comparative value, any notion why Shakespeare is better than the television movie. In my opinion value-judgments in literature should not be hurried. It does a student little good to be told that A is better than B, especially if he prefers B at the time. He has to feel values for himself, and should follow his individual rhythm in doing so. In the meantime, he can read almost anything in any order, just as he can eat mixtures of food that would have his elders reaching for the baking soda. A sensible teacher or librarian can soon learn how to give guidance to a youth's reading that allows for undeveloped taste and still doesn't turn him into a gourmet or a dyspeptic before his time.

It's important too that everything that has a story, such as a myth, should be read or listened to purely as a story. Many people grow up without really understanding the difference between imaginative and discursive writing. On the rare occasions when they encounter poems, or even pictures, they treat them exactly as though they were intended to be pieces of more or less disguised information. Their questions are all based on this assumption. What is he trying to get across? What am I supposed to get out of it? Why doesn't somebody explain it to me? Why couldn't he have written it in a different way so I could understand him? The art of listening to stories is a basic training for the imagination. You don't start arguing with the writer: you accept his postulates, even if he tells you that the cow jumped over the moon, and you don't react until you've taken in all of what he has to say. If Bertrand Russell is right in saying that suspension of judgment is one of the essential operations of the mind, the benefits of learning to do this go far beyond literature. And even then what you react to is the total structure of the story as a whole, not to some message or moral or Great Thought that you can snatch out of it and run away with. Equal in importance to this training is that of getting the student to write himself. No matter how little of this he does, he's bound to have the experience sooner or later of feeling he's said something that he can't explain except in exactly the same way that he's said it. That should help to make him more tolerant about difficulties he encounters in his reading, although the benefits of trying to express oneself in different literary ways naturally extend a lot further than mere tolerance.

I have to cover a good deal of ground in this talk, so I can only suggest briefly that the study of English has two contexts which must be in place for the student if his study is to have any reality. There is, first, the context of languages other than English, and there is, second, the context of the arts other than literature. The people who call themselves humanists, and who include students of literature, have always been primarily people who studied other languages. The basis of the cultural heritage of English-speaking peoples is not in English; it's in Latin and Greek and Hebrew. This basis has to be given the young student in translation, although no translation of anything worth reading is of much use except as a crib to the original. Nowadays the modern languages take a more prominent place in education than the Classical ones, and it's often said that we ought to learn other languages as a kind of painful political duty. There's that, certainly, but there's also the fact that all our mental processes connected with words tend to follow the structure of the language we're thinking in. We can't use our minds at full capacity unless we have some idea of how much of what we think we're thinking is really thought, and how much is just familiar words running along their own familiar tracks. Nearly everyone does enough talking, at least, to become fairly fluent in his own language, and at that point there's always the danger of automatic fluency, turning on a tap and letting a lot of platitudinous bumble emerge. The best check on this so far discovered is some knowledge of other languages, where at least the bumble has to fit into a different set of grammatical grooves. I have a friend who was chairman of a commission that had to turn in a complicated report, where things had to be put clearly and precisely. Over and over again he'd turn to a French Canadian on the committee and ask him to say it in French, and he'd get his lead from that. This is an example of why the humanists have always insisted that you don't learn to think wholly from one language: you learn to think better from linguistic conflict, from bouncing one language off another.

And just as it's easy to confuse thinking with the habitual associations of language, so it's easy to confuse thinking with thinking in words. I've even heard it said that thought is inner speech, though how you'd apply that statement to what Beethoven was doing when he was thinking about his ninth symphony I don't know. But the study of other arts, such as painting and music, has many values for literary training apart from their value as subjects in themselves. Everything man does that's worth doing is some kind of construction, and the imagination is the constructive power of the mind set free to work on pure construction, construction for its own sake. The units don't have to be words; they can be numbers or tones or colours or bricks or pieces of marble. It's hardly possible to understand what the imagination is doing with words without seeing how it operates with some of these other units.

As the student gets older, he reads more complicated literature, and this usually means literature concerned largely or exclusively with human situations and conflicts. The old primitive association of human and natural worlds is still there in the background, but in, say, a novel of Henry James it's a long way in the background. We often feel that certain types of literature, such as fairy tales, are somehow good for the imagination: the reason is that they restore the primitive perspective that mythology has. So does modern poetry, on the whole, as compared with fiction. At this point a third context of literature begins to take shape: the relation of literature to other subjects, such as history and philosophy and the social sciences, that are built out of words.

In every properly taught subject, we start at the centre and work outwards. To try to teach literature by starting with the applied use of words, or "effective communication," as it's often called, then gradually work into literature through the more documentary forms of prose fiction and finally into poetry, seems to me a futile procedure. If literature is to be properly taught, we have to start at its centre, which is poetry, then work outwards to literary prose, then outwards from there to the applied languages of business and professions and ordinary life. Poetry is the most direct and simple means of expressing oneself in words: the most primitive nations have poetry, but only quite well developed civilizations can produce good prose. So don't think of poetry as a perverse and unnatural way of distorting ordinary prose statements: prose is a much less natural way of speaking than poetry is. If you listen to small children, and to the amount of chanting and singsong in their speech, you'll see what I mean. Some languages, such as Chinese, have kept differences of pitch in the spoken word: where Canadians got the monotone honk that you're listening to now I don't know—probably from the Canada goose.

What poetry can give the student is, first of all, the sense of physical movement. Poetry is not irregular lines in a book, but something very close to dance and song, something to walk down the street keeping time to. Even if the rhythm is free it's still something to be declaimed. The surge and sweep of Homer and the sinewy springing rhythm of Shakespeare have much the same origin: they were written that way partly because they had to be bellowed at a restless audience. Modern poets work very hard at trying to convince people in cafés or even in parks on Sunday that poetry can be performed and listened to, like a concert. There are quieter effects in poetry, of course, but a lot even of them have to do with physical movement, such as the effect of wit that we get from strict meter, from hearing words stepping along in an ordered marching rhythm. From poetry one can go on to prose, and if one's literary education is sound the first thing one should demand from prose is rhythm. My own teacher, Pelham Edgar, once told me that if the rhythm of a sentence was right, its sense could look after itself. Of course I was at university then, and I admit that this would be a dangerous thing to say to a ten-year-old. But it said one thing that was true. We're often told that to write we must have something to say, but that in its turn means having a certain potential of verbal energy.

Besides rhythm, the imagery and diction of poetry should be carried out into other modes of English. The preference of poetry for concrete and simple words, for metaphor and simile and all the figures of associative language, and its ability to contain great reserves of meaning in the simple forms that we call myths and read as stories, are equally important. The study of literature, we've been saying, revolves around certain classics or models, which the student gradually learns to read for himself. There are many reasons why certain works of literature are classics, and most of them are purely literary reasons. But there's another reason too: a great work of literature is also a place in which the whole cultural history of the nation that produced it comes into focus. I've mentioned Robinson Crusoe: you can get from that book a kind of detached vision of the British Empire, imposing its own pattern wherever it goes, catching its man Friday and trying to turn him into an eighteenth-century Nonconformist, never dreaming of "going native," that history alone would hardly give. If you read *Anna and the King of Siam* or saw *The King and I*, you remember the story of the Victorian lady in an Oriental country which had never had any tradition of chivalry or deference to women. She expected to be treated like a Victorian lady, but she didn't so much say so as express by her whole bearing and attitude that nothing else was possible, and eventually Siam fell into line. As you read or see that story, the shadow of an even greater Victorian lady appears behind her: Alice in Wonderland, remembering the manners her governess taught her, politely starting topics of conversation and pausing for a reply, unperturbed by the fact that what she's talking to may be a mock turtle or a caterpillar, surprised only by any rudeness or similar failure to conform to the proper standards of behaviour.

This aspect of literature in which it's a kind of imaginative key to history is particularly clear in the novel, and more elusive and difficult in Shakespeare or Milton. American literature falls mainly in the period of fiction, and in such books as *Huckleberry Finn, The Scarlet Letter, Moby Dick, Walden, Uncle Tom's Cabin*, a great deal of American social life, history, religion and cultural mythology is reflected. I think it's a mistake to approach such books inside out, as is often done, starting with the history and sociology and the rest of it and treating the book as though it were an allegory of such things. The book itself is a literary form, descended from and related to other literary forms: everything else follows from that.

The constructs of the imagination tell us things about human life that we don't get in any other way. That's why it's important for Canadians to pay particular attention to Canadian literature, even when the imported brands are better seasoned. I often think of a passage in Lincoln's Gettysburg address: "The world will little note nor long remember what we say here, but it can never forget what they did here." The Gettysburg address is a great poem, and poets have been saying ever since Homer's time that they were just following after the great deeds of the heroes, and that it was the deeds which were important and not what they said about them. So it was right, in a way, that is, it was traditional, and tradition is very important in literature, for Lincoln to say what he did. And yet it isn't really true. Nobody can remember the names and dates of battles unless they make some appeal to the imagination: that is, unless there is some literary reason for doing so. Everything that happens in time vanishes in time: it's only the imagination that, like Proust, whom I quoted earlier, can see men as "giants in time."

What is true of the relation of literature to history is also true of the relation of literature to thought. I said in my first talk that literature, being one of the arts, is concerned with the home and not the environment of man: it lives in a simple, man-centred world and describes the nature around it in the kind of associative language that relates it to human concerns. We notice that this man-centered perspective is in ordinary speech as well: in ordinary speech we are all bad poets. We think of things as up or down, for example, so habitually that we often forget they're just metaphors. Religious language is so full of metaphors of ascent, like "lift up your hearts," and so full of traditional associations with the sky, that Mr. Krushchev still thinks he's made quite a point when he tells us that his astronauts can't find any trace of God in outer space. If we're being realistic instead of religious, we prefer to descend, to get "down" to the facts (or to "brass tacks," which is rhyming slang for the same thing). We speak of a subconscious mind which we assume is underneath the conscious mind, although so far as I know it's only a spatial metaphor that puts it there. We line up arguments facing each other like football teams: on the one hand there's this and on the other hand there's that.

All this is familiar enough, but it isn't often thought of as directly connected with one's education in literature. Still, it takes me to a point at which I can perhaps venture a suggestion about what the real place of literature in education is. I think it has somewhat the same relationship to the studies built out of words, history, philosophy, the social sciences, law, and theology, that mathematics has to the physical sciences. The pure mathematician proceeds by making postulates and assumptions and seeing what comes out of them, and what the poet or novelist does is rather similar. The great mathematical geniuses often do their best work in early life, like most of the great lyrical poets. Pure mathematics enters into and gives form to the physical sciences, and I have a notion that the myths and images of literature also enter into and give form to all the structures we build out of words.

In literature we have both a theory and a practice. The practice is the production of literature by writers of all types, from geniuses to hacks, from those who write out the deepest agonies of the spirit to those who write for fun. The theory of literature is what I mean by criticism, the activity of uniting literature with society, and with the different contexts that literature itself has, some of which we've been looking at. The great bulk of criticism is teaching, at all levels from kindergarten to graduate school. A small part of it is reviewing, or introducing current literature to its public, and a still smaller, though of course central, part of it is scholarship and research. The importance of criticism, in this sense, has increased prodigiously in the last century or so, the reason being simply the increase in the proportion of people that education is trying to reach. If we think of any period in the past—say eighteenth-century England—we think of the writers and scholars and artists, Fielding and Johnson and Hogarth and Adam Smith and a hundred more, and the cultivated and educated audience which made their work possible. But these writers and artists and their entire public, added all together, would make up only a minute fraction of the total population of England at that time—so minute that my guess is we'd hardly believe the statistics if we had them. In these days we're in a hare-and-tortoise race between mob rule and education: to avoid collapsing into mob rule we have to try to educate a minority that'll stand out against it. The fable says the tortoise won in the end, which is consoling, but the hare shows a good deal of speed and few signs of tiring.

In my third talk I tried to distinguish the world of imagination from the world of belief and action. The first, I said, was a vision of possibilities, which expands the horizon of belief and makes it both more tolerant and more efficient. I have now tried to trace the progress of literary education to the point at which the student has acquired something of this vision and is ready to carry what he has of it into society. It's clear that the end of literary teaching is not simply the admiration of literature; it's something more like the transfer of imaginative energy from literature to the student. The student's response to this transfer of energy may be to become a writer himself, but the great majority of students will do other things with it. In my last talk I want to consider the educated imagination and what it does as it goes to work in society.

Northrop Frye, "Verticals of Adam," *The Educated Imagination* (Toronto: CBC Publications, 1963).

JAMES REANEY

Perhaps the drive behind this magazine might be found in the following cluster: (a) The most exciting thing about this century is the number of poems that cannot be understood unless the reader quite reorganizes his way of looking at things or "rouses his faculties" as Blake would say. *Finnegans Wake* and Dylan Thomas' "Altarwise by owl-light" sonnet sequence are good examples here. These works cannot be enjoyed to anywhere near their fullest unless one rouses one's heart, belly and mind to grasp their secret alphabet or iconography or language of symbols and myths. A grasping such as is involved here leads to a more powerful inner life, of Blake's "Jerusalem's wall." Besides which it's a hell of a lot of fun. It seems quite natural, then, in this century and particularly in this country, which could stand some more Jerusalem's wall, that there should be a journal of some sort devoted to iconography. After all Ernest Cassirer defines man as a symbol-making animal.

But (b) there had to be more than this general feeling of our time. There had to be the particular pressure of friends, teachers and even scoffers also interested in symbolism in one way or another. I can remember about twelve years ago at Toronto feeling the final clutch of the so-called scientific world. Metaphors seemed lies. Poetry seemed to have no use at all. The moon looked enchanting through the trees on Charles Street, but the enchantment was really nothing but an illusion of clouds and fantasy covering up a hide-out pock-marked spherical desert. When I told this part of my problem to a friend, whose work appears in this issue, he showed me a passage from the *Marriage of Heaven and Hell* which had the effect of starting me back to the belief I had held as a child that metaphor is reality. Those were the months when young men and women sat up all night reading *Fearful Symmetry* which had just come out. I think I have been present at more conversations about the Fall than even Adam could have thrown a certain withered apple core at, and assuredly more speculations concerning Leviathan than Job scratched his boils to. Here in your hands lies one of the effects of those conversations—a small secret looking book devoted to the proposition that it is very interesting mankind should answer the terrors of the inner and the outer world with a symbolic fruit and an iconic sea-beast. Interest increases with exploration. This attitude is to me one of the most stimulating areas of intellectual life in Canada. A traveller from abroad would immediately pick it out. *Ils ont parlé toute la nuit de baleines blanches!* So base a mag on this fact, actually personally observed, this fact of our cultural life. It's a sturdy fact too; why else so much opposition? The tactics of the anti-symbol, anti-analogy gang could only be described by making up titles for their mags, such as : *Anti-Rot, ExeJesus, Values, The Lampman Review* and *True Feelers.* However.

And (c) there was the desire to do the same delightful thing I had watched *here and now,* also *Northern Review,* do: publish real poems and real stories in a format and an area of subtle zoning that created a memorable effect (as distinct as a taste) on readers and also "placed" the poems and stories to their advantage. This must be one of the happiest of civilized activities, akin to the proper arrangement of flowers. It was Kleiman's story I first felt I must see published; it was so imaginative and no one was doing a thing about it. No really live focus appeared to put the story in until a juxtaposition, mind and social, occurred: Jay Macpherson read a paper on myth at the English Club (part of it appears on pages within) and afterwards there was a party at an apartment on Yorkville. Here Hope Lee told the stories about being a twin that we've also printed. It suddenly came to me that here was proof that life reflected art. The myth of Narcissus reaches out and touches with a clarifying ray the street scene where the two human beings glide by also in the toils of reflection. That's how poetry works: it weaves street scenes and twins around swans in legendary pools. Let us make a form out of this: documentary on one side and myth on the other: Life & Art. In this form we can put anything and the magnet we have set up will arrange it for us.

Two years later (printing lessons, typesetting, waiting for t's to come from Toronto, balancing trays of type on buses rolling in blizzards) here it is.

James Reaney, Editorial from *Alphabet,* No. 1, September 1960.

ELI MANDEL

As George Orwell reminds us in 1984, the equation for tyranny is terrifyingly simple· "Orthodoxy is unconsciousness." The tyrant, then, like the conformist, hates poetry, for poetry is the antithesis of unconsciousness. Against the witless rigidities of society and personality, it employs the strategies of the lively mind: ironic perspectives, the masks of comedy, tragedy and anarchy, new dramas of voice and imagery. Terror of the organization man, its vitality suggests to him chaos; its energy, destructiveness; its perceptiveness, obscurity: he calls its morality, immorality; its humanity, brutality; its compassion, obscenity. And, fearing its huge demands for comprehension, he longs for the single stupidity of hate.

A lively poetry shatters limitations. It refuses to be contained by officialdom (even by the most insidious officialdom of all: the orthodoxies of selection, reputation, respectability and success) for the simple reason that its life is change. And the present character of Canadian poetry is, above all, liveliness. Probably the most striking feature of contemporary Canadian poetry is its range of activity. It is now sufficiently varied to be represented in any number of ways—from the point of view of its articulate myth-makers, its passionate metaphysicians or its eloquent anarchists—and yet it leaves no impression that its energy is being dissipated in diversity. If anything, the opposite: one senses in it a gathering of forces for the performance of some unprecedented and enormously significant drama of the mind.

Such vitality demands elbow room. It demands, for one thing, that we suspend judgment about official versions of the contemporary scene until all the evidence is in. It demands, for another, that new work receive wider circulation than it can get in its experimental workshops in little magazines. It demands simultaneous representation of established modes and new ones so that their relationship can be understood—to the benefit of both poets and readers. In short, it demands a new (perhaps a new kind of) anthology.

This anthology has been created in response to those demands. It is not retrospective—no work in it has appeared before in book form. It does not seek to be inclusive, and it need not be, since it is hoped that this volume will be followed by others which should provide something close to a comprehensive view of the contemporary scene. It is an attempt to introduce new poets in the company of established poets, especially in the company of the new work of established poets (though, it should be noted here, the selection in this context could hardly be anything but arbitrary). At the cost of appearing eccentric, then, the anthology is selective of few rather than many; but in this is meets the most insistent demand of the new poetry, that where it is represented it should be represented substantially and that it should have room for the long poems which its vitality seems especially able to produce. Above all, the series begins here with the belief that the new poetry will win its own audience, that it will continue to demand representation and that it is considerably bigger than any one editor's taste, critical judgment or prejudices. Succeeding volumes, edited by others, should make that clear.

Nothing indicates more strongly the need for this anthology than the wide interest it already has aroused among poets and critics and the whole-hearted support which the editors have received from them. Mr. Jean-Guy Pilon, of course, is primarily responsible for the selection of French poetry, and I must say that without his enthusiastic support this volume could not have been produced. I have to thank also for their advice and encouragement Jay Macpherson, Louis Dudek and Raymond Souster—though the English selection is in the end my own responsibility; and to Rowland McMaster in particular I owe thanks for his constant help with the manuscript and for his critical comments.

Eli Mandel, Preface to *Poetry 62* (Toronto: Ryerson, 1961).

VII

THE LITTLE MAGAZINES

The Little Magazines

The little magazine in Canada has been the most important single factor behind the rise and continued progress of modernism in Canadian poetry. The history of the little magazine covers a period of some forty years and closely parallels the development of modern poetry itself from the mid-1920s to the present time. All the important events in poetry and most of the initiating manifestoes and examples of change are to be found in the little magazines.

There is no exact count of all the little magazines which have come and gone during this period in Canada, but a fair estimate would seem to indicate that about eighty periodicals in some way related to the little magazine movement have existed, and of this number some ten or so have a permanent place in the literary history of Canada.

The little magazine here began at least a decade later than its counterparts in England and America. It took its inspiration from the experiments of F. R. Scott and A. J. M. Smith with the *McGill Fortnightly Review,* 1925-27. From that point, and the short-lived *Canadian Mercury* which grew, indirectly, out of the *McGill Fortnightly Review,* the little magazine in Canada shows a clear and consistent development.

Whatever the interpretation of the role and function of such magazines, they provide the setting where new poetry and new poets have their beginning. The key developments of modern poetry in Canada take place on this makeshift stage—usually a very unpretentious, modestly-printed (or even mimeographed) periodical, edited by beginning writers of no standing and having little relation to the general reading public or the large-circulation media of communication. The little magazine is a form of semi-private publication which aims at public success and eventual victory over whatever is established in literary taste.

In the little magazines the editor or the editorial board is the key factor. (Ezra Pound, the American impresario of little magazines, has said that no magazine can be better than its editor.) If we divide the Canadian little magazines into broad categories or groups, from the point of view of their editorial direction, we see that they fall into three essential types. In the first place, there is the little magazine with a small *cénacle* or group of like-minded young writers forming the editorial board. This normally results in a loose-knit programme or body of ideas and a rather aggressive or militant role in getting the new programme across. The little magazine is then a proselytizing agent and a subject of acrid debate with other magazines and groups. Some of the most important little magazines—*The Canadian Mercury, Preview, First Statement, Tish*—were of this kind. In the second group, and this is perhaps the largest category, we have the uncommitted or eclectic magazines, still usually edited by an editorial group, but leaving their pages open to submissions from all literary lines, and publishing material from a wide range of sources and styles. Good literature is their pious hope. A notable example of this type of little magazine was Alan Crawley's *Contemporary Verse*; and in general, campus literary magazines fall into this category. Finally, we have the little magazine directed by a single personality. This is normally a personal magazine, and serves as the vehicle for a single writer's views and ideas. *Northern Review* (in its later years), *Delta, Contact, Combustion* and *Island* were of this kind.

Historically, it may be argued that little magazines in Canada begin with the first type, the coterie magazine, and move later into magazines of the second and third type, the eclectic and personal magazines. The development seems to be natural, tracing the history of modern poetry from its beginning to a stage of variety and confidence: first, as the new poetry calls for a campaign of literary action, we see a moderate and tolerant group tentatively organizing an advance in the direction of modernism, mainly at war with the old Victorian standards. This is the enterprise of F. R. Scott, A. J. M. Smith, and their group in the 1920s and thirties. But as this poetry becomes more confident, better entrenched, and as the pattern of modern expression becomes diversified, the eclectic magazine appears on the scene, as in Alan Crawley's *Contemporary Verse,* and later in *Tamarack Review.* Finally, with the appearance of flourishing personalities, either confident young men carrying on with new experiments, or older poets developed to a greater independence, we get the personal magazine—*Island* edited by Victor Coleman, or *Delta* edited by Louis Dudek. Thus, when a large new movement is in its beginning, we would expect a group magazine to arise, as in the case of *Tish* in Vancouver. And in later stages one would expect the other types to appear in succession, as in the case of Frank Davey's *Open Letter,* and George Bowering's *Imago.* Vancouver's *Prism,* in fact, is struggling with difficulty to establish itself as a quality eclectic magazine.

The articles included in this section complement one another in the matter of information and the view of historical significance of little magazines, but they differ in some interesting ways in their interpretation of the role of the magazines in general, and also in their account of the particular magazines discussed. Louis Dudek, in his article from the *Canadian Forum*, sees the little magazine phenomenon within the wider problem of the corruption of culture by the commercial press; he interprets and evaluates each magazine as a would-be engagement in the continuing battle for literary integrity. As a result, he seems reluctant to include the literary periodicals of the 1920s and 30s in his list of true little magazines. Michael Gnarowski, on the other hand, sees the little magazine primarily as the cultural revolt of an intellectual minority in Canada against an Anglo-colonial tradition; he too emphasizes the militant character of the little magazines, but he interprets this in terms of social dynamics and positive social change. Frank Davey, however, speaks from the point of view of a specific poetry movement in Vancouver centred around the magazine *Tish*. Some of the points made in the first two articles are therefore illustrated in the tone and bearing of his argument. (The omission of any mention of two current Montreal magazines not aligned with the *Tish* movement, *Yes* and *Delta,* is perhaps significant.) The very absence of the earlier criteria for little magazines is worth noting in Frank Davey's account; instead, his view of the situation is determined by a sense of opposition to the literary establishment and a firm view of the new directions which poetry is taking in the magazines he describes. All three articles, of course, contribute to a definition of the essential drives which move groups or individuals to participate in the little magazine movement, and through these magazines to contribute to the shaping of a diverse and mature culture.

LOUIS DUDEK

The little magazine is a recognizable and peculiar phenomenon associated with the growth of the modern poetry movement in this century. In Canada, this type of magazine can be said to have appeared only after 1940, although a number of forerunners having some claim to be ranked as little magazines appeared earlier. It is with the period after 1940 that the kind of literary activity and movement-poetry that had arisen in England just before World War I and in America during the 1920s began to flourish in Canada. A clear idea of the real nature of this type of magazine and of its role in Canadian literary developments is certainly preliminary to the understanding of our poetry and some of its motives.

The literary magazine of this type marks a stage in the history of printing, a retreat into intimate, or *cénacle* publication, after the extreme extension of literacy and printing for mass audiences: it is also the stage at which printing and paper become economically available for such private and limited publication. In literary terms, it is the embattled literary reaction of intellectual minority groups to the commercial middle-class magazines of fiction and advertising which had evolved in the nineteenth century.

The profit motive as a drive in periodical and newspaper publishing had, by the beginning of this century, outbalanced and displaced the literary and scholarly values that had normally entered into the act of publication in the past; money had taken the rudder of editorial taste into its own hands, and in the notorious work of Harmsworth and Newnes—not to mention American publishers like W. R. Hearst —newspapers had become sensational mass entertainment media designed to season the advertising matter that provided their main source of income. Magazines had taken the same direction as newspapers, although the full effect of such popularization was not to appear until after 1920. The quality magazines of the educated middle class, such as *Harper's* and the *Atlantic,* if uncontaminated directly, drifted into a state of ineffectual dotage—so far as publishing poetry or imaginative prose is concerned—since they were oblivious to the nature of the spreading corruption and published only a small quantity of epigonic poetry and story-telling, when more vociferous writing was needed. It is against this advertising-dominated journalism of the twentieth century and its decadent quality-magazine culture that the little magazines of literature arose. "To hell with *Harper's* and the magazine touch," wrote Ezra Pound when *Poetry* (Chicago) was in its early months. He defined the new poetry and the central drive of the new movement—away from the popular culture shaped by the big magazines and newspapers.

The Canadian part of this revolt against the tyranny of the subjugated majority came, like most Canadian artistic contributions, late and with some confusion of intent. Our first modern poets, A. J. M. Smith and F. R. Scott, were more concerned with learning a fashion from Eliot, Yeats and presently Auden, than in expressing their own aroused resistance on native grounds; and A. M. Klein was partly withdrawn into a parochial idea. Smith and Scott started the *McGill Fortnightly* (1925-1927), in some sense a little magazine, but one whose very name identifies it with the staid journalism of the nineteenth century (the English *Fortnightly,* edited by G. H. Lewes, John

Morley, etc. founded in 1865) not with the new intellectual bohemian fringe (cf. *Blast, Exile, Transition*). *The Canadian Mercury* (1928-1929), *The Canadian Forum* (1920-   ) and *The Canadian Bookman* (1919-1939), by and large have followed the same pattern: they are not little magazines. As for *Canadian Poetry Magazine*, the official organ of the Canadian Author's Association, that is the kind of magazine that is antithetical to the "little magazine": it publishes the poetry of appeasement, of gullible sentimentality.

The depression carried the new poetry in Canada into political channels of a conventional kind; and Scott especially, as we know, became a sharp and effective proponent of social action against Canada's lethargic and outdated colonial capitalism; but as poets, not one of our moderns, Scott, Smith or Klein, committed himself entirely to poetry, and therefore could not draw upon a personal drama displaying the pain or indignation of a poet in a world of barbarism (the drama of Eliot's and Pound's poetry), though Klein came nearest to expressing this drama in his "Portrait of the Poet as a Nobody" (later retitled "Portrait of the Poet as a Landscape"). Smith voices a personal malaise which is the correlative of such a subject matter; and Scott has all the subject matter in his social satires without any of the malaise or dramatic involvement.

Nor did these poets as yet take full action in producing the magazines and books which are everywhere a part of the intellectual resistance to advertising journalism and to "popular" or "mass" culture. It was only in their college days that they undertook the abortive *Fortnightly,* and of such campus by-products every university has a certain supply. In 1936, too, Scott and Smith persuaded the Ryerson Press* to bring out a thin book, *New Provinces,* containing somewhat pale modernist work by six contributors. But it was fifteen years or more [i.e., after the *Fortnightly*] before Scott, Smith, or Klein were each to bring out a separate book of poetry. In short, Canada in the 1930s had no "little magazine" or "little press" movement: no magazines of poetry and experiment representing the rebellion of the creative minority against the profit-motive literature of mass-readership and cultural appeasement.

The long delay in the appearance of such a movement in Canada has been attributed usually to the Depression of the 1930s. A point of note, also, was the departure of A. J. M. Smith to teach in the United States: he should have been sought out by some brilliant college president and given a post in Canada. The conservatism of Toronto publishers has also been remarked, though in fact the Ryerson Press alone has done more to advance our literature than any

New Provinces was published by Macmillan not Ryerson.

other single force. More real than any such explanations must be the bare fact that our modernist poets had not yet fully awakened to the nature and requirements of the job they had undertaken. The new poetry was—and still is—an active campaign of the poets themselves against the machinery of publication and the mortified mind of the existing arbiters of taste: it demands a special kind of enterprise on the part of poets, such as had been shown by Margaret Anderson, Harriet Monroe, Harold Monroe, Amy Lowell, Ezra Pound, T. S. Eliot (with Faber and the *Criterion*), and a whole army of editors of little magazines in England and America. Our Canadian poets—"the meticulous moderns," as I have sometimes called them—published no such poetry magazines, nor did they even publish their own separate books, until the next generation came on the scene in 1940.

Contemporary Verse (1941-1952) in Vancouver broke the ice. This magazine, a true little poetry magazine on the American pattern, was edited by Alan Crawley, who was handicapped by blindness and cornered in the far west; but a group of leftist poets, Dorothy Livesay, Anne Marriott, and Floris McLaren, had initiated the scheme, invited Crawley to edit, and continued to collaborate in the production. The defect, however, was that *Contemporary Verse* was not a fighting magazine with a policy; it was concerned only with publishing "good poetry"—which, in itself, can embody an affirmation—but it did not in addition work out any program of ideas which this poetry could fire. It lasted for ten years, however, carrying sparks from any source which might show a flicker in that period.

A more aggressive "second stage" was reached in Montreal. Almost at the same time, and without any relation to the Vancouver magazine, *Preview* (1942-1945) was launched by a group of young people in Montreal. The characteristic impulse and direction was given to that magazine by Patrick Anderson, an Englishman who had come to Montreal via New York and Columbia University, from Oxford, bringing with him a mellifluous and hyper-eloquent manner of speech (that overwhelmed our literati) and a fertility of imagination that soon became the model or emulation for the poets writing in *Preview*. Of the younger poets attached to the magazine, P. K. Page, Bruce Ruddick, and Neufville Shaw seemed to close the list; while, of the earlier generation, Scott, and even Klein, contributed to the ferment. The magazine, though mimeographed only, was ambitious, in its literary and political aims, and in its intellectual intensity; it was exclusive (the list of permanent contributors appeared on the printed cover) and oriented toward a strongly Left political line. (Anderson suggests in his recent autobiographical fantasy, *Search Me*, that it was actually run off somewhere on a Communist underground machine; but as we know, there were clear differences between members of the group, certainly between Scott and Anderson.) The magazine was soon hailed in Chicago as "brilliant"; it was "read by Auden" in New York; it was the admiration of Canadian critics

In retrospect, it seems that *Preview,* although it was a real "little magazine" and a magazine of protest, was still derivative, in its leaning on Auden, in its excessive adulation of the Oxford-English Ideal in Patrick Anderson, and in its esoteric unawareness of the need for local literary stimulus, for variety, for native expression. Such a native product appeared on the scene when *Preview* turned down some poems by John Sutherland, then just out of college, and he turned to the launching of a new magazine of his own, *First Statement* (1942-1956),* which was to outlast *Preview* by more than a decade. His first assistants were Audrey Aikman (later Mrs. Sutherland) and Robert Simpson; soon these were joined by Irving Layton and myself, and strengthened by contributions from new poets in Toronto, Miriam and Patrick Waddington, and Raymond Souster.

The poets writing in *First Statement* were often rough and crude in expression ("lumpen intellectuals" in contrast to the "meticulous moderns"), and their aims perhaps were less formulated, less doctrinaire, than those of *Preview;* but their work was more visceral, their convictions hotter and more truly expressive of the pressures of life: they were working-class poets. The magazine, also, was open to new writers. It had many of the characteristics of fringe literature: anarchic attitudes of rejection, anti-literary leanings, a certain irresponsibility combined with a puritanical conviction in the prime virtue of integrity. Obviously unwashed behind the ears, our *First Statement* at least had a shining morning face.

After a few years of struggle (these magazines are always expensive to the editors and never profitable except to the soul), the *Preview* and *First Statement* groups combined to form *Northern Review* under a grand joint Editorial Board. The main fact, however, was the demise of *Preview* under this arrangement. Within a few months, editorial disagreement over a review by Sutherland led to a complete break-up and *Northern Review* proceeded under the management of Sutherland and Layton. In the days of *First Statement* we had acquired a printing press and had gradually improved the production; in Sutherland's hands, and with the support of his wife, the magazine grew to be a reputable literary review. But the new poetry movement had by this time broken up.

*1942-1956 spans the combined lives of *First Statement* (1942-1945) and of *Northern Review* which continued *First Statement* and *Preview* from 1945 to 1956.

It had all been generated by the release of the war, the end of Depression, and the loosening of Canadian lethargies after 1939. Even in the midst of war, Raymond Souster with the help of Bill Goldberg, both of them Air Force men, had been able to edit their own mimeo magazine, *Direction,* from various outposts. Another offshoot, *Elan,* ran for a time in Montreal. *Reading,* a guide to good books, was edited for a few issues by Robert Simpson. But during and after the war, the poets of the *Preview-First-Statement* axis had scattered somewhat—P. K. Page to Ottawa, myself to New York, Anderson back to England—so that the sense of exciting activity subsided. Layton resigned from *Northern Review,* as Sutherland became convinced that the movement had been a complete failure, that all modern poetry was misdirected, that the truth lay in Roy Campbell and in the Roman Catholic Church.

In the meantime, other enterprising magazines of the genuine "little mag" variety continued to arise: *Impression* in the mid-west, *Protocol* in Newfoundland, *P.M.* in Vancouver (where Earle Birney was now active), and a very expensive adventure in Toronto, *Here & Now.* Clearly a vigorous movement of modern poetry had been set going by the Montreal magazines and by *Contemporary Verse.* In the West Coast area, Earle Birney, Roy Daniells, Phyllis Webb, Anne Marriott, Dorothy Livesay, Al Purdy and Daryl Hine were to emerge through the medium of magazines. In Toronto, James Reaney, Anne Wilkinson, Souster, the Waddingtons, W. W. E. Ross (resurrected), and more recently Jay Macpherson, Peter Miller and Kenneth McRobbie, have appeared. And in Montreal, the poets already mentioned: in fact Montreal became a virtual centre to which poets from all parts of Canada congregated; Mandel, Hine, the Waddingtons, Miss Webb, Purdy, Miss Macpherson, all settled here for a time. Fredericton, N.B., also has added to the activity by the publication of *Fiddlehead,* by the critical writing of Desmond Pacey and the poetry of Fred Cogswell, Robert Rogers, Elizabeth Brewster and others.

After about 1950, the retreat of John Sutherland into Catholicism and into literary conservatism began to be countered by a resurgence of independent magazines backed or begotten by members of the old *First Statement* group. Souster has edited two mimeo magazines, *Contact,* and recently *Combustion,* mainly intended for poets; these cultivate translation (especially from the French, including Canadian), contact with American young poets, and a poetry of iconoclastic forthrightness and honesty of statement. In Montreal, *CIV/n* (code word for "Civilization"), edited by Aileen Collins, published seven memorable numbers of a magazine of fine vigour and aggressiveness:

it brought out Leonard Cohen, Eli Mandel, and other new poets. *Yes* (still in action), edited jointly by Mike Gnarowski, Glen Siebrasse, and John Lachs—all of whom write poetry—has added to the ferment, struggling toward an affirmation in the midst of disorder. *Delta,* a quarterly now in its fourth number, of which I am the editor, publishes a complex of poetry from all quarters of Canada interlarded with prose that aims to shake up the conventional subject matter of verse.

In Toronto, *Tamarack Review* has for the past two years supplemented the ancient reliable *Canadian Forum* by publishing both prose and poetry in an impressive and distinguished format. Though not as extravagant in this as was the magazine *Here & Now* (or the recent beautiful UBC campus publication *Raven*), it is probably too expensive to be practicable in the long run; and its contents confirm an ambiguous definition of aim. *Tamarack Review,* as Robert Weaver, one of its editors, recently noted, is "not a little magazine"; in format and editorial direction it resembles an English quarterly, a quality journal of literature and ideas.

With this we can return to our original purpose, which was to define the aim and the role of the little magazine in Canada. This type of magazine is not simply a repository of the best that is being thought and said. That role would be a misty illusion in this century, if we accept the cultural analysis of our best poets and critics; it is a role, for example, that is proposed to be filled by such journals as the *Times Literary Supplement* and the dull pot-bellied quarterlies of our universities. Such periodicals are holding to old standards in an alien and chaotic new world. The representative magazines of present-day culture are of course *Look, Life, Time,* and their English counterparts, *Sketch, Everybody's, Illustrated, John Bull* and the rest. The veritable "little magazine" of literature is a vociferous reaction to this latter form of readership; also to the radio, movies, and TV, that supplement and now replace the printed page; and to any deaf traditionalism that hopes to carry on without immersing in the destructive element of reality.

Canadian literary magazines which have most directly attacked this problem have only appeared since 1940; and in Canada there is very little understanding as yet of what the whole quarrel is about. It is about the issue in Allen Tate's statement a few years ago that "the central literary tradition is being fostered today by three or four journals whose combined circulation does not exceed three thousand." It is about the same issue described by T. S. Eliot when he closed the files of the *Criterion*: "For this immediate future, perhaps for a long way ahead, the continuity of culture may have to be maintained by . . . the small and obscure papers and reviews, those which hardly are read by anyone but their own contributors." (He does not mention the quarterlies, the quality weeklies, the university publications stuffed with culture and "scholarship.") In Canada such "small and obscure papers and reviews" are continuing at present on several fronts, and they promise quietly to create a vital literature of salutary value for this country before they run their course. They have few readers; but their eventual influence will be measured by the survey of Canadian Literature in A.D. 2000, not by the readers they had within their time.

Louis Dudek, "The Role of Little Magazines in Canada," *Canadian Forum*, July 1958.

MICHAEL GNAROWSKI

The little magazines of Montreal, have by now reached that stage where they enjoy a vague and somewhat respectable history. They figure prominently in any serious consideration of modern Canadian poetry written in English, and some of their names are so familiar that they have a kind of legendary aura, plus all the usual accretions of anecdotal myth about them. As a matter of fact the significant thing about these little magazines is that they have not only performed the functions which are expected of such publications, but have gone, because of the peculiar circumstances of Canadian poetry in the last thirty years, beyond the routine services expected of advance guard periodicals. It is quite obvious that the "little magazine" has seen fulfillment in the fullest sense of the word only in the United States. There it has experienced the widest range of publishing experiment, a process which has justified itself by the discovery of almost all the major literary figures of these times. The "little magazine" has been defined as a periodical intended to print artistic work which for any one of several reasons is considered unprintable or unacceptable in commercially oriented presses or periodicals. Someone else in a more grandiose but equally true pronouncement has stated that the "little magazines" of America have pressed defiantly in the front ranks of the battle for a mature literature. Statistics tend to support this latter statement since, as was mentioned earlier, something like eighty per cent of established modern writers have been discovered by and introduced to their audiences by the "little magazine." In some respects the Canadian experience has been analogous, although the effect of the little magazine has been felt primarily in poetry. Major novelists and writers of short stories as a rule, have sought outlets and recognition for their creative expression in foreign media or through agencies, publishing houses and large magazines which could assure them of some kind of tangible income, and a much wider if less select and discriminating audience. The Canadian critical performance as well has tended to stay outside the immediate area of little magazines, and we have not had any such publication which can claim a sustained and significant critical life. The vortex of literary activity in Canada has chosen to spin in Montreal, and it is there that the Canadian little magazine saw its inception. Those early little magazines which based themselves on Montreal have proved to be generally more conservative than one would normally expect. The reason for this is that it has been axiomatic, although it is rapidly becoming less so, that a little magazine in Canada was invariably destined to function as a national magazine. As a consequence, the influence of such a little magazine has tended to be uncommonly large. Until the last few years, there have been blessedly few little magazines published in this country, so much so that the small interested group which has supported this creative enterprise, has been kept informed of literary developments and of its own life chiefly through the medium of these little magazines, which have thus performed the task of liaison and borne the burden of an unusual national responsibility.

It is also a noteworthy fact that the influence of Canadian little magazines, although it has been appreciably diluted by the presence of a larger number of these publications on the scene, as well as by a growing awareness on the part of the public which now has recourse to other less recherché but equally interested media of artistic expression, witness some of the excellent programming, poetry readings, etc., of the Canadian Broadcasting Corporation, still remains a vital and significant factor in the slow progress of our literary development. This is due to the fact that one may still, at the price of a near nominal expenditure of twenty dollars subscribe to all the little magazines of Canada, an amount which could hardly purchase subscriptions to half the little magazines published on the Eastern Seaboard of the United States alone. This is a comparison which is meant to illustrate only one thing, that an interested individual can keep in touch with all the trends which may be developing in the area of little magazines in Canada and by extension be kept informed of the direction the nation's poetry has chosen to follow. One may also add that there has been manifested a greater sense of balance and less of the outré and the extremist in the overall tendencies of Canadian little magazines. There is detectable in most cases, perhaps an unconscious but nevertheless a refreshing determination which has succeeded in preserving our little magazines from much of the regionalism, the editorial clamour and pretension and the sheer eccentricity which have become synonymous with the notion of the "little magazine." In this continuing effort at staid editorial sense the Canadian little magazine movement has inched immeasurably closer to that defiant front rank which, in the rich world of scholarly imagination is battling for a mature literature.

In such a mood, and in the warm glow of a modest albeit true self-congratulation, one proceeds to the actual discussion of the nature and role of the little magazines of Montreal. Seniority has been ceded by general critical and historical agreement to *The McGill Fortnightly Review,* published from 1925 to 1927. One is inclined to challenge this opinion on the grounds that *The McGill Fortnightly Review* was not a little magazine in the strict sense and meaning of the term. This publication differed profoundly from the usual little magazine in its intent, its editorial policy, its outlook, its contents, and even its format. This was a magazine edited by university students in tenuous association with the student paper, aimed primarily at the student body, and with the avowed intention of devoting itself essentially to the intellectual life and the news of a university community. In spite of this restricted orientation, *The McGill Fortnightly Review* did have a very profound bearing on the future of little magazine publishing in Montreal and in Canada. Its fundamental and most significant achievement was simply that of creating a climate of assurance for its editors. It proved to Scott, Smith, Edel and others that it was possible to publish a literary magazine on an independent basis, and that this was an exciting and rewarding experience. The fact that the editors of *The McGill Fortnightly* chose a name for their publication which resembled so closely that of a much more influential magazine, specifically *The Fortnightly* published every month by Courtney in London, is in this estimation further evidence that the young editors were lacking in that original assurance—or perhaps one should say the originality and bravado—which is elementary equipment for prospective editors of little magazines. The success of *The McGill Fortnightly Review,* and in this case, a pattern of survival and a limited run of two years, established and guaranteed some kind of a little magazine tradition in Canada. It had proved not only to its own editors, but to other writers outside of McGill as well, that one could not only publish one's own magazine, but that one could experiment in publishing ventures on a limited scale. It must also be said that while *The McGill Fortnightly Review* may have required the crutch of direct association with the University in order to begin and to survive, it also achieved the much more important and independent purpose of coalescing a literary group with obvious potential, of training its own editors, and finally in preparing them for bolder more individualistic ventures in the future. Existing comment on little magazines stresses the "manifesto" element which these periodicals invariably contain. They are supposed to sound a clarion call as a very necessary part of their coming into this world. If the fire of their opening editorials can be taken as a good indication of the spirit of their founders, then the opening editorial of *The McGill Fortnightly* is disappointingly sedate. Hoffmann, Allen and Ulrich in the introduction to their history and bibliography of the little magazine, have defined the little magazine editor as follows:

. . . a man stimulated by some form of discontent—whether with the constraint of his world or the negligence of publishers, at any rate with something he considers unjust, boring or ridiculous.[1]

They also state that one of the great, if not the greatest values of little magazines lies in its spirit of conscientious revolt against the guardians of public taste. The opening editorial of *The McGill Fortnightly Review* read in part as follows:

The Review is an independent journal and, as such, it has a right to an independent opinion of its own on all matters. The Editors will express that opinion in the editorial columns. But this emphatically does not mean that we shall suppress the contributions of those who disagree with us. We shall be glad to receive and publish articles taking any attitude whatever. We reserve only that they shall be of sufficient literary merit. The body of *The McGill Fortnightly Review* will be devoted to purely literary, artistic and scientific matter, but space will also be reserved to do duty as an open forum wherein students of McGill may voice their thoughts on the affairs of the student body, saying freely whatever they may feel.[2]

The rest of this measured editorial consists of a collection of snippets of comment on everything from reading by Bliss Carman to some quibble over the refereeing of a football game. All this, is of course, in keeping with what one would expect of a university student magazine, and is in striking contrast with what one has come to expect of little magazines. As an example one can cite an editorial statement from *The New Talent*. It reads in part:

[Writers of avant-garde literature are motivated by] the spirit of revolt . . . against artificial boundaries of so-called good taste, against hypocritical sweetness and light, against formalistic strictures of language. . . .[3]

[1] Frederick J. Hoffman et al, *The Little Magazine: A History and a Bibliography* (Princeton U.P., 1946), p. 3.
[2] Editorial, *The McGill Fortnightly Review*, I, 1, 1925.
[3] E. G. Arnold, Editorial, *The New Talent*, IX, July/September, 1935, pp. 1-2.

Or from *Impromptu* (Jan./April 1931), "A magazine pledged to interpret and elaborate a philosophy of the creator as an anti-mechanical corrective to our age." Or from *Nativity* (1930-1931), "A magazine devoted to the direct attack upon the most obnoxious of all American cults, the cult of respectability."

Among other tendencies shown by *The McGill Fortnightly Review* which may be described as being alien to the nature of a true little magazine, is the heavy emphasis on material which we may consider as being non-literary: or more appropriately as belonging in the quieter limbo of more respectable and scholarly periodicals. An average number of the review could be expected to contain more or less the following material. Say a total of five poems, all written by Scott and Smith, and appearing under various thin but dashing pseudonyms such as Brian Tuke, Michael Gard or Vincent Starr. These poems were tucked away between various pieces of prose, the best of which was usually work by Leacock, while the most sober dealt with "The Theory of a Stationary World Population"; or again "Science and Happiness"; or a review of a concert at the Montreal Forum. In no sense therefore, even though Smith, Scott and Klein, pseudonyms and all, made frequent appearances in its pages, can we call *The McGill Fortnightly Review* a truly self-willed little magazine. Its historic value is lodged in the fact that it brought a group of promising poets together, gave them editorial experience and finally pointed them in the right direction, thus starting a literary movement on its way. In this latter connection it may be pointed out that the little magazines of Montreal have been instrumental in originating and have supported not what a recent trend in Canadian literary criticism has called a school of poetry but a full-fledged literary movement. They are and have always been the expression of a state of mind of responsible, anxious writers and their small but appreciative audience. This state of mind has been self-perpetuating; and it has gone out in an ever-widening ripple producing an almost uninterrupted series of little magazines which have involved most of the major poets of Canada. In a final understanding of the role played by these individualistic periodicals it will become apparent, that beside performing the expected function of providing an outlet, a forum and a focal point of literary activity, these magazines supplied as well, those elements of motive energy and of literary continuity which are considered to be the essential constituents of a literary movement.

The cessation of publication of *The McGill Fortnightly Review* was followed by a brief lull; a period which saw the regrouping of editorial talent and the making of plans for a new magazine. *The Canadian Mercury* had Frank Scott and Leo Kennedy among its editors, with Leon Edel and A. J. M. Smith serving in the posts of Paris correspondent and contributor from Edinburgh respectively. Although *The Canadian Mercury* could not really be considered a little magazine, it is obvious that it was much nearer to the ideals of a little magazine than its immediate predecessor. It ran for seven numbers from December 1928 to June 1929, as a self-confessed liberal journal of opinion. *The Canadian Mercury,* short-lived though it was, and though it quite obviously attempted to survive commercially, presents evidence in itself of the establishment of real literary and social horizons for a larger, more active, more conscious and more involved group of young writers. It is also in the pages of *The Canadian Mercury* that one may discover hints of that cosmopolitan attitude or outlook which is later going to characterize the spirit of *Preview*. It would appear that the true significance of *The Canadian Mercury* both as a precursor of the little magazine, and as an organ of intellectual and social awareness has been either ignored or underestimated. Its opening editorial is a stinging, slightly anarchic declaration of independence and purposeful intent in the best tradition of little magazines.

To quote:

EDITORIAL

It is idle to say that in this considerable Canada of ours there is no place for a journal of the genre of *The Canadian Mercury*—no place, in effect, for a Journal of Literature and Opinion conducted along the necessarily liberal lines of an open forum. Nevertheless it is true that during the months of labor which prefaced our appearance this criticism was most prevalent, greatly enhancing the normal difficulties of organization. This attitude did not interrupt preparation . . . it stimulated to further effort the few young people whose preoccupation with some definite standards of literary criticism and the development of a Canadian literature had led them to stake purse and aggregate intelligence on the venture. From a minority, however, we received nods of encouragement, and it is to these cordial and generous persons in particular that we hasten to dedicate our first issue.

The Canadian Mercury then, with nothing between it and the eyes of the judiciary but an ingenious and rather ribald colophon, appears, determined to preserve its policies in spite of all reactionary opposition; intent on offering the more thoughtful Canadian public the best available matter on subjects immediately concerning that public; demanding as we have said, a higher and more adequate standard of literary criticism in Canada, and striving to contribute in so far as it is possible to the consummation of that graceful ideal, the emancipation of Canadian literature from the state of amiable mediocrity and insipidity in which it now languishes.

To change the image, Canadian Literature is a lusty but quite inarticulate brat constrained in a too-tight swaddling; you will know him by his red Mounted Policeman's jacket, and his half-breed guide's racoonskin cap. He has been sired by Decorum out of Claptrap . . . and we are not resigned. He has not the faculty of self-expression which may be found in his adolescent American cousin; he has not reaped the benefits arising from an extensive immigration policy. He has retained the stifling qualities of Nordic consciousness and is likely, by present symptoms, to become idiot. We do not approve of this, and therefore gather behind our colophon, which at least symbolizes vigour and a modicum of intellectual health.

We must add that we have no affiliation whatsoever: we owe no allegiance to the Canadian Authors' Association, the Canadian Manufacturers Association, the Young Communist League of Canada, the IODE, the YMCA, the UF of A, or the CPR.

In brief, it may be said that with exception of a spinster aunt in London and a wild uncle in America, neither of whom would claim relationship—*The Canadian Mercury* is individual . . . and again we revert to our hobby. We have no preconceived idea of Canadian literature which we are endeavouring to propagate; our faith rests in the spirit which is at last beginning to brood upon our literary chaos. We believe that an order will come out of the void, an order of a distinct type, reflecting, as modern Canadian painting has begun to do, a unique experience of nature and life.

Above all, *The Canadian Mercury* is intended primarily for the younger writers in this country. The editors are all well under thirty and intend to remain so. We seek to ally with ourselves all those whose literary schooling has survived the Confederation, and whose thought and verse is not afraid of being called free.[4]

The Editors.

There is, of course implicit in the above editorial a direct challenge to the Canadian public to find itself, and thereby to discover a purpose for the existence of a national literature. As far as content is concerned, there is a noticeable increase in the volume of poetry appearing in the pages of the magazine. There is also a greatly enlarged group of permanent poets contributing material, as well as the usual quota of apparently promising writers who invariably bob up to the surface of a little magazine and after a clever stab or two vanish from the scene. One cannot help but notice as well that *The Canadian Mercury,* liberal opinions and all, is oriented essentially in the direction of literature—Canadian literature.

In the course of seven numbers, the editors managed to produce two articles on Canadian literature—Leacock on "The Problem of Canadian Literature" in Vol. I, No. 1, and Leo Kennedy on "The Future of Canadian Literature" in Vol. I, No. 5-6. Among other

4Editorial, *The Canadian Mercury,* I, 1, December 1928, p. 3.

items which indicate a deeper involvement and interest in contemporary poetry and literature is a perceptive and sympathetic article on Elinor Wylie and a review of "John Brown's Body" by Frank Scott. Edel writing his newsletter from Montparnasse in Vol. I, No. 2, mentions Joyce's "Work in Progress" and belabours the hordes of imitators who were then springing up. He also manages to be mildly disparaging of Gertrude Stein besides attacking *transition*, and making passing mention of *Dial*. *The Canadian Mercury*, therefore, is very definitely, both in its mental attitude and in the material which it chose to print, an avant-garde literary periodical. It is also here that we see the recurring appearance of Dorothy Livesay, A. M. Klein, Leo Kennedy, and of course Smith and Scott. A stable of regular writers has been established, and in keeping with the ferment of the times certain liberal stances are taken. As a matter of fact this growing sense of militant liberalism is characteristic and indicative of the sense of social responsibility which the writers and intellectuals of the time had assumed. Curiously enough this political soul-searching and the mood of social duty experienced by many was incidental to and part and parcel of some of the best poetry of the late twenties and the early thirties. *The Canadian Mercury* struck several curious poses, and espoused several burning but unpopular causes. It is odd in its anti-Anglo-Saxon tone, and intense in its comment on the Sacco and Vanzetti case. In general its stance was one which on the highest principles defended the cause of all foreigners, immigrants and proletarians against the forces of reaction and racial bigotry which in those years had a virulent hold on this country.

From this point of view of literature, however, greater importance must be attached to certain trends which were even then discernible in its pages. These were indications that the poets of the late twenties were definitely moving to that social awareness which would motivate and typify both the angry work of *First Statement* and the slightly more sophisticated tone and the controlled irony of *Preview*.

Following the death of *The Canadian Mercury* in 1929, there was a period roughly of ten years when little magazine publishing seems to have temporarily lost its impetus. Those poets and writers who had been most intimately connected with *The Canadian Mercury* seem to have taken time off to settle into the routine of professions for themselves, as well as to try their work on publications in which they wielded no editorial power or influence. Creative energies, however, had suffered no relapse, and there was no real lull in the actual writing of poetry. In 1936 all the activity which may be said to have begun with *The McGill Fortnightly Review* was brought into focus in an anthology entitled *New Provinces*. This collection confronted the Canadian reader with the first substantial body of work from the pens of Canada's most promising and perhaps even prominent young poets. The most encouraging element in this anthology was that the hard core of Montreal poets consisting of Scott, Smith, Klein and Kennedy were brought together with Robert Finch and E. J. Pratt. It was evident that modernism had become the dominant mood of Canadian Poetry.

With the launching of *Preview*, quickly followed by an irate *First Statement* we have the first examples of the genuine little magazine in operation in Montreal. These two pioneer periodicals were also the last to gather substantial groups of writers around them, and to function as the organs of expression of these groups. Later developments in little magazine publishing, beginning notably with the merging of *Preview* and *First Statement* into the *Northern Review* would herald a new approach to this editorial art. We note, with the gradual growth of the authority of John Sutherland on the *Northern Review*, a very definite movement away from the wider scope and the free-wheeling policies of the older little magazines, and a corresponding concentration of editorial power in smaller and smaller groupings and increasingly tighter cliques. This has of course culminated in such purely personal ventures as Dudek's *Delta*. No longer would writers be joined in a loose association of common purposes which would seek expression in the publication of a little magazine. The fact was and still is, that with the number of little magazines increasing appreciably, poets had many more ready outlets for their work and much less reason to edit their own periodicals. As a matter of fact with *Northern Review* we have moved into the field of the little magazine edited by someone (not necessarily a poet) for the young writer. We also find that little magazines have passed more and more into the hands of friends and associates of poets; people who have willingly assumed the chores of publication.

Preview was published primarily as an outlet for the work of an influential group of young writers which had now come to include Patrick Anderson, Neufville Shaw, P. K. Page and Bruce Ruddick; poets who cultivated a kind of distinguished commitment to modern poetry, an attitude which acted as an irritant for the soon-to-be-formed *First Statement* group, and which was later labelled "the cosmopolitan tradition." Of these two little magazines, and of the two literary groups which had formed behind them, the poets who were associated with *First Statement*, young, gauche and raw as they were, were obviously destined for the greater achievement. A strangely tense yet respectful entente existed between the elder statesmen of *Preview* and the turbulent turks of *First Statement*. The most worthwhile by-product of the friction which naturally developed between the two groups was the two distinct kinds of poetry being written in Montreal. The first of these had its roots in that tradition of the thirties which had seen Canadian poetry as part of a universal content of ideas lodged in an English-language culture, dominated by a social theme which could be best expressed in the cosmopolitan language of the intelligence. The second believed in a coarser and more militant approach to poetry. Leaning heavily on a leftist interpretation of society, this group, which gathered its strength in *Other Canadians*, carried the social theme to greater extremes and larger significance in its poetry.

The *Northern Review* did not represent a simple merger of two periodicals of similar purpose. The merger is evidence of a loss of interest and influence on the part of those associated with *Preview*, and the emergence of a more virile grouping among the poets of Montreal. The leadership which John Sutherland assumed in connection with the *Northern Review* proved, in the final analysis, to be an unfortunate development in the life of this and other little magazines. *Northern Review* became progressively the vehicle for the opinions of one man, and set a pattern for that trend in little magazines which can be best described as limited editorial participation. More and more, with magazines like *Direction, CIV/n, Yes, Delta*, et cetera, the little magazine of Montreal was published not so much by as for the young poet. The new function of the little magazine was to publish as much as possible of the material made available to it.

One of the most important contributions to Canadian poetry made by *Northern Review*, besides an unusual volume of consistent literary criticism which appeared in its pages, was the sponsorship of *First Statement's* New Writers Series. This invaluable collection included the work of Layton, Anderson, Miriam Waddington, Souster and others, and gave these poets that important first book which may have made them acceptable to commercial publishing houses.

During the latter part of the Second War, there was besides *Preview* and *First Statement*, and latterly *Northern Review*, a mimeographed little magazine called *Direction*. It was published by a kind of splinter group consisting of William Goldberg, David Mullen and Raymond Souster. This magazine was the child of military life, and it is only by a kind of imaginative extension that we call it a Montreal little mag. The editors were stationed at various bases, mainly in the Maritimes, and issued the magazine from these locations. Our interest is drawn by the fact that we have here a periodical which devoted itself to work that was usually the result of the boredom and the privation of military service; prosy, hard-hitting poetry in which the social theme is submerged by the presence of war. There is also noticeable an optimism which can look forward to a post-war world—a world which will and must be set right. *Direction* had a respectable list of contributing poets, most of whom had made a name for themselves in *First Statement*, *Preview* and *Northern Review*. An interesting sidelight on the vigorous and open-minded editorial policy of this magazine is the fact that in *Direction* No. 7 we note what was probably the first attempt to publish selections from Henry Miller's *Tropic of Cancer* in this country. *Direction* ran for ten numbers from November, 1943 to February 1946, and may have been the spiritual ancestor of *Contact* which appeared in Toronto in 1952.

Recent little magazine activity in Montreal has tended to emphasize the fragmentation rather than the cohesion of poetic attitudes in that city. The existence of at least three very different periodicals is also indicative of the fact that while Montreal may be responsible for a movement in Canadian literature, it is certainly not the center of a specific school of poetry.

Michael Gnarowski, "The Role of 'Little Magazines' in the Development of Poetry in English in Montreal," *Culture*, XXIV, No. 3, September 1963.

FRANK DAVEY

Historically, little magazines have sprung up whenever new, animated, and serious writing cannot find a market. Thus these magazines are usually managed and edited by writers—writers who are anything but reluctant to publish their own works. The annoyance that gets such writers into the magazine business is, of course, that in any period both the commercial outlets—whether "literary" mags or publishing houses—and the glossy-paged scholarly quarterlies cater chiefly to established writers. A new group or school of writers cannot possibly get a sufficient quantity of its work published to make its presence felt. Some of the semi-professional literary quarterlies, such as Canada's *Tamarack Review*, tend to become coterie magazines, depending for almost fifty per cent of their material on a particular fixed circle of writers—again writers whose reputations the magazine knows are safe and established. Which is, of course, a sensible commercial policy, particularly in a country which has tended to be a graveyard for literary magazines.

Little magazines, on the other hand, never have to depend on "name" writers, their mimeo expenses being low enough to keep their losses at a minimum. But this is only a minor difference. The major one is still·that little mags are published by *engaged* writers, not by semi-interested onlookers. Whereas the commercial magazine or glossy-paged quarterly usually reflects one man's desire to be an editor, or a group's wish that their town, university, or whatever, have a "literary" mag, the little magazine nearly always reflects genuine writing activity and interest. While the editors of the *Tamaracks* and the *Prisms* seldom have any new work of their own to exhibit, seldom are engaged in creation with any excitement or persistence (but rather go altruistically or parasitically to those that are), the editors of little magazines are usually so absorbed in and dedicated to their own writing that they feel they *must* found a mag—in order that their work may receive at least some attention and criticism. Often, if not always, the little magazine reflects the presence of a group of writers of similar interests who are meeting, arguing, fighting, writing, almost every day—a group charged with literary energy that seems to keep continually overflowing into and out of their mimeographed pages.

One could take the founding of Vancouver's *Tish* as an example of the birth of a little magazine. All of its five editors had been writing for some time; George Bowering had been getting poems published in eastern Canada—though, he says, never the ones he wished to have published. With two visits from the U.S. poet Robert Duncan their bi-monthly meetings to discuss their own work became weekly meetings of intensive study of Charles Olson, Duncan, Creeley, Pound, and Williams. In no time literary theories and poems began filling the air, covering the desks, and some quick and dependable outlet for quantities of material had to be found. Even the established magazines willing to publish some of this work could not be relied on; they were too slow, and by the time one's poems were published one wished to disown them, ideas had changed so. Thus *Tish*, Vancouver's poetry newsletter, was born, and the energy, the intensive literary study and creation that began it show no sign of abating. If it did, of course, there would be no reason for *Tish* to continue, for, in order to be worthwhile, any little magazine must have this inspiring energy. Evidence of such energy is perhaps the prime criterion for judging its value.

Magazines with no energy whatsoever are, naturally, one of the other minor but important causes of the founding of little magazines. In Canada there are a large number of very low-energy literary mags with no particular policy; for example, *Prism's* often nondescript collections, *Canadian Poetry Magazine's* usual dilettante sprawl, and *Fiddlehead's* custom of printing so nearly an equal number of bad poems to good ones that a writer begins to doubt the value of publication there.

All of which will tend to make the new little magazine editor angry and belligerent. He will be so proud of his strong direction and sense of development that he will often make a point of countering the petrified standards of the professional outlets with work initially as shocking as important. He will counter the nebulous—if even existent —editorial policies of the *Fiddleheads* and *Prisms* with an editorial line or bias strict enough to exclude almost all of the—to him— mysteriously-established establishment. It can almost be said that, to be true to the energy that has got him writing and publishing, the new little magazines editor must be of necessity rebellious—else have his magazine redundant.

Again historically, such ventures have often been successes. Writers such as Hemingway, W. C. Williams, Pound, and Aldington, to name a few, all began their careers in little magazines that have now either disappeared or evolved to unrecognizable forms. Since the last war little magazines such as Canada's *Combustion* and *Contact*, and the U.S.'s *Black Mountain Review*, *Origin*, *Migrant*, *Measure*, and *Yugen*, spawned most of the writers now finding recognition in Grove Press and New Directions publications and in professional magazines such as *The Outsider* and *The Evergreen Review*. At present in the States Robert Kelly's *Trobar*, Cid Corman's second series of *Origin*, and Le Roi Jones and Diane Di Prima's *The Floating Bear* are carrying on the fight for the acceptance of new writers, the last with undoubtedly the most vigour.

In Canada too we are witnessing a new crop of little magazines. In the last two years *Moment, Mountain, Evidence, Cataract, Tish* and *Motion* have all appeared. In Vancouver alone three new ones are projected: *Recall*, a new non-commercial mag of *Kenyon Review* tastes, *Spasm*, one probably in the "beat" tradition, and *Q*, "a quizzical monthly of satire and other social criticism." University magazines, such as Waterloo's *Chiaroscuro,* UBC's *Raven*, and Acadia's *Amethyst*, continue, but only as "student" publications— seldom with any attempt at absolute excellence.

Of the new and ambitious little magazines Toronto's *Evidence* is the only one to get above the usual mimeo format. Alan Bevan, the writer-editor, says that it "was born out of the conviction that there is a good deal of serious writing being done for which there is no adequate outlet in Canada." This is, of course, the best and only excuse for the founding of a little magazine, and so far Mr. Bevan has been able to find interesting writing. There have been frequent weaknesses, especially in the critical articles, but *Evidence* has still been superior to *Tamarack's* seemingly endless issues of unexcitement. Bevan's magazine can be lively—see No. 3's provocatively accurate article on marijuana—but, in order to counteract its cold, almost malicious reception by the Toronto establishment, should become even more boisterous and militant, and its editor should take a more prominent part in its revolutionary trends. *Evidence* does not seem to be the product of an active group; it looks like a one-man job, and, unless Bevan himself gets more lively, I foresee a dull future for his magazine.

Montreal's *Cataract* is certainly militant. Which is perhaps the best thing one can say about it. Militancy is fine when one has something to be militant about; *Cataract's* most obvious trouble is that its writer-editors seem to spend more time thumbing their noses than they do writing poetry. Irving Layton's "Open Letter to Louis Dudek" in No. 2 shows more concern for Layton's own waning reputation (see his defensive and high-schoolish "To a Lily" here too) than for Dudek's. But *Cataract* is the product of a group intensely active and outspoken in writing; it has a distinct direction. And it has had good poems (ignore Avi Boxer); Sydney Aster has had several lucky hits, and K. V. Hertz and Henry Moscovitch have consistently shown much talent and potentiality. *Cataract* is certainly not a pretentious magazine— it even belabours its non-academic roots, and is definitely worth "bothering" with.

Moment is a Toronto mimeo poetry magazine at one time edited by poets Milton Acorn and Al Purdy, now edited by Acorn and his wife, Gwendolyn MacEwen. Like *Cataract* it is squarely in the little magazine tradition of being founded by cooperating poets to publish poetry that might not be accepted by the established markets. The poetry of Miss MacEwen is often "poetic" and esoteric, and at times beautiful and real; Acorn's is rougher, probably less poetic by anyone's standards. The outside poetry is diverse, both in quality and manner, and, with the lack of similarity between Acorn and MacEwen, the magazine thus appears to have little unity of policy. It is probably held together more by marriage than by literary interest. From what I have seen *Moment* is not dull and not lively, not consistently experimental and not quite reactionary, not sufficiently discriminating and not actually careless. It does have its triumphs, though—such as the Al Purdy poem in No. 6. A Toronto magazine.

David McFadden's *Mountain* from Hamilton is probably in one way the most ambitious and comprehensive little magazine in Canada. Its purpose seems to be not so much to announce something new, as to bring together and reannounce all of the new things that have happened recently in Canadian poetry. A sort of poor man's *Evergreen*

Review, although one cannot call Padraig O Broin's poetry new, or John Robert Colombo's lines poetry. Still the first issue of *Mountain* marked the first time a Canadian reader could see together in one place most of his country's important new writers. With possibly only two exceptions, all of the writers were under twenty-seven years of age.

McFadden announced in No. 1 that *"Mountain* has very definite and rigid editorial standards, but they change from day to day," and they must in such an eclectic mag. The only demands McFadden appears to have made of his writers are youth and quality, and even these he has very clearly lifted at times. In the next issues perhaps some direction will become apparent, maybe not from Hamilton activity but from McFadden's consciousness of the energies of young Canadian poets as a group. A long hope, but still even as merely "a lively review of current poetry," *Mountain* is indispensable.

Tish and *Motion* are two Vancouver mimeo "newsletters." *Tish*, the poetry newsletter, is now in its twelfth issue, and seems to have crystallized its determination to re-make poetry a natural and spontaneous human occupation and rid it of the obscure and obviously "poetic" creations of would-be "artists." Man not art, and the universality of human experience, are two of its battle-cries, and battle-cries they are, for its editors seem to have made a fetish out of belligerency. A lot of their poetry seems weak and irrelevant, yet some of it is powerful and does show that their attempts at "natural" poetry have enabled them to write skilled and complex poems with the craft totally submerged and unobtrusive.

Motion, the prose newsletter, seems also to be working in favour of unpretentious style and subtlety of effect. However, with only two issues out the question is still whether *Motion* has work that should be published despite the rejections of established magazines, or merely would like to think it has. Either in Canada or the U.S. I know of no magazine with which to compare *Motion*; the idea of a monthly prose newsletter seems to have been totally neglected, possibly because of the large amount of work necessary to provide sufficient material.

There is one other mimeo little magazine in Canada: another Toronto one, Padraig O Broin's rather harmless *Téangadoir*, now in its 39th issue. It claims to be a magazine of current Canadian poetry, and is, exactly, and is thus all over the map. O Broin himself will never pretend to be experimental, yet side by side with his own traditional lyrics he will publish even such uncontrolled ones as those by G. C. Miller. *Téangadoir* is an interesting little magazine, but not a vital one. There is obviously no group of fermenting young poets behind it; most likely it is a hobby to O Broin, who does not seem to have much difficulty getting his poetry published elsewhere.

These little magazines really comprise most of what is happening in Canadian poetry. The so-called "quality or mass magazines," the established glossy literary quarterlies, continue to grind on, but most of the changes that slowly but eventually occur in them are generated elsewhere between the rollers of someone's rusty Gestetner. Canada is fortunate to have such a large number of little magazines that the commercial literary outlets are never allowed the peace to become permanently stultified. What is sad is that most of these mags do not take sufficient advantage of their unique position—no one asks them to be responsible, and money is never available enough to be an objective—to further shake up the commercial world and speed the evolution of writing. As I said before, a little magazine must be either bold or redundant. *Cataract*, *Mountain*, and *Tish* are each in their own way somewhat brash, but *Evidence, Moment, Motion*, and especially *Téangadoir,* could all stand acquiring some reason for additional chips on their shoulders. An affable little magazine cannot help but be worthless.

Frank Davey, "Anything but Reluctant: Canada's Little Magazines," *Canadian Literature*, No. 13, Summer 1962.

VIII

WIDER HORIZONS

Poetry Finds A Public

Modern poetry in general, whether in England, the United States, or Canada, has represented a withdrawal from the middle-class public. In the tradition of Flaubert and Mallarmé, fierce anti-bourgeois critics, modern writers like T. S. Eliot, James Joyce and Ezra Pound wrote for a select audience of erudite intellectuals (the elite of modern literature), and their aesthetic principles excluded the reading public engrossed by commercial journalism and the best-sellers.

Canadian poetry in its major phase from 1925 to 1955 was largely oriented in the same way toward a select audience, resisting commercial influences and the popular media, and accountable only to the standards of modern poetry abroad. A. J. M. Smith, Canadian spokesman for *l'art pour l'art*, occasional translator of Théophile Gautier and Mallarmé, was our representative anthologist, and E. K. Brown and W. E. Collin were the first scholarly critics of the new literature. There was a certain current of dissent from these mandarin standards—in poets like A. M. Klein and the First Statementers—but on the whole all poets belonged to the same minority culture of embattled intellectuals.

A radical change from this condition began to take place around 1956, dating from William Carlos Williams' Introduction to Irving Layton's *The Improved Binoculars* (1956). Not that this Introduction, or Irving Layton's subsequent growing reputation, are central to the dynamics of this change, but they mark conveniently the beginning of a new direction and must in fact be explained by this transition.

The shift in Canadian poetry is really part of the larger movement in recent literature represented by the Beats in America and the Angry Young Men in England. This postwar movement, in general, abandoned the position of intense exclusiveness typical of modern poetry and gave vent to open rage and revolt. A decade of silence was broken by the wail of Allen Ginsberg's "Howl" (1956), and the caperings of *Lucky Jim* (1954). Colin Wilson's *The Outsider* (1956) explained the new attitudes of youth in protest. In Canada, this new literature of protest and platform rhetoric in poetry coincided with the emergence of a bright young talent in Leonard Cohen; it produced poets like George Ellenbogen, Daryl Hine, Michael Malus and Dave Solway in Montreal; it brought Al Purdy, Milton Acorn and Alden Nowlan to public notice, and, a bit later in Vancouver, the *Tish* group had its beginnings in 1961.

Leonard Cohen seems to be the key figure for the understanding of this stage of development. A poet of the postwar generation (born in 1934), he belongs to the period of affluence combined with anxiety which has marked the last twenty years. The disaffected teenagers of this time may be either a pampered generation of rebels or a tragic generation of young idealists, depending on the view we take of their dilemma. They have not known either the War of the Forties or the World Depression of the Thirties, and in a time of economic prosperity they are threatened by atomic annihilation or by technological conformity, all of which results in profound discontent and gestures of erratic protest.

The same period of relative peace and affluence has brought literature and the arts to a wider public. Arts centers and modern auditoriums have arisen in all the major cities and universities; popular magazines and news media have turned to art as a possible ornament for a materially rewarding life. This has combined with the maturing of a taste for modern poetry and the acceptance of this poetry by the general public. T. S. Eliot's "Waste Land," once the esoteric poem of the moderns, is now studied in freshman English courses. A new generation of radio broadcasters and newspaper and magazine editors, men like Robert Weaver or Robert Fulford, following the William Arthur Deacons and S. Morgan Powells of the past, have partly opened the mass media to a kind of literature which met with extreme prejudice in the 1920s and 30s. The CBC, started in 1932, has had a marked effect on the growing prestige and acceptance of modern poetry. The moderns became fairly acceptable. By the end of the 1950s, poetry and news of poetry began to appear regularly in the popular media, in the metropolitan daily and weekly press, in magazines like *Maclean's* and *Time*, as well as on radio and television.

The articles in this section provide a few samples of this new and popular kind of writing on contemporary poetry. They show a current recognition of poetry at the journalistic level in two ways: recognition of the human interest potential in the bohemiam or eccentric behaviour of poets; and belated acceptance of genuine poetic achievement. Irving Layton's reputation, for example, may owe something to both possibilities. Poets like Raymond Souster and F. R. Scott, clearly, have received public honours in recent years after long neglect; while Leonard Cohen and Alfred Purdy have gained considerable publicity as personalities and subjects of news interest. Whether this fanfare and fame are good for poetry in the long run only the future can tell; the strength of modern literature has depended largely upon isolation from the idols of the market-place; but then, all true literature aims at universality. By reading the essays that follow, and those which have preceded, the issues involved will emerge with increasing clarity.

WILLIAM CARLOS WILLIAMS

What else are you going to say about a man whose work you whole-heartedly admire than that he is a good poet? If you consider yourself a critic of poetry, which I do, all the more reason for speaking with all the force you can command in his support. You would be a fool to do less.

When I first clapped eyes on the poems of Irving Layton, two years ago, I let out a yell of joy. He was bawdy but that wasn't why I gave him my recognition. But for the way he greeted the world he was celebrating, head up, eyes propped wide, his gaze roving round a wide perimeter—which merely happened to see some sights that had never been disclosed to me so nakedly or so well.

In writing of a good new poet for the first time the words come crowding to my mind, jostling together in their eagerness to be put down: He inhabits the medium and is at home in it, passionately; luxurious freedom, as of a huge creature immersed in an ocean that he knows he will never plumb and need never fear to reach the bottom of. This is poetry in which he lives unchecked. And he has eyes and he has power to penetrate wherever its lust leads him to satisfy its hungers. More moral men will fly off from a dish which is his natural food and which he takes with a laugh. May he never grow too delicate to take his fill of it and speak of his joy in it with a full appetite. That he is a man, and therefore must be guarded, he knows also. He laughs from a full belly. Not to be confined by a metaphor—he has been to the university and sat grinning and with moist eyes among his peers. He knows the Puritans and what they do and have done. He knows at least two religious beliefs, and how to practice all ten of them. In fact he knows the colors of the spectrum, and how all the colors are split off from it. If you want him to be true to yellow, he will be true to red; and if green, he will be true to purple or brown or black or the most heavenly blue. He has an unrivalled choice of words; an unusual vocabulary and the ability to use it. As far as deftness in the craft of a poet, I think he can do anything he wants to—except confuse himself with the mere sound of his own mouthings or delicate mincings or weighty sounding apostrophes. He is modest in facing the opinions of others—an enormous and increasingly rare virtue. He even respects Ezra Pound but has no inclination to imitate him. He despises Canada (being a Canadian), and loves and would give his heart for it. He loves women and speaks of it freely. They enjoy him also and doublecross and abandon him—and all this his poems show and speak of in the most meticulous English. He uses as much slang as suits his fancy or his need, and no more. He is not bound by the twentieth century if he does not find its language fitting to his purpose, and defies anyone who would blind him to that use. His structure of the poetic phrase is eclectic; that is to say, he does what he pleases with it, and there he possibly goes wrong. But what difference does it make, if he writes well? He has a quick and dogged wit which does not shun to soil its hands; in other words, he can be downright dirty if the occasion calls for it—as it frequently does in dealing with the nicer present-day wits of the United States. The metaphysicians, men and women who want to abandon a British or American way of talking, he is indifferent to—but the same is common with all present-day poets if they are worthy of the name.

Irving Layton has written profusely, pouring out his verses without check. That is the way to write, correcting one's self in the act of writing, the words, held as it were, in solution, latent, eternally in process of being formed. No constipation here—though the action of writing can be repeated and repeated in multiple draughts until, by sheer repetition, it finally becomes fluid. But that doesn't appear to be his way.

In short, I believe this poet to be capable of anything. He's a backwoodsman with a tremendous power to do anything he wants to with verse. I have seen modern verse written in French and in the local dialects of the United States before which he must stand in awe. Lucky for such writers that he exists, for he will not be idle, but attack with his unsated egotism until he has subdued their challenges. There will, if I am not mistaken, be a battle: Layton against the rest of the world. With his vigor and abilities who shall not say that Canada will not have produced one of the west's most famous poets?

Can't say that it is my practice to read or to quote Blake, but I agree with him and with Layton, *"Praise is the practice of art."*

William Carlos Williams, "A Note on Layton," *The Improved Binoculars* (Highlands, N.C.: Jonathan Williams, 1956).

JOAN FINNIGAN

Two men whose opinions carry authority declared last year that if English-Canadian poetry has ever had a golden age, it is with us now.

The speakers were Desmond Pacey, professor of English at the University of New Brunswick, and Ralph Gustafson, a Canadian poet who has lived for many years in New York. Though their assessment might be over-enthusiastic and perhaps premature, it does seem fair to say that Canadian poetry is coming of age in the 1960s. More Canadian poets are being heard, seen and—most of all—read, than ever before. There are now more doors in which to put a literary foot than poets even dreamed of 20 years ago.

The readings at the Canadian Conference of the Arts, held at O'Keefe Center in May, last year, attest to the new popularity of Canadian poetry. Take away the socialites, hangers-on, "culturettes" and merely curious, and it might still safely be claimed that the remaining crowd of earnest listeners was one of the largest live audiences ever faced by Canadian poets. Earle Birney, Gilles Henault, Jay Macpherson, Irving Layton and Leonard Cohen read from their own works, and Cohen also read selections from Anne Hébert.

Layton, as usual, stole the day. First, he delivered a pithy off-the-cuff dissertation on the boring pomposity of the speakers who had opened the conference. Then he read some of his most valid poems, such as "The Bull Calf." Finally, he delighted his audience with a new poem, *Why I don't make love to the First Lady*, a eulogy to Jacqueline Kennedy, which ends:

> A president must stay up night after
>> night
> Deliberating such matters;
> My lovely unlucky Jacqueline!
> Still, when a husband
> Is so harrassed,
> Shall I add to his burdens
> by running off with his attractive
>> wife?
> Not I, not Irving Layton;
> I'll wait until
> the international situation has cleared;
> After that it's every poet for himself!

The conference was one indication of the new winds which, whether they blow from the Atlantic or the Pacific, are providing a more favorable climate for the poetic muse in Canada. For one thing, more and more Canadian poets are being listened to.

During the past 10 years, the Canadian Broadcasting Corporation has spread a substantial feast of poetic fare, with executive producer Robert Weaver as master chef. During this period, says Weaver, "almost all our better poets have given readings on the radio shows Anthology or Wednesday Night." Ventures into dramatic verse and verse documentaries have been more ambitious and increasingly successful.

Several of E. J. Pratt's narrative poems, such as *The Titanic*, have been adapted and broadcast by the CBC as dramatic readings. Earle Birney, a professor of English at the University of British Columbia, had his verse play, *Trial of a City*, dramatized on the same series. John Reeves, a CBC staffer, wrote the play *A Beach of Strangers*, in verse and prose, for the Wednesday Night show and won the $3,300 Italia prize for radio writing. James Reaney of the University of Western Ontario won a radio award in the United States for his verse documentary *A Message to Winnipeg*; his *Message to Stratford* coincided with the beginning of the Stratford Festival last June.

For the past five years, monthly poetry readings have been held in Toronto, the first three years in the Isaacs Gallery, in 1960 at the Young Men's & Young Women's Hebrew Association on Spadina Avenue, and last year again at the Isaacs Gallery.

A highlight of the 1960 program was Margaret Avison's reading, just a few days after she had won the Governor-General's Award for *Winter Sun*. Hailed almost unanimously by the critics, *Winter Sun* is not a collection for those who regard the rustic simplicity and lucid reflectiveness of Archibald Lampman, Bliss Carman and Duncan Campbell Scott as the highest level of Canadian poetry. For those who prefer poetry that is difficult and full of challenge there are lines such as these from her poem "Butterfly Bones," or "Sonnet Against Sonnets":

> What law and wonder the museum
>   spectres
> bespeak is cryptic for the shivery
>   wings,
> the world cut-diamond-eyed, those
>   eyes' reflectors,
> or herbal grass, sunned motes, fierce
>   listening,
> Might sheened and rigid trophies
>   strike men blind
> like Adam's lexicon locked in the
>   mind?

Aided by a Canada Council grant, the series of readings in the 1961/62 season at the Isaacs Gallery has included poets Robert

Creeley, Miriam Waddington, Peter Miller, Louis Dudek, Eli Mandel, Gael Turnbull, Charles Olson, Frank O'Hara and James Reaney.

In late 1960 poet-professor D. G. Jones, formerly at the Ontario Agricultural College and now at University of Bishop's College, did some poetical pioneering as librettist for the Guelph Light Opera Company's production *This Happy Land*, a solidly Canadian production without any blatant strewing of maple leaves, and good enough to seriously interest Stratford and the CBC. If the show is performed professionally, Jones (whether he likes it or not) may be the first Canadian poet to be heard on jukeboxes, with such catchy lyrics as:

> My love is like a lonely bird,
> Goes crying through the skies,
> No answer to his cry is heard,
> No voice of love replies.

Jones is also one of the very few Canadian poets to achieve the prestige of publication by the University of Toronto Press, which has received a Canada Council grant to assist in the publication of his third volume of poetry, *The Sun is Axeman*.

As well as being heard in various ways, Canadian poets are also being seen by the general public. Many have appeared on television, among them George Johnston, the late Anne Wilkinson, George Whalley and Gwen MacEwen. Such appearances serve to destroy the public's conception of what poets look like. The men, it usually turns out, are not passive, emaciated, long-haired esthetes; the women are not usually pale, frail, spinster types.

Furthermore, though it may be true that many of them scribble away in the ivory towers of our universities, many others are contributing to society in diverse and unexpected ways.

R. A. D. Ford is Canadian ambassador to the United Arab Republic and the Sudan, and Douglas Le Pan, now on the staff of Queen's University, was formerly a member of the Department of External Affairs. P. K. Page is the wife of W. A. Irwin, ambassador to Mexico and Guatemala; Dorothy Livesay teaches at a high school in Vancouver; W. E. Ross is a geophysicist with the Agincourt Magnetic Observatory near Toronto; Miriam Waddington is a Montreal social worker; F. R. Scott is Dean of the Faculty of Law at McGill University, and the man who recently defended the novel *Lady Chatterley's Lover* against charges of obscenity in Quebec.

Scott is perhaps best known for satiric verse, such as these lines from *Lest We Forget*:

> The British troops at the Dardanelles
> Were blown to bits by British shells
> Sold to the Turks by Vickers.

But another side of Scott is revealed in fine love lyrics such as *Message,* which ends:

> And some lead outward from the
> wood,
> Dropping to roads and planted fields
> Where houses stand whose quiet mood
> Of love is seasoned. He would lose
> In choosing, what he did not choose.

Of course, that earnest rebel Irving Layton has, with his frequent appearances on television, done the most to upset the public stereotype of the Canadian poet. This may be one reason his book *A Red Carpet for the Sun* is one of the most-sold collections of Canadian poetry.

Last, and perhaps most important, Canadian poets are being read as never before. Peter Martin, president of the struggling 2,500 member Readers' Club of Canada in Toronto, says that "for the first year or so of the club's existence, we were astonished at the success we had every time we offered a volume of poetry; now we are no longer astonished—we have come to expect the reaction we get, and we have yet to be disappointed."

Indeed, readers of Canadian poetry are increasing so rapidly that in 1960 that finely tuned sensometer, the Oxford University Press, saw fit to publish a 500-page anthology of Canadian poetry, ranging from Standish O'Grady's bitter depiction of a pioneer winter in Lower Canada to the lush symbolism of the talented newcomer Daryl Hine. The Canadian poet A. J. M. Smith, now a professor of English at Michigan State University, was editor.

Ryerson Press of Toronto, so long a stalwart benefactor of Canadian poetry through the publication every year of five or six critic's bane chapbooks, decided to concentrate on fewer but larger and more expensive volumes. In 1961 it published two authors — Dorothy Roberts (*Twice to Flame*) and Alden Nowlan (*Under the Ice*).

In 1952, Ryerson Press was joined in the field when an enterprising group of poets headed by Louis Dudek and Irving Layton banded together in a cooperative effort called Contact Press, dedicated to higher printing standards for Canadian poetry and the presentation of first-rate and avant-garde poets. Its list includes the first volumes of Peter Miller, Eli Mandel, Sylvia Barnard and George Walton and further works of Phyllis Webb, George Ellenbogen, Gael Turnbull, R. G. Everson, D. G. Jones, F. R. Scott and Louis Dudek.

With the encouragement of a Canada Council grant, McClelland and Stewart of Toronto has also begun a poetry series, the first volume of which was 1960's *Rivers Among Rocks* by Ralph Gustafson, a superbly printed work illustrated with wood-block prints. In December, 1961, Ryerson Press published the first of its biennial anthologies of Canadian poetry, and that indefatigable supporter of the arts, Avrom Isaacs, has produced the first of the Gallery Editions series, Kenneth McRobbie's *Eyes Without a Face.*

For many years, the Canadian poet's market in the magazine field was limited to the staid and conservative university quarterlies, the most receptive of which have continued to be the Queen's University Quarterly and the University of New Brunswick's *Fiddlehead,* one of the oldest literary magazines; and the *Canadian Poetry Magazine,* which owes much of its longevity to a Canadian Authors Association subsidy. It is probably the only Canadian poetry magazine the general public is aware of.

Round and about these old standbys there have come and gone a number of "little mags"—*Yes, Contact, CIV/n, Combustion,* the West Coast's *Contemporary Verse*; *Here & Now,* the most ambitious and therefore short-lived (three issues)* poetry magazine ever to appear on the Canadian literary scene; and the late John Sutherland's *Northern Review,* which had a record run of 13 years out of Montreal.†

Since the late 1940s there has been a resurgence of the little magazines. Toronto's *Tamarack Review* has recently swung a Canada Council grant and set a precedent by announcing it will pay its contributors. *Alphabet,* is a one-man show, printed, published, edited and partly written by James Reaney, twice winner of the Governor-General's Award for poetry. There are Milton Acorn's courageous publication *Moment,* and the West Coast's *Canadian Literature,* which was highly commended by the O'Leary Royal Commission on Publications. British Columbia's *Prism* has published western poets such as Anne Marriott, Dorothy Livesay, Earle Birney, George Walton and such newcomers as Marya Fiamengo, whose first volume, *The Quality of Halves,* reveals a young poet worth watching.

In a class by themselves are two other publications, *Canadian Forum* and *Delta.*

Published in Toronto since 1920 by "an unobtrusive company of shareholders," the volatile and uninhibited *Canadian Forum* is exactly as it states on its masthead: An independent journal of opinion and the arts, a publication in which the social, economic and political overlap with the cultural and artistic. Recently the recipient of a $2,800 Canada Council grant, *Canadian Forum* has always been a

---

*There were four issues of *Here & Now.*
†*Northern Review* existed under that name for a period of a little more than ten years, exactly from December-January of 1945-1946 to September of 1956.

market for poets, ranging from the young unknown to the professional, and like its century-wise and richer counterpart in Boston, it is one of the few markets in the country for the serious short story.

Delta magazine, devoted to poetry and criticism, is a three-and-a-half-year-old monument to the dedicated spirit of McGill University's Louis Dudek, a man who combines the qualities of creator and critic. One of Canada's best-known poets, he not only writes volumes of poetry and books on Canadian printing and publishing, but also manages a blithe exchange of letters and criticism which enlivens *Delta* and puts upon it the imprint of his humor and perspicacity. Like his friend, Ezra Pound, he advises and encourages talented young poets and helps get their work printed.

He is also the writer of award-winning poetry, such as this from "Europe":

> Beauty is ordered in nature
> > as the wind and sea
> shape for each other for pleasure;
> > as the just
> know, who learn of happiness
> from the report of their own actions.

Dudek is one of the poets who have been aided by a Canada Council scholarship. Among the others are Leonard Cohen, Eloi De Grandmont, Irving Layton, Gaston Miron, Alain Grandbois, Michele Lalonde and Alfred Purdy, all of Montreal; Philip Child, Toronto; Ralph Gustafson, New York.

Dudek's *Delta,* John Robert Colombo's poetry monographs from Toronto, the readings of John Harney and Douglas Jones in Guelph's public library—all these are signs of the coming of age of poetry in Canada.

Still, it should be recalled that when Ralph Gustafson's Penguin Book of *Canadian Verse* went on the market in 1958, it was bought by only 3,000 Canadians though it was called vital (New York *Times*), vigorous (London *Times*), strong and mature (Sydney *Morning Herald*). The *Saturday Review of Literature* felt that Canada "was enjoying a flowering within which everything is possible."

Things may never have been better for poets in Canada, but we are still a long way from a Golden age in the Greek sense of the words.

Joan Finnigan, "Canadian Poetry Finds Its Voice in a Golden Age," *Globe and Mail*, January 20, 1962.

THE PRIVATE WORLD OF RAYMOND SOUSTER

Precisely at noon, the bank clerk emerges from the huge basement vault of the Canadian Imperial Bank of Commerce at King and Bay. Every day he goes to the company cafeteria for the same chicken or fruit salad lunch, and then melts into the crowd of other grey-suited, grey-faced clerks for a half-hour stroll in Toronto's financial district. He is apt to notice, with the intensity of a sympathetic child, a crippled news-vendor, or a sun-blinded rubbydub who has just lurched out of the Metropole Tavern. But he also glances frequently at his watch, because, "of course, I only have one hour for lunch." He sometimes reflects: "It would be nice to be a branch manager, but however the Bank wants to make use of me, I'm there."

It is difficult to imagine that Bank Clerk Raymond Holmes Souster, 43, is also a leading Canadian poet. But that is fully confirmed by a new selection of Souster's poems, *The Colour of the Times* (Ryerson Press, $4.95). *Colour* is partly black-and-white snapshots of Souster's Toronto. Here is "a city surrounded /by water no fish can live in," peopled with "unshaved, unpaid, unloved" men. They live in "the sprawling darkness of streets," or in a squat tenement that seems on a hot summer evening a "tin-roofed sweat-box/on the lower slopes of Hell."

Found Wanting. He is an oddly neglected poet, though his fans range from Northrop Frye to Irving Layton. His productivity—twelve volumes since 1946—is vast, and he has been a quiet mentor of such younger poets as Leonard Cohen and Gwendolyn MacEwen in his underground little magazines *Contact* (1952-55)* and *Combustion* (1957-60). Yet Souster also happens to be about the only major Canadian poet today who is not a university teacher, and academic critics tend to find him a hard man to write about. They feel that Souster is just a straightforward social realist, somewhat dated and unsubtle, and lacking in poetic craftsmanship.

But Souster's poems of social protest are neither flatly realistic nor ideological. They are personal outcries in which the poet tries—and sometimes fails—to express universal images of loneliness.

> The six-quart basket
> one side gone
> half the handle torn off
>
> sits in the center of the lawn
> and slowly fills up
> with the white fruits of the snow.

Often enough, Souster escapes from the seamy side of the street to a "kingdom, shining and far away,/where there's no darkness of

Contact magazine appeared between January 1952 and March 1954 for a total of ten issues.

city or of mind." He discovers exotic places where "wild ducks/ floated on the talking waters" and "blue horses toss/riderless and proud." One of the first Canadian poets to write in a spare American idiom, Souster is certainly no lyricist. Yet he can go on outrageous excursions into comedy. One is "Flight of the Roller Coaster," which "as many witnesses reported," decided to rise off its rail, swoop over the shooting-galleries and beach of the amusement park and fly out to sea. The playful "Rainbow over Lake Simcoe," dazing the local aldermen, sucks up half of Lake Simcoe and, "after once around the horseshoe," deposits it gently into Lake Couchiching.

High-strung. In all his poetry, once the surface placidity is penetrated, Souster seems to be reaching for high-strung tensions and counter-tensions. On "Easter Sunday"

> The day begins
> too well. The wind
> summer's, out
> of season,
> the sun, shy
> behind clouds,
> surely will burst through
> in brilliance
> soon.
>
> But rain with thunder
> before evening.
> Behind the stone
> rolled away
> another and another
> without end.

Now that Raymond Souster has retired from the infield in the Bankers' Softball League, he stays mostly at home with his wife, a part-time bank teller, and his mother-in-law. They live in a red brick semi-detached house in Swansea, six blocks from the one where Souster was raised. The Souster home is covered with ivy, the postage-stamp lawn flourishing with spirea bushes. "I don't go out very much," Souster says. "I'm a little bit of a hermit." He writes in a schoolboy scribble at an old kitchen table in an upstairs room. He watches television in a little living room filled with red-plush furniture and antimacassars. The only unusual note is a framed letter from the late William Carlos Williams.

It says: "I read Irving Layton, but try as I may it doesn't come off. Maybe the age is at fault. But somehow when I read you, I am moved. Have confidence in yourself. You've got it."

[Anonymous], "The Private World of Raymond Souster," *Time* (Canada Edition), June 12, 1964.

THE PURDY PIGMENT

> after a while the eyes
>   digest a country and
> the belly perceives
>   a mapmaker's vision
> in dust and dirt
>   on the face and hands

—From Alfred Purdy's "Transient"

After two decades, Canadian academe has perceived in the unpretentious verse of Alfred Purdy what Poet Phyllis Webb, in 1963, called "one of the few important voices in Canadian poetry." Purdy's latest volume, *Cariboo Horses* (McClelland & Stewart; hard cover $4.50, paperback $2.50), is the first moneymaker among seven he has published since 1944. It has also made so much stir on campus that, reports that *Tamarack Review's* Editor Robert Weaver, Purdy is "the hottest poet in the country at the moment."

This week Purdy is about to set out on a Canada Council travel grant. Though home is the last place Canadian poets usually think of when they win council grants, Purdy will spend his $4,000 to see the isolated Eastern Arctic. "I wouldn't write much," he shrugs, "sitting in a Paris *café*."

Fossils & Bears. Rawboned Al Purdy would seem as out of place in a chic bistro as his poetry beside the stylistically clever, self-confidently iconoclastic school identified with Montreal's Irving Layton. The best of Purdy's *Cariboo Horses* is spare, maturely reflective, with a self-deprecating humor that establishes him as a refreshingly unobtrusive painter of man and his metaphysical landscape.

Above the apparent eternities of the British Columbia seacoast, Purdy's modern seagulls cry "louder than ever in a noisy masquerade /of permanence." His reminders of human vanity are cutting, yet wistful. A 92-year-old rubbydub struts out of a tavern "young as a newborn fossil"; a young factory worker, crushed by the Machines, manages to retain "a stupid dignity/like a bear smeared with garbage."

At 46, Purdy still publishes careless work, allowing the commonplace to mar his verse with sentimental clichés like "the undulating green waves of time" and the "echoing rooms of yesterday." Nor has he fully mastered meter. One of the best *Cariboo* poems should be "The Country North of Belleville," a harsh landscape of Purdy's native rural Ontario. It is "a country of quiescence and still distance," "the country of defeat" for his pioneer ancestors. Their homesteads have reverted to a wasteland of weathered fences among overgrown brush, their moss-covered stone markers have "lost meaning under a meaningless sky." Then, abruptly, the fine image goes lurching off the page:

> And where the farms are it's
> as if a man stuck
> both thumbs in the stony earth
>   and pulled
> it apart to make room
> enough between the trees

On the Road. The lapses in *Cariboo Horses* are understandable to Purdy's friends. Critic John Robert Colombo affectionately describes him as "United Empire Loyalist stock gone to seed. He's decadent, slouching and shabby, and you can almost sense the dirt under his fingernails." Purdy knows about dirt under the fingernails. He was raised by his mother, the widow of an Ontario fruit farmer, in a house in Trenton (pop. 10,000) near the paper mills, grimy coal piles and smoking roundhouses of the Bay of Quinte. After two years in high school during the Dirty Thirties, Purdy "got out of Trenton and discovered just how awful things were."

For years he rode the rails as a hobo. Later, scribbling poetry on scraps of paper, he took whatever jobs he could get—on construction gangs and wheat farms, in shoe and mattress factories, as a taxi driver, storekeeper and peddler of science-fiction magazines. An RCAF airman during the war, Purdy was busted from NCO rank because "I didn't like other people telling me what to do." In 1941, he married quiet-spoken, 17-year-old Eurithe Parkhurst. She devotedly insists that the only thing she knows about poets is that "they're no different from other people." Yet only now is Eurithe completing her last year of high school, largely because she has been working to help Al write ever since they were married.

The poet's Arctic jaunt, "writing and playing it by ear," will probably last a full year. The Arctic will surely be a congenial place to Al Purdy,

> where a man might have some
> opinion of what beauty
> is and none deny him
> for miles

[Anonymous], "The Purdy Pigment," *Time* (Canada Edition), May 28, 1965.

ROBERT FULFORD

Perhaps it's appropriate, in some hideously local way, that the only Toronto poet in the city of Toronto is mostly ignored by Torontonians. Raymond Souster's books sell few copies, the magazines in which his poems appear are read by few people, and only the odd newspaper reviewer bothers to notice that he exists. The Toronto city council has struck him no medals, and on great civic occasions no one asks him to compose an appropriate verse. Souster probably likes it this way: he enjoys his privacy, and I believe that some of the people he works with in a downtown bank are entirely unaware that when he goes home at night he publishes books, edits magazines, and writes poems that are among the most engaging and (my guess) most lasting of this generation in Canada. In this period in history, of course, poets tend to be anonymous creatures, their verse lost in the mass of printed matter that surrounds us (unless, of course, they happen to be sick and miserable alcoholics, in which case they come to be known as very funny fellows). Raymond Souster is especially easy to overlook. His conversation is so unaggressive and unpretentious that you could talk to him for hours without realizing he was anything other than a bank employee of modest ambition; it would be hard to guess that he would *read* poetry, much less write it. Nor does he seek a reputation—he doesn't write book reviews, or even appear on TV to denounce the suburbs. Like any poet he's absorbed by the human condition, but with him this absorption is as likely as not to manifest itself in a casual interest in jazz or baseball.

Souster is now forty-two. He has been writing verse since he was a teenager and publishing it since 1945. His new volume, *The Colour of the Times: The Collected Poems of Raymond Souster*, draws together what he thinks is the best poetry he has published over the last nineteen years in his own books and in anthologies. Over these years, Souster has edited the little magazines *Contact* and *Combustion* and has helped organize the poetry books published by Contact Press, an enterprise in which he has worked with poets like Louis Dudek and Irving Layton. Souster's own poetry may at times have been overshadowed by the flamboyance of other Canadian poets, or by his own promotional activities on other poets' behalf, but this new book makes it clear, if it was not clear before, that Souster is a remarkable and valuable poet.

He is not, of course, "a Toronto poet" in any self-conscious sense. His themes are love, death and loneliness, but his setting is Toronto and some of his best poems are crammed with local landmarks like the Don River, Massey Hall, Grenadier Pond, Casa Loma and public places like the Colonial and Town jazz bars and Angelo's restaurant. In one poem Souster writes "what are poems for but for celebration/ of our time on/earth, years behind us/and ahead?" and yet much of his verse is a cry of anguish rather than of celebration:

> and age does not wither us decently
> it rips us, desolates us
> opens a door
> on nothing
> on darkness

In his introduction to an earlier Souster volume, Louis Dudek referred to "his sordid and wondrous city, Toronto." Looking around this city, Souster finds in it images of loneliness, isolation and corruption:

> Haven't you seen the river before,
>   did you know it runs and smells like a sewer,
> haven't you choked on the smoke from these
>   factories
> looking in the night like the tombs of many
>   ghosts?
>
> . . .
> where beauty and truth have been burned out,
>   slugged out,
> given the gate forever?

Much of Souster's verse depends on ironic contrast, as in one piece about an injured victim of the Second World War: "The historians say/Mr. King saved Canada/As for Steve/he gets a pension/and may learn in time/to walk without a cane." More often it leans on tension between "poetic" language and either slang or absolutely blunt speech:

> It's cold in the streets, winter's coming.
> The white whip of winter waits
> to be swung with a crack
>   in our stupid, grinning faces.

Souster would be as good a poet if he lived in Winnipeg or San Francisco, of course: Toronto provides for him only a familiar situation in which he can comment in his direct but resonant way; the city is merely the background and point of reference for his highly personal poetry. Still, it seems a pity that Torontonians hardly know he is there.

Robert Fulford, "On Raymond Souster: A Good Toronto Poet Toronto Never Discovered," *Maclean's*, LXXVII, No. 8, April 18, 1964.

Relations with French Writing in Canada

There has always been a sense of distance and separation between English and French writing in Canada. This has resulted in the rise and development of two separate literatures having the common denominator of one national and social context. In fact, relations between the two literatures, as well as any mutual influence or impact between them, have by now become matters of self-congratulation, and each of the two literatures constitutes a special subject of study in itself. This section of our anthology dips very tentatively into the obscure and difficult no-man's-land of bicultural relationships in Canada.

The historical separation of English and French-Canadian writing has been aggravated by the practice of literary historians. Anthologies and literary histories have usually presented these two literatures in separate language compartments and have treated one or the other in isolation. English-Canadian scholars and writers have found themselves reluctant or ill-equipped to write about French-Canadian literature, and *vice versa*; attempts to integrate the two literatures under the umbrella of a common literary history of Canada have been extremely modest and rare. Edmond Lareau's *Histoire de la littérature Canadienne* (1874) comes to mind as one of the earliest and noblest of efforts to deal with both literatures together as a coherent, organic whole; that is, as two branches of literature having separate identities but many parallel developments and relationships between them. Lorne Pierce's *An Outline of Canadian Literature* (1927) is a good example of a gesture of the same kind from the English side. But these books failed to establish a historical procedure. The teaching of Canadian literature both in the schools and universities has treated each literature separately, and thus has further contributed to the division of Canadian literary expression into two separate bodies. We should be forewarned, perhaps, that a separation of literatures implies separate national identities. Only an interrelation between the two literary traditions, at the level of deep experience and of critical understanding, can prevent Canada from remaining segregated into distinct culture compounds, or prevent the fatal split into separate nationalities.

Since Canadians are not in the majority bilingual, translation has emerged as a possible bridge over the gap of language between English and French Canadian writing. But while the ideal solution to the problem in this form would seem to be obvious—the systematic translation of major works from one language into the other—in fact translation of literature in Canada has been very slow in coming, and what there has been, especially in the nineteenth century, has been haphazard and uncertain. The translation of nineteenth century books either way seems to have been arbitrary and capricious, reflecting mainly the private interests and personal initiative of individual translators and *amateurs*, not the concerted effort of well-directed scholarship. Thus we have Mrs. J. L. Leprohon's *The Manor House of the Villerai* translated into French in 1861, and John Talon Lespérance's *The Bastonnais* in 1896; but there is no translation of Haliburton, Richardson, or Gilbert Parker, and certainly none of the poetry of Carman or Lampman. Nor do we have the poetry of Crémazie or the poets of the *terroir* translated into English. On the credit side, there is Philippe Aubert de Gaspé's *Les Anciens Canadiens* translated in 1884 and again (by Charles G. D. Roberts) in 1890; *The Golden Dog* in 1884 (translated by poets Pamphile Le May and Louis Fréchette); Francois-Xavier Garneau's *Histoire du Canada* in 1860; also selections from Louis Fréchette in the Warner's Library of the World's Best Literature, and his *Le Noel au Canada* translated by Charles G. D. Roberts in 1899—but these are the only works of any importance to be translated.

For a century no complete and reliable translations of the work of our most important writers—Fréchette or Crémazie, Haliburton or Carman—were made available. Thus the experience of one-half of our burgeoning literature was denied to a great number of Canadians in the other language culture, and no consistent effort was made to bridge the language gap or to unite the divided literary life of the country.

Since the turn of the century there has been a gradual improvement in the situation. An increasing number of titles have been translated as modern literature has developed in importance and interest. A gradual increase in the number of translations is already visible from about 1920, but it becomes quite impressive with the stirrings of the so-called Quiet Revolution after 1955. There are obviously two distinct motives for the great increase in translations in recent years: there is the natural stimulus of the market for books in a time of extraordinary modern development—best-sellers are made available no matter what language they started in; and there are the political anxieties of the present which have no doubt roused English-speaking Canadians to make up somewhat for the deficiencies of the past. (A corresponding zeal from the French side has not appeared, since the political discontent is too sharp at present to allow for a cooperative spirit.) Foundations, universities, the Canada Council—and more recently the Centennial Commission—have encouraged and subsidized translations. A few translations and studies of English Canadian writers have also appeared. But the commercial stimulus seems to be self-sufficient on the French side, in such instances as translations of the work of Mazo de la Roche, Leacock's *Literary Lapses* (1953), Gwethalyn Graham's *Earth and High Heaven* (1946), Hugh MacLennan's *Two Solitudes* (1963), and Mordecai Richler's *The Apprenticeship of Duddy Kravitz* (1960). On the other hand, this does not guarantee the translation of poetry or of work of a more esoteric quality. In English we have not only the translation of many popular works, such as Gabrielle Roy's *Bonheur d'Occasion* (*The Tin Flute*, 1955) and Gratien Gélina's *Bousille et les Justes* (1961), but also the poetry of Anne Hébert and Saint-Denys Garneau (F. R. Scott's translations, 1962), the poetry of Emile Nelligan (P. F. Widdows translation, 1960), the Journal of Saint-Denys Garneau by John Glassco (1962), Peter Miller's translations of Alain Grandbois (1964) and Anne Hébert (1967), and G. R. Roy's *Twelve French-Canadian Poets* (1959). John Glassco is at present preparing a comprehensive anthology of French-Canadian poetry translated by several hands.

It is only in very recent years, the last ten or so years in fact, that poetry in translation in any serious quantity has begun to appear; and because of its inherent nature, this has touched a depth of possible communication between French and English Canada that is quite new in our experience. It must be noted, however, that this phase of literary activity has come very largely as a product of the initiative of interested individuals. Foundations only assist in publication where the spade-work has already been done, as a rule. The educational and publishing machinery of the country is not yet adjusted to serve the day-to-day needs of a dual culture.

By and large, the literary periodicals and little magazines still neglect the writers of the partner culture, whether in French or English. Some notice of French-Canadian literature in English newspapers, or in periodicals such as *Canadian Literature* and *Tamarack Review* has begun to appear, but it is still of a token nature; and the reverse compliment from the French side is even more minimal. The only exceptions with any kind of consistency of policy have been the rather special magazines *Gants du ciel* and *Culture*. *Gants du ciel* (1943-1946) was especially active in trying to make a whole range of English Canadian literary thought and criticism available to French readers. *Culture* (1940-) has sought to cover both literatures by publishing articles and reviews in both languages dealing with French and English writing in Canada.

The selections which appear in this section provide a chronological account of current views and problems. The paper of Jean-Charles Bonenfant is a statement about French attitudes to English-Canadian literature which confirms much that we have long suspected: as yet there is little real interest in English-Canadian writing among the French-Canadian intellectuals. Bonenfant's paper dates from 1956; a short time later, A. J. M. Smith made a significant bid to bring the poetry of the two literatures together in *The Oxford Book of Canadian Verse* (1960). The approach was fresh and original. (The two earlier anthologies of this kind are worth noting: Lorne Pierce and Bliss Carman's *Our Canadian Literature* (1935), which contained a generous representation of both French and English poetry; and W. D. Lightall's *Songs of the Great Dominion* (1889), which included at least a token sampling of poetry in French.) One can foresee that the bilingual anthology will take its place as a standard Canadian publication.

F. R. Scott's brief article on "The Poets in Quebec To-day" is interesting as a document on the situation in 1963, as well as an expression of his own convictions on the bi-cultural needs of Canada. As a member of the Royal Commission on Bilingualism and Biculturalism he has worked hard to document the present state of our dual isolation in two compartments of language and culture.

A. J. M. SMITH

The earliest French poetry in Canada was produced in the city of Quebec before the conquest. It was minor occasional poetry in the neo-classic tradition. From the beginning it went hand in hand with journalism and had a social and often political function. After the victory of the English, the political function became a national one, religious and even racial in its scope. The habitants, led by European- and American-inspired intellectuals, tried to win the struggle for survival by force of arms in 1837 and 1838, and lost. They were to win it instead, as the century developed, by industry and the arts of peace. The study of the heroic past in the work of a national historian, François-Xavier Garneau, and a national poet, Octave Crémazie, gave an impetus to French-Canadian patriotism at the very moment it had become essential to survival. The national pride of the defeated and, as they felt, abandoned colonists of New France was stimulated and their wounds to some extent salved by the glowing pages of Garneau and the impassioned verse of Crémazie.

Crémazie is acknowledged to be the father of French-Canadian poetry. He was a man of wide culture, and though the theme of faithfulness to the courtly and Catholic ideals of pre-Revolutionary France was his chief inspiration, he was not himself provincial or even only national. He was well read in English and French, and like some later poets he studied Sanskrit. His first verses, published in 1854, hailed the partnership of Britain and France in the Crimean War. The immense enthusiasm aroused in Quebec, and indeed throughout the whole of Canada, by the visit of the French corvette *La Capricieuse* in 1856, marking the first time the flag of France had appeared in the St. Lawrence since the fall of New France, was shared also by Crémazie, and he wrote the first of a series of ambitious patriotic poems of which "Le Drapeau de Carillon" is the most famous and the best.

Crémazie, however, was too intelligent a critic and too modest a man not to recognize the limitations and weaknesses of purely patriotic poetry, where rhetoric and hyperbole are the most effective instruments, and in his later years which he spent as a kind of Canadian exile in France, whence he had fled in 1862 from the financial catastrophe that had overtaken his efforts as a bookseller, he analysed with considerable acumen the difficulties, chiefly economic, of the writer in a colony and was able to make fun of his own popular and in French Canada very influential verses. "Il faut bien le dire", he wrote to his friend Abbé Casgrain, literary critic and editor, in 1867,

Il faut bien le dire, dans notre pays on n'a pas le goût très délicat en matière de poésie. Faites rimer un certain nombre de fois *gloire* avec *victoire*, *aïeux* avec *glorieux*, *France* avec *espérance*, entremêlez ces rimes de quelques mots sonores comme notre *religion*, notre *patrie*, notre *langue*, nos *lois*, le *sang de nos pères*; faites chauffer le tout à la flamme du patriotisme, et servez chaud. Tout le monde vous dira que c'est magnifique.

Crémazie outlined here not only his own worst defects, but those of one long-lived school of French-Canadian poetry. Only a very good poet can make something permanently valuable out of such material, and though it was his patriotic poetry that gave Crémazie his fame and his influence it is the melancholy "Les Morts," in spite of echoes of Hugo and Lamartine, that testifies best to his poetic power. Perhaps the most satisfying example of early French-Canadian nationalism in poetry is the briefest and the simplest, the folk-song-like lyric by the novelist Antoine Gérin-Lajoie, "Le Canadien errant," which celebrates the devotion of the exiled *patriotes* of 1837.

The mantle of Crémazie, who died in Le Havre in 1879, descended upon Louis Fréchette, a young law student of Lévis, across the river from Quebec. Fréchette associated with the older poet in his bookshop in Quebec City and published his first volume *Mes Loisirs* in 1865, poems emphasizing, as Crémazie had, the glorious past of French Canada. For three years in the late sixties Fréchette sought his fortune in Chicago and in *Voix d'un Exilé* he published some bitter attacks on the conditions that forced a young Canadian to leave his home for the more prosperous States. Later, after his return to Quebec, his participation in Canadian politics, and the acceptance of his poetry by his compatriots, he bought up and destroyed this volume. His poems published in Canada and in Paris during the late seventies were crowned by the French Academy, and it seemed at last as if something done in the North American dominion was meritorious enough to place beside the masterpieces of the old world. Fréchette acquired enormous prestige among his countrymen —English as well as French. He was winning recognition outside the narrow confines of his own province at the very moment that English-speaking poets in the Maritimes and Ontario—Roberts, Carman, Lampman, and Duncan Campbell Scott—were about to achieve something of the same sort of success in London and Boston. Fréchette's finest work was his *Légende d'un Peuple* (1887), which utilized the method of Victor Hugo to depict the heroic passages in the history of French Canada.

It is clear that both Crémazie and Fréchette had a divided aim and were attempting to do two somewhat incompatible things at once. They wished to express and interpret their native French-Canadian scene and to write a kind of Genesis and book of heroes; at the same time, they wished to demonstrate that poetry as good as, and therefore like, that produced in France could come out of the lost colony. It was this objective that prevented them from achieving a genuinely contemporary expression of the individual life of the province and limited their work, as so much of the thought and feeling of Quebec has been limited, to a nostalgic and static evocation of an idealized past. Nearly all of the contemporaries, rivals, and successors of Fréchette continued, as he did, the patriotic tradition of Crémazie, but all of them, in part of their work, developed a school of sober realism devoted to the minute delineation of the hard and homely life of the farmer and of the virtues of integrity and endurance that were really a part of the make-up of the *habitant*. Among these were Pamphile LeMay, the founder of the *terroir* school, William Chapman, and Nérée Beauchemin. Beauchemin had written in the vein of Crémazie in the nineties, but his best work was reserved for a volume of sonnets and lyrics of the soil published as late as 1928 and demonstrating the continuing vitality of the *terroir* poetry.

. . .

In French poetry also, the decade of the nineties was a sort of "golden age," and here its influence was to extend fruitfully into the two first decades of the new century. Beginning with the establishment in 1895 of the *École Littéraire de Montréal* the patriotic themes of the Quebec masters Crémazie and Fréchette were replaced by a more cosmopolitan emphasis on craftsmanship, personal emotion, and variety. The Montreal School was established by two young law students, Jean Charbonneau and Paul de Martigny, and regular meetings of poets, critics, scholars, and journalists were soon being held in the Château de Ramezay, the old headquarters of the French governors of Montreal. The proceedings of some of the meetings and new work by the poets belonging to the group were published in 1900, including also a contribution by Fréchette, who was honoured if not imitated by the succeeding generation. The new poets were inspired in their experiments with form and in their more emotional and original themes by the various poetic movements in France, particularly Parnassianism and Symbolism. Among these poets must be named Gonzalve Désaulniers, one of the oldest, who much later, in 1930, turned back to the homely task of depicting in brief realistic descriptions the scenes of his native province; Charles Gill, the painter poet who planned a series of ambitious descriptive and historical tableaux of the river St. Lawrence; the critical and sceptical Charles Dantin; the invalid Albert Lozeau; and the tragic figure of Emile Nelligan. The last two made the most impressive and enduring contribution to Canadian poetry.

From the age of eighteen Lozeau had been confined to his bed with a form of spinal paralysis. Forced to relinquish any attempt to interpet the life of his *beau pays Canadien,* which he confessed he did not and could not know, he became instead the poet of the closed-in life. With great elegance, charm, and modesty—"Je suis resté neuf ans les pieds à la hauteur de la tête," he wrote once, "cela m'a enseigné l'humilité"—he developed a narrow but pure talent for the inner life of sensibility and reverie, which provided him with material for three volumes of verse between 1907 and 1916.

The career of Emile Nelligan was briefer and more brilliant. His poetry, which introduced Baudelairism and Verlainism into the opening circles of the French-Canadian literary consciousness, was hailed with enthusiasm by the poets and critics of the Montreal School, and the reciting by the young poet of his "Romance du vin" at one of the *soirées* of the Château de Ramezay was a memorable event. Technical virtuosity, aspirations of more than local scope, and a passionate, if feverish, sensibility combined to produce some of the finest poems ever written in Canada. A new, surprising, and, for French Canada, extremely salutary movement was being inaugurated at the moment it could be most useful, a movement that was at once aesthetic, passionate, cosmopolitan, and exotic, and that gave an immense impetus to the *other,* the non-native tradition in Canadian literature. It was later poets, however, Paul Morin and René Chopin particularly, who were to carry on the movement. Nelligan, like Chatterton or Rimbaud, was a marvellous boy, whose work was done before he reached twenty. In 1899 his mind collapsed, and though he did not die until 1941 he remained hopelessly insane, one of the most tragic figures in the history of North American letters.

One or two poets of lesser stature belonging to the Montreal School indicate almost as clearly as Lozeau and Nelligan the new winds that were blowing into the closed garden of Quebec culture. Louis Dantin, in such ambiguous poems as "Noël intime," sounds the familiar note of religious scepticism, a scepticism, however, which is actually a painful, if inescapable, shadow of faith. Albert Ferland, who later, however, was to become a poet of the French-Canadian soil, wrote with bitter irony in "La Patrie au poète" what amounts to a repudiation of the earlier school of patriotic poetry:

> Va, Barde primitif des vierges Laurentides,
> Va-t'en pleurer ton cœur comme un fou dans le bois,
> Fidèle au souvenir des héros d'autrefois,
> Tandis que l'or vainqueur fait les hommes avides!
>
> Poète, mon enfant, tu me chantes en vain.
> Je suis la Terre ingrate où rêva Crémazie;
> Célèbre si tu veux ma grave poésie;
> Mais pour toi, mon enfant, je n'aurai pas de pain!

Joseph-Arthur Lapointe, at one time president of l'École de Montréal, produced in the nine lines of "Les Pauvres" a poem of social indignation and pity worthy of Thomas Hardy. Paul Morin, who published two volumes, *Le Paon d'émail* in 1911 and *Poèmes de Cendre et d'Or* in 1922, was a leader of the aesthetic and exotic school. He had frequented the salon of la Comtesse de Noailles in Paris and had travelled in Greece, the Levant, and North Africa. His poetry was polished, brightly coloured, heavily jewelled, and with a Byzantine glitter that was in itself something of a criticism of the provincialism and piety of so much French-Canadian poetry. Morin was accused of dilettantism and coldness, of exoticism and paganism; but the perfection of his forms and the dedicated spirit of his devotion to art answered for him even more effectively than his own humble reply in the poem "A ceux de mon pays."

.　　.　　.

There is a good deal of psychological subtlety in the work of all [these] English-Canadian poets of the forties and fifties, but for spiritual insight we must turn to two of their French compatriots, Saint-Denys-Garneau, a descendant of Canada's first historian, and his cousin, Anne Hébert. Saint-Denys-Garneau, who was born in 1916 and died in 1943, was the master of an abstract and symbolic poetry that mirrors a metaphysical anguish. The poems in his *Régards et jeux dans l'espace* (1938), though they have an affinity with the *method* of Rimbaud and recall sometimes the *subject* of Rilke or Kafka, are nevertheless quite individual and original. Their unifying theme is the problem of responsibility and guilt. The perceptions of childhood, of nature, and finally of death and nothingness are explored in an effort to recover lost innocence. Anne Hébert is perhaps less adventurous, but her sensibility and her style are even purer, if that is possible. Her poems collected in *Les Songes en équilibre* (1942) and *Le Tombeau des rois* (1953) deal also with childhood, loneliness, memory, and death. They show an awareness that sometimes approaches mysticism. Solitude, reverie, and the enclosed life are valued in their personal aspect. In some of her poems, however, notably "Vie de Château," she expresses a sense of the stifling atmosphere created by the enclosed, backward-looking, ancestor-worshipping, earthbound spirit of French-Canadian nationalism. It is a new and more critical attitude that is replacing the patriotic and religious poetry of the school of *le terroir* in the work of the French poets of the forties and fifties. Sometimes the transcending of provincial limitations is found in the cosmopolitan modernism of the technique rather than explicitly in the subject-matter—Pierre Trottier's "Femme aux couleurs de mon pays" is a good illustration of this—and certain poets, notably Alain Grandbois, have introduced the methods of surrealism into Canadian poetry. His "Fermons l'armoire" is explicit enough in its rejection of the old spirit, and so are the later poems of François Hertel, a Jesuit priest who, having for a number of years in the late thirties and forties exercised a considerable influence as poet, critic, and editor, underwent a spiritual crisis, came to doubt his vocation and even his faith, and exiled himself to France, a colonial, a hopeless outsider, proclaiming himself in his prose memoirs a new *Canadien errant,* "porc parmi les porcs." Of the many young French poets of the new cosmopolitanism Gilles Hénault, Roland Giguère, and Jean-Guy Pilon may be allowed to represent the adventurousness of style and the resolute seeking for a new faith to replace the old, no longer satisfying, objects of respect.

A. J. M. Smith, Sections II, IV and part of VI of the Introduction to *The Oxford-Book of Canadian Verse* (Toronto: Oxford University Press, 1960).

JEAN-CHARLES BONENFANT

Aux yeux d'un Canadien français cultivé, qu'est-ce que la littérature canadienne-anglaise? Pour vous le dire, je n'ai pu me livrer à une enquête approfondie et méthodique; je n'ai pas distribué un questionnaire, quoique le procédé mériterait peut-être utilisé; je n'ai pas examiné la circulation des livres canadiens-anglais dans les bibliothèques. Je crois toute-fois pouvoir esquisser une première réponse à ma question en référant à un ouvrage qui a connu avec raison une certaine popularité en anglais aussi bien qu'en français, celui de M. Jean Bruchési, *Canada Réalités d'hier et d'aujourd'hui.*[1] Ce livre, né de conférences données à la Sorbonne au printemps de 1948, a été louangé par la critique et il a été répandu dans le monde entier pour former chez plusieurs l'image synthétique qu'ils ont de notre pays. L'auteur a l'habitude de voir au delà des frontières de la province de Québec et il a été président de la Société Royale du Canada. Ses informations pourraient être relativement à la page, car la dernière édition de son ouvrage est de 1954. Eh bien! pour M. Bruchési, la littérature canadienne-anglaise, et je comprends sous cette appellation, la poésie, le roman et la critique, c'est ceci:

Les Canadiens de langue anglaise, écrit-il, ont aussi leurs poètes: des romantiques comme Bliss Carman, le plus célèbre de tous peut-être, dont la manière évoque Shelley, comme Duncan Scott et Charles Roberts, des lyriques comme Arthur Smith, Robert Finch ou le brillant et sérieux Moses Klein, des poètes épiques tel Edwin-John Pratt dont l'œuvre maîtresse, *Brébeuf and his brethren,* passe à just titre pour être « le plus grand, le plus achevé des poèmes narratifs canadiens ». Tous, ils continuent la tradition anglaise du XIXe siècle,

[1] Jean Bruchési, *Canada: Réalités d'hier et d'aujourd'hui,* Montréal, 1948; Jean Bruchési, *A History of Canada,* transl. from the French by R. W. W. Robertson, Toronto, 1950.

mais, même lorsqu'ils s'en échappent, ils parviennent rarement, en dépit d'une réelle habileté technique, à donner des œuvres originales ou de forme parfaite.[2]

Plus loin, M. Bruchési rappelle et je cite:

Cinq ou six noms d'écrivains canadiens de langue anglaise, celui du conteur William-Henry Drummond, de la célèbre romancière Mazo de la Roche, de romanciers Hugh MacLennan, Gwethalyn Graham, Grace Campbell et de l'humoriste Stephen Leacock. Pour ceux-là aussi, moins que pour les Canadiens de langue française, toutefois, ajoute M. Bruchési, le problème est de s'intégrer dans la littérature universelle, sans perdre leur originalité de Canadiens, de combattre un étroit provincialisme, de répudier toute conception coloniale de la culture et de viser à l'œuvre d'art en recherchant, avec la perfection de la forme, l'image sensible et véridique de l'éternel cœur humain.[3]

De la critique, M. Bruchési ne dit pas un mot.

Cette vision incomplète évidemment, dans un livre écrit non pas sur le Canada français, mais sur le Canada tout entier, me semble révélatrice. En réalité, la littérature canadienne-anglaise n'existe guère pour les Canadiens de langue française. C'est d'abord ce que je voudrais essayer de vous démontrer. Dans une seconde partie de ma communication, j'essaierai ensuite d'analyser les causes de cette situation. Nous terminerons en jetant un coup d'œil sur l'avenir pour deviner s'il s'annonce meilleur et pour tenter de le transformer par quelques efforts de bonne volonté.

Il faut d'abord admettre que pour nous Canadiens de langue française, la littérature canadienne-anglaise est une littérature étrangère. Et ici pour donner plus de force à mon affirmation, j'emploierais volontiers deux mots anglais que sir Wilfrid Laurier confondit naguère dans un lapsus volontaire ou involontaire en les appliquant à un général anglais: «it is a foreigner» plutôt que «a stranger». C'est un littérature étrangère dont nous éprouvons la curiosité par coquetterie de culture ou par manie d'érudition et non par un besoin pressant de mieux nous connaître nous-mêmes. Un peuple possède véritablement une littérature lorsqu'il se retrouve et s'approfondit en elle et, pour nous de langue française, c'est vraiment notre chance et notre joie depuis quelques années avec des romanciers comme Roger Lemelin, Gabrielle Roy, André Giroux, André Langevin, Robert Elie. J'ai assez bien pratiqué les romanciers canadiens-anglais et aucun sauf peut-être Hugh MacLennan dans *Two Solitudes*, n'a répondu substantiellement je ne dis pas à mes préoccupations de Canadien français mais simplement de Canadien.

[2]*Op. cit.*, pp. 304-305.
[3]*Ibid.*, p. 307.

Cela ne signifie pas que je n'ai pas pris de plaisir à lire Earle Birney, Edward A. McCourt, Thomas Raddall, W. S. Hardy, Morley Callaghan, Eric Nicol, David Walker, pour ne citer que mes principaux auteurs préférés. Ils m'ont aidé à pénétrer l'homme en moi, car toute lecture est une découverte de soi-même, mais ils l'ont fait surtout comme auteurs étrangers à la façon des romanciers russes, polonais ou américains.

Regardée par les Canadiens français comme étrangère, la littérature canadienne-anglaise court beaucoup de risques de se voir préférer d'autres littératures plus célébres et plus fécondes. Il y a énormément de gens dans la province de Québec qui lisent en anglais par goût ou par système pour perfectionner leur connaissance d'une langue seconde. Ils vont plus naturellement aux livres anglais ou américains qu'aux livres canadiens-anglais avec d'ailleurs cette impression parfois fausse qu'ils trouveront mieux à Londres ou à New-York qu'à Toronto ou à Vancouver. Je le dis sans crainte de froisser qui que ce soit, car les Canadiens de langue anglaise ont souvent manifesté un dédain analogue pour la littérature canadienne-française sûrs qu'ils étaient, souvent avec raison, que le centre de la culture française est à Paris et non à Montréal ou à Québec.

Une littérature étrangère peut se révéler par l'enseignement, la critique et la lecture. Dans nos collèges classiques, les étudiants s'initient aux grandes lignes de la littérature anglaise, ils expliquent quelques textes de Shakespeare, Macaulay ou même Chesterton, mais seule l'initiative d'un professeur pourrait leur révéler quelques échantillons de la littérature canadienne-anglaise. Mais le maître le plus intelligent et le plus dévoué ne peut parler de ce qu'il ne connaît pas, et c'est pourquoi le problème de l'enseignement de la littérature canadienne-anglaise me semble plutôt se poser au niveau des universités, dans les facultés des lettres où se forment les futurs professeurs des établissements secondaires. Or, si j'ouvre l'Annuaire de la Faculté des Lettres, 1956-1957, de l'Université Laval, aux cours d'anglaise, je ne trouve rien qui puisse nous intéresser si ce n'est dans un cours intitulé *Histoire de la langue anglaise*, la mention qu'à la fin on étudiera «la langue anglaise au Canada, en Australie et aux Etats-Unis». Quant à l'Annuaire de la Faculté des Lettres, 1956-57, de l'Université de Montréal, il annonce un «Seminar in Canadian literature» avec «Discussion of some major Canadian poets» et de la «comparative research in French-Canadian literature», mais cela ne semble pas une étude très poussée des principaux écrivains canadiens de langue anglaise.

D'ailleurs ma présence ici est déjà révélatrice du peu d'intérêt que les universités canadiennes-françaises portent à la littérature canadienne-anglaise. Normalement, c'est un professeur de la littérature anglaise dans une université canadienne-française qui aurait dû présenter ce travail et non un bibliothécaire et un professeur de droit et d'histoire qui ne pratique les lettres que par amusement ou tout au plus comme critique.

Il y a quatre ans, dans une communication présentée devant vous et intitulée *Le rôle comparé de la critique littéraire au Canada anglais et français,*[4] je soulignais que notre critique des livres canadiens-anglais était assez pauvre et surtout que nous ne possédions rien en français de comparable à la série de *Letters in Canada*. Ces dernières années Guy Sylvestre et Roger Duhamel ont parfois parlé dans leurs chroniques de livres canadiens-anglais, mais je crois sans vantardise avoir contribué plus que tout autre à faire connaître aux gens de langue française cet aspect important de la vie canadienne. Ce fut par hasard et l'aventure mérite peut-être d'être racontée pour vous montrer la pauvreté d'une improvisation individuelle et vous faire soupçonner en même temps la fécondité possible d'initiatives plus officielles.

En 1945, la section française du service international sur ondes courtes me confia une chronique hebdomadaire des livres publiés au Canada. C'étaient de modestes recensions destinées à mieux faire connaître à l'étranger la vie intellectuelle de notre pays. Pendant quelques mois, je ne parlai que de livres écrits en français. Un jour, manquant de livres intéressants et en même temps désireux de plaire à un ancien employé du service international qui avait publié un livre en anglais, je l'analysai. Puis je convainquis facilement les directeurs du service international que notre pays étant bilingue il convenait d'alterner de semaine en semaine. Pendant quelques années, j'étudiai ainsi méthodiquement la production littéraire canadienne-anglaise et j'y pris intérêt. Mais toutes mes analyses étaient pour l'étranger, pour des auditeurs parfois très hypothétiques si on en croit certaines critiques qui furent formulées à l'égard du service canadien sur ondes courtes.

C'est encore le hasard qui devait me permettre de communiquer à mes compatriotes le fruit de mes études. En effet, le directeur de la *Revue de l'Université Laval* m'ayant invité à collaborer à sa revue, je tirai du fond de mon tiroir mes chroniques radiophoniques que je transformai et complétai pour rédiger une trentaine d'articles sur la littérature canadienne-anglaise. La revue les aurait peut-être tout aussi bien acceptés s'ils avaient été consacrés à la littérature de la

⁴*Culture*, 1952, pp. 266-276.

Chine ou à celle de l'Amérique du Sud. Je dois avouer cependant, avec toute la modestie possible, que plusieurs lecteurs prétendirent s'intéresser à mes articles qui leur révélaient des livres à la fois si proches et si lointains. J'ai dû interrompre ma collaboration à la *Revue de l'Université* car d'autres disciplines occupaient tout mon temps et d'ailleurs je ne pouvais plus m'alimenter dans mes chroniques radiophoniques qui avaient cessé. Je crois, comme nous le verrons tout à l'heure, que l'expérience mérite d'être reprise mais plus sérieusement.

Mais la meilleure façon pour une littérature de se répandre, c'est encore d'être lue, d'être lue par les intellectuels et le commun des mortels. Sans pouvoir vous apporter des statistiques précises, je suis sûr que les livres canadiens-anglais ne sont pas lus par les Canadiens français. Il y a bien Mazo de la Roche qui nous revient par le truchement de traductions faites et publiées en France mais admettons que la fréquentation de Jalna est une très modeste initiation aux lettres canadiennes-anglaises.

Quant aux écrivains canadiens-français, connaissant assez bien parfaitement les meilleurs d'entre eux, je crois pouvoir affirmer qu'ils ne doivent rien à la littérature canadienne-anglaise. La plupart l'ignorent et elle ne les intéresse pas. Tout au plus commencent-ils à comprendre que leurs compatriotes d'une autre langue ont les mêmes problèmes qu'eux et qu'un dialogue profond pourrait s'engager au-dessus des races.

Mais aujourd'hui, pour ma part, je répéterais volontiers en ne m'occupant que de l'aspect qui m'intéresse, ce qu'écrivait il y a quelques années M. Desmond Pacey: « There is still a wide gulf between the cultures of French and English Canada, and few indeed are the bridges over it ». M. Pacey citait ensuite la prédiction faite en 1877 par William Kirby, savoir qu'un jour au Canada les traditions littéraires de la France et de l'Angleterre seraient « united in one grand flood stream of Canadian Literature ». Et il concluait avec raison: « That time is not yet; indeed there was more basis for the hope in 1877 than there is in 1950».[5]

La comparaison avec le passé lointain ne m'intéresse guère, car ses éléments tirés de deux littératures plutôt pauvres me semblent trop accidentels. Je me contenterai maintenant dans une seconde partie de ma communication de tenter d'analyser les raisons d'une de nos deux solitudes en commun.

Je mets de côté les motifs matériels, renseignements pauvres, distribution mauvaise, me réservant toutefois la liberté de vous parler

[5]Desmond Pacey, *Creative Writing in Canada*, (Toronto: Ryerson, 1952), p. 5.

tout à l'heure de l'absence de traductions. Il y a des raisons plus profonds à notre apathie. J'en ai esquissé une tout à l'heure que je veux maintenant souligner: les Canadiens français qui lisent l'anglais croient qu'il vaut mieux puiser leur nourriture en Angleterre ou aux Etats-Unis. Ne vous en scandalisez point, car vous de langue anglaise êtes naturellement portés à agir de la même façon à l'égard des livres français, mais je crois cependant que depuis quelques années vous manifestez plus d'intérêt pour nos lettres que nous en témoignons pour les vôtres. Roger Lemelin et André Langevin me semblent mieux connus des Canadiens anglais que Morley Callaghan et David Walker le sont des Canadiens français. Vos moyens d'approche, revues et chaires d'universités ont été plus puissants que les nôtres et peut-être, permettez-moi de le dire franchement, offrions-nous plus d'intérêt pour vous que vous à notre égard. L'existence d'un groupe français en Amérique anglo-saxonne, un groupe dont la lutte pour la survivance et dont la transformation sont riches d'inspiration littéraire, pique la curiosité des anthropologues, des sociologues et des hommes de lettres. Bien des Canadiens anglais en sortant du colonialisme et en redoutant l'écrasement par les Etats-Unis voisins ont aussi été heureux de retrouver dans la jeune littérature canadienne-française un canadianisme profond qui s'explique par des raisons historiques.

La traduction y a aidé puissamment. Les meilleurs livres canadiens-français ont été traduits en anglais alors que très peu de livres canadiens-anglais l'ont été en français. Certes plusieurs Canadiens français lisent facilement en anglais, mais c'est toujours pour eux une langue seconde et il en est une foule, dans les campagnes surtout, qui ne pourront fréquenter qu'en français les romanciers canadiens-anglais.

Encore faut-il qu'ils en vaillent la peine! Nous touchons là un problème essentiel de la connaissance réciproque de nos deux littératures. Dans ce domaine, la sympathie, l'amabilité, l'esprit de bonne entente et ce que j'appellerais le complex de l'achat chez nous ne peuvent avoir que des effets artificiels qui ne durent pas. Seules comptent les qualités humaines et artistiques. Les livres canadiens-anglais seront connus et aimés au Canada français s'ils le méritent et s'ils apportent quelque chose de nouveau comme livres canadiens ou livres universels. Et comme une littérature ne vit pas artificielle-ment mais doit être toujours entée sur la réalité nous en arrivons à une question bien importante: existe-t-il des traits canadiens communs que des lecteurs canadiens-français aimeraient trouver dans les livres canadiens-anglais?

Le Canada est aujourd'hui un pays souverain, mais les textes constitutionnels ne donnent pas nécessairement l'unité et la maturité surtout dans Etat général si divers par la géographie, les langues, les religions et les origines de ses habitants.

Cependant, on peut affirmer que déjà un type canadien est né. Qu'il soit de langue anglaise ou de langue française, à quelque religion qu'il appartienne, que sa famille compte au pays une ou plusieurs générations, le Canadien subit une foule d'influences qu'on ne retrouve pas en Europe et qui diffèrent de celles qu'on observe au États-Unis. Certaines images évoquent pour lui la patrie. Dans un livre qu'il a publié il y a quelques années, le gouverneur général actuel du Canada, Monsieur Vincent Massey, avait dressé une liste d'images essentiellement canadiennes dont voici l'énumération: un homme de la gendarmerie royale, une gerbe de blé Marquis, une peau de castor, un clocher argenté d'église au Canada français, un lingot de nickel, une paire de mocassins, le monument éléve à Wolfe et à Montcalm à Québec, une ampoule d'insuline, un totem, une calèche, un pain de sucre d'érable, la chanson Alouette, un bâton de hockey, une paire de raquettes, un renard argenté, un bison, la Citadelle de Québec, l'ouverture du Parlement, en hiver, à Ottawa.[6] Il y en a bien d'autres que vous pourriez vous-mêmes énumérer et qui sont pour vous le symbole de notre pays.

D'autres traits communs sont plus essentiels mais plus confus comme notre caractère religieux ou tout au moins notre religiosité, notre conservatisme, notre colonialisme au sens très large du mot qui comprend notre attitude à l'égard de l'influence américaine et peut-être aussi notre satisfaction d'une agréable médiocrité.

Certains romans canadiens-anglais permettraient jusqu'à un certain point aux Canadiens de langue française de mieux approfondir ce qu'ils ont en eux de canadien. Je ne veux pas dresser ici un palmarès mais quelques exemples peuvent être donnés. Dans l'œuvre de Hugh MacLennan, je laisse de côté *Two Solitudes* qui pour des raisons spéciales doit intéresser tous les Canadiens, mais je crois qu'un Canadien français trouvera dans *The Precipice* plusieurs de ses propres réactions à l'égard des Etats-Unis, *Turvey* de Earle Birney aurait pu être un soldat populaire auprès des Canadiens français si son langage avait été traduisible. Je n'ai pas oublié le Montréal de *The Loved and the Lost* de Morley Callaghan. La solitude de Norah dans *Home Is the Stranger* de Edward McCourt m'a profondément touché. Dans *Blaze of Noon* de Jeanne Beattie les deux jeunes Canadiennes presque provinciales transplantées subitement dans le milieu cosmopolite de la grande ville américaine auraient pu être de langue

[6]Vincent Massey, *On Being a Canadian* (Toronto, 1948).

française. En lisant *The Unfulfilled* de W. S. Hardy, j'ai compris bien des différences entre le Canada et les Etats-Unis. J'ai transporté facilement dans la province de Québec *The Provincials* de John Cornish. Enfin, lorsque j'ai lu *Least of All Saints* de Grace Irwin j'ai pu imaginer un pretre catholique canadien-français connaissant le drame du ministre méthodiste.

Je pourrais continuer longtemps ainsi. J'aurais pu préparer un travail assez fastidieux et assez pédant dans lequel j'aurais recherché dans les livres canadiens-anglais que j'ai lus tous les traits qui m'ont frappé comme Canadien français et comme homme. Pour le moment, cela demeure limité et cela ne se développera qu'avec la croissance naturelle des deux littératures canadiennes ou des deux expressions d'une littérature canadienne, car ce n'est qu'une question de mots. Le Canada est peut-être à l'heure actuelle trop jeune, trop médiocre, trop incapable de s'analyser pour produire de grandes œuvres d'art aussi bien en Anglais qu'en Français. Mais ce que vous nous offrez, vous de langue anglaise, est déjà fort intéressant et mérite d'être connu. J'espère que vous pensez un peu la même chose à notre égard.

Il existe tout de même quelques moyens matériels qui pourraient être pris pour mieux nous connaître. Je voudrais en énumérer quelques-uns avant de terminer.

Les revues et le journaux canadiens de langue française devraient parler davantage des livres canadiens-anglais. Des chroniques régulières devraient être tenues ne serait-ce que pour signaler à titre d'événements canadiens la publication et le succès de certains ouvrages. Par exemple, les prix annuels du gouverneur général mériteraient plus qu'une brève dépêche dans le journaux. Je crois que le réseau français de Radio-Canada pourrait aussi faire une plus large part à la littérature canadienne-anglaise.

J'ai pensé naguère que les traductions de livres canadiens-anglais étaient inutiles parce que de nombreux Canadiens français lisent l'anglais, mais j'ai changé d'idée. Je souhaite que ces traductions se multiplient et comme le marché de la province de Québec est plutôt restreint, elles pourraient aussi s'adresser à la France. J'ai eu l'occasion, l'an dernier, à Paris, de constater que des spécialistes français de la littérature anglo-saxonne ignoraient tout de la production canadienne si on oublie Mazo de la Roche bien entendu. Par ailleurs, ils étaient désireux de connaître les livres canadiens-anglais.

Je souhaite aussi que les sections anglaises de nos facultés des lettres se souviennent qu'il existe des écrivains canadiens-anglais et leur accordent dans les programmes une place qui s'élargira avec le temps.

Je souhaite surtout que nous vieillissions et que notre littérature ou nos littératures deviennent adultes. Dans une étude préparée pour la Commission Royale d'Enquête sur l'avancement des arts, lettres et sciences au Canada, René Garneau a écrit, et on l'a cité dans le Rapporte:

Une littérature ne peut être considérée comme l'expression originale d'une nation qu'à partir du moment où cette littérature compte en tant que témoignage auprès des autres nations. Ce serait donc lorsqu'elle a prise sur l'universel, lorsqu'elle a assez de résonance humaine et de valeur esthétique pour éveiller l'intérêt et susciter l'admiration des autres peuples, et qu'elle sait en même temps exprimer le tempérament particulier du peuple dont elle est l'émanation, et c'est seulement à partir du moment où elle remplit toutes ces conditions q'une littérature peut être dite nationale.[7]

Mais ce programme difficile doit s'accomplir au sein d'un pays bilingue. Comme le note le rapport Massey:

Le fait du bilinguisme canadien, sans être un empêchement définitif à l'avènement d'une littérature nationale, peut être considéré au moins comme une cause de retard dans son élaboration, en tous cas comme l'une des nombreuses difficultés auxquelles notre littérature doit faire face.

Mais toujours sous le rapport Massey:

Le bilinguisme et reconnu comme une donnée permanente de notre civilisation canadienne au même titre que l'étendue géographique du pays, la formule confédérative, etc.[8]

Nous sommes donc destinés à vivre éternellement ensemble. Cherchons ce que nous avons de commun entre nous dans tous les domaines et en particulier dans les lettres. Cela vaudra mieux que tous les discours académiques de bonne entente.

[7]*Rapport de la Commission Royale d'Enquête sur l'avancement des arts, lettres et sciences au Canada* (Ottawa: Queen's Printer, 1951), p. 259.
[8]*Id.*, p. 259.

Jean-Charles Bonenfant, "L'influence de la littérature canadienne-anglaise au Canada français," *Culture*, XVII, No. 3, September 1956.

F. R. SCOTT

Like other leaders of the seminars at the Conference, I am writing down months later from a few notes what I think I said at the time. Since that actually cannot be exactly recalled, I shall not hesitate to enlarge on ideas that are relevant to the topic and which are in the spirit of our discussion.

The title, "The Poet in Quebec Today," is in one sense absurd. The absurdity would be more evident if we changed the title to read "The Poet in Brome County." The poet's only role is to be as good a poet as his talent allows him to be, wherever he may be, whether in Brome County or Timbuctoo. Nevertheless if we take the title to mean "What role in fact does the poet play in Quebec?" then there is a serious question to be answered. For it is evident that the social environment of the poet, as well as the geography of his country, are almost certain to affect in some degree the kind of poetry he will write. It is obvious that Quebec contains poets who write in English and poets who write in French, to mention the two major groups only, because that is the nature of our community.

Let me speak for a moment of myself as a poet who has written in Quebec. My early poetry was very influenced by the geography of Quebec. Coming back from Oxford, where for the first time in my life I was brought into direct contact with the European tradition, in which one soaked up the human achievements of great individuals and great nations past and present, and where always one was drawn back toward antiquity, I found Quebec presented a totally different kind of challenge. Here nothing great seemed to have been achieved in human terms. I was shocked by the ugliness of the cities and buildings by comparison with those that I had recently lived in, and there seemed so little that one wished to praise or draw inspiration from in our social environment or past history. But the Laurentian country was wonderful, open, empty, vast, and speaking a kind of eternal language in its mountains, rivers and lakes. I knew that these were the oldest mountains in the world, and that their rounded valleys and peaks were the result of long submersion under continents of ice. Geologic time made ancient civilizations seem but yesterday's picnic. This caught my imagination and I tried to express some of this feeling in what I call my Laurentian poems. It was a form of "internalization of the wilderness," and it sufficed me at first for poetic inspiration.

As I became more involved in the human society about me, particularly after the great financial crash of 1929, the ensuing depression, and the emergence of revolutionary and reform political movements in which I participated, I found that I reacted negatively in my writing and turned easily to satire. The satire was the holding up of the existing society against standards one was formulating in one's mind for a more perfect society. It was not revolutionary poetry; it was satiric poetry, which is quite a different thing, though somewhat allied.

I have been fascinated in reading French-Canadian poetry to see its relationship to the community in which the poets lived and wrote. The first book of poetry in the French language published in Quebec was written by a man called Bibaud and published in 1830. It is filled with political satire. One of the liveliest pieces is a diatribe against the Act of Union proposed in 1822 by the English minority in Quebec for the uniting of Upper and Lower Canada in the hope that this would enable them to obtain their will in the Legislature. It was proposed in the Bill to reduce the French language to second rank—an idea that emerged later in the union Act of 1840. Bibaud has this verse in his poem:

> Que si malgré notre précaution,
> Quelque Français veut faire une harangue,
> Faut qu'il renonce à sa prétention;
> Nous leur ôtons l'usage de leur langue.

Bibaud was not a vigorous or revolutionary critic of political movements, but he related himself to them.

Much of the early French-Canadian poetry that followed is completely devoid of satire and becomes sentimentally patriotic. What is known as the poetry of *Le Terroir* expresses the love of the land and family and church institutions, which constituted so much of the total life in Quebec during the long years when there was little in the way of social change. This poetry was folkloric and nostalgic. Its spirit found its most characteristic prose expression in Hémon's *Maria Chapdelaine*. There are other movements and schools of French-Canadian poetry, but not till St-Denys Garneau can it be said that Quebec poets entered the twentieth century—and there is a touch of the *fin de siècle* about Garneau.

I find that in the poets like Garneau and Anne Hébert and in younger ones like Giguère, Pilon and others who followed, there is a considerable amount of poetry which exposes the hollowness, hypocrisy and immobility of French-Canadian society as it then was. Less so in Garneau, who wrestled with his internal philosophy and beliefs, though even he shows the beginnings of this condemnation:

> De l'amour de la tendresse qui donc oserait en douter
> Mais pas deux sous de respect pour l'ordre établi

In Hébert, Giguère and others the condemnation is far more clearly developed. Hébert's poem "Vie de château" contains the following descriptive lines (I use my own translation):

> Here is an ancestral manor
> Without a table or fire
> Or dust or carpets
>
> The perverse enchantment of these rooms
> Lies wholly in their polished mirrors.
>
> The only possible thing to do here
> Is to look at oneself in the mirror day and night.

Giguère's poem "Saisons polaires" fixes the image of a stagnant society most vividly:

> No flame. No warmth.
> It was a cold life, the heart gripped in a ring of ice.
>
> The sun had withdrawn its rays and finally left the
> humans who had insulted it for so long. They had
> spat in its face, in broad daylight; they had violated
> love like a whore, right on the street; they had
> dragged liberty through the mud and barbed wire.
> The noblest reasons for living torn to shreds under
> our windows and thrown to the four winds.
>
> In autumn, we watched the dead leaves fall and,
> mentally, counted them among the green ones that
> we should not forget the colour of our hope. In our
> deepest selves, secretly and timidly, there still
> wavered the idea of the dignity of man.
>
> But the centre of the earth was growing colder
> and colder . . .
>
> No flame. No warmth.
> It was a cold life, the heart gripped in a ring
> of ice.
>
> . . . . . .
>
> Silently, we sought a new horizon on which to find
> a foothold for a new life, to start all over again,
> to reinvent everything beginning with ourselves.

Then there is this little poem by Pilon, "L'étranger d'ici," written (he told me) after Duplessis had won another of his smashing electoral victories:

> He came from a country of devout pirates
> Where indifference was taken for dogma
> The idiot for master
> The sick man for the seer

It was a country of useless struggles
And magnificent ruins
A country eaten out by vermin

When he wished to shout out his rage
They would not allow it

They hardly allowed him to die

I do not mean of course to imply that these poems were the most important that these poets wrote, or even constituted the major part of their work. Far from it. However, we do find that where the poet moves out from his own internal self-expression to the contemplation of the society about him at this period, the poetry showed an awareness of the end of an era long before the politicians started to try to deal with it.

It is quite evident that the poets, as usual, got there first. Quebec is in the midst of a period of "accelerated history" if not of actual social revolution. Are we to expect that poets will more directly express this revolutionary feeling? I would think that not only is this kind of poetry bound to emerge but that in fact it is already emerging. It is too early yet to know what will be distilled out of the turmoil and self-analysis. The very titles of poems appearing in little magazines like *Liberté* and *Parti Pris* show that the furore has reached the younger writers. Paul Chamberland writes an "Ode au guerrier de la joie," introduces it with a quotation from the Russian revolutionary poet Maiakovsky, and puts in it this verse:

O l'extase de ton sang par la scansion de l'Hymne
rouge dressant les troups prolétaires aux marches
des cités sans maîtres, l'extase hors des caries de
l'ordre cadenassé.

(Incidentally, if the "troupes prolétaires" are the organized workers in Quebec, they strongly oppose the separatism that Mr. Chamberland preaches.) The same poet publishes a poem in *Parti Pris* called "Poème de l'anté-révolution." André Brochu's poem in *Liberté, Printemps '63,* ends with the naïve and rather touching cry:

Et les anglais
à la potence

As an "anglais" I feel somehow called upon to help, and I am reminded of how Buddha, in a previous incarnation, is said to have given himself to a starving tiger just to appease his appetite, and thereby to have attained much grace. These youthful outbursts at least show an involvement in the "tranquil révolution" that is taking place. To quote Jean Ethier-Blais, "Today, the poets of twenty to thirty are writing about a classless, socialist, Rousseauist society that they imagine is a natural flowering of Quebec's history."

I do not find any sentiment of this kind in the English language poetry of Quebec. Though living in the same province, its writers do not appear to feel that it is their revolution which is taking place. On the other hand one could cite many examples among them of poets who have written bitter social satire, who have vigorously attacked the commercial and bourgeois values that deny and frustrate the creative spirit in man, and who have, therefore, participated in the changing of the society. For them, however, as for their French counterparts, the poetic function is by no means confined to this particular kind of expression and their poetry ranges over varying aspects of man's emotion and sensibility.

F. R. Scott, "The Poet in Quebec Today," *English Poetry in Quebec*, ed. John Glassco, (Montreal: McGill University Press, 1965).

Modern Poetry Across Canada

In the early stages of modernism in Canadian poetry Montreal and Toronto provided the central axis. Montreal in fact, was the centre of activity. By the 1950s, however, the attention began to shift toward Toronto: James Reaney's *The Red Heart* appeared in 1949; Souster founded *Contact* magazine in 1952; John Sutherland moved *Northern Review* to Toronto. But this drift was really part of a much wider dissemination of the new poetry. In the early fifties, *The Fiddlehead* of Fredericton, New Brunswick, emerged on the national scene; *The Waterloo Review* (Waterloo, Ont.) was started in 1958 (succeeded by *Alphabet* in 1960, from London, Ont.), and *Prism* began to publish in Vancouver in 1959. By the early 1960s modern poetry in Canada was firmly and widely established.

But one may ask, what do we mean by modern poetry in Canada? Is it merely an echo of poetry in England and America? As A. J. M. Smith wrote in 1960 in his Introduction to *The Oxford Book of Canadian Verse,* "Canadian poetry is a branch of English and French poetry and to some extent also, particularly in the work of contemporary writers, of American poetry." Is this branch, however, merely a development of the parent trunk, or is it unique and original in itself?

Comparison of contemporary Canadian poets with their colleagues abroad will show that there is no significant identity between the major poets either on thematic or formal grounds. We do not find that Smith, Scott or Klein are concerned with religion and modern man in the way that Eliot is, or with Art and Culture in the manner of Pound, or with the norms of nature as in Frost, or with the Romantic conception of poetry as in Yeats. The real relevance of Canadian poetry must be found in its relation to Canadian experience and history.

In this direction modern Canadian poetry has moved through several stages. We have had the satire of F. R. Scott liberating us from Victorian saintliness and Imperial bondage; Smith adapting Symbolism to Canadian needs and providing Canadian writing with a sense of high art; and Klein with characteristic exuberance reaching deep into Canadian experience.

This process of realistic enlargement of poetry has continued to the present time. The movement of the 1940s and 50s only extended to stronger and freer modes of expression, with possibly antithetical developments in poets like James Reaney and Jay Macpherson. By the 1960s an identifiably Canadian form of modern poetry has taken hold in several centres of literary activity in Canada.

The article "Patterns of Recent Canadian Poetry" offers a useful general summary of the situation in 1958, though it leaves many points open to debate. George Woodcock's Introduction *cum* Editorial to the first number of *Canadian Literature* marks an important event: the beginning of the first critical journal devoted entirely to Canadian writing. Items by George Bowering and Frank Davey relating to *Tish* magazine illustrate the kind of theoretical discussion typical of that magazine and its poets. The articles from *Evidence* and from *Moment* show the range and variety of recent critical writing. Souster's Introduction to *New Wave Canada,* a collection of young poets of 1966, insists on the importance of the American influence, and again shows the relevance of this central fact in Canadian writing.

LOUIS DUDEK

In a recent count of book-publishing poets writing in Canada in English I was able to put down no less than fifty names. In making up this list, simply in the act of writing down names in their geographical, chronological, or various literary orders, a series of patterns seemed to emerge, a map of the current literary scene. Looking at these patterns and groups, one could easily see relations between them; our poetry is more self-contained and unified at present than either English or American poetry can be, partly because we are a small community. (The one real divide is between the French and English language literatures; but we are even now in the midst of setting up closer relations with French-Canadian poets, e.g. through the translations of Turnbull, Scott, Glassco and others.) So that an outline of this group picture—though it may prove only a superficial method of classification—should prove helpful to the general reader of Canadian poetry, especially for the understanding of any of the new recent developments.

The first group that seems to fall into place on the page is that of what I would like to call, with a niggling motive, our Inactive Older Poets. These include well-known poets such as Leo Kennedy,

Robert Finch, A. M. Klein, our G.O.M. Dr. E. J. Pratt (through illness), A. J. M. Smith and F. R. Scott. There will probably be a roar of objection as I mention some of these names; but the making of anthologies (which is Mr. Smith's special province) is not equivalent to writing new poetry; and Professor Scott's *Eye of the Needle,* valuable though it may be in getting him into heaven, is really a compilation of his best satirical poetry of some time ago. There is no knowing what some of our poets may be doing in secret; there is a difference at any rate between the occasional new poem one sees from these defunct poets and the constant stream of new work that any Canadian editor gets from the next group, which I call our Active Older Poets.

This second group consists of some poets who have been on the literary scene for several decades, and others who, despite their age, are newcomers. In the former class, we have W. W. E. Ross, a prolific and active wit, who first appeared in the 1920s, in Marianne Moore's *Dial,* published two books in the early thirties, then contributed frequently to John Sutherland's *Northern Review* and Crawley's *Contemporary Verse,* and now sends poetry to the magazines, *Yes, Delta,* and others. Such creative continuity seems to contradict the Canadian tradition, whereby poets become sclerotic with their thirtieth year. (F. R. Scott, of course, has been praised for a similar record of writing and doing; but his poetic output has been more spotty and sporadic than critics admit, and I have put him in the Inactive group as a disciplinary measure.) At any rate, here is a bit of *recent* Ross poetry:

> Why worry about
> the world or the bomb
> while the well heeled, the wealthy,
> preserve their aplomb?
> Let outer storms swirl
> let seas toss and pitch
> here God's in his heaven;
> all's well with the rich!
> It was almost as if
> a saintliness
> (preempted by Eliot)
> descended to bless
> the eager expectant
> multitude
> condemned, though deserving
> to ways that are rude.
> Do murky clouds hover?
> Are seas black as pitch?
> Is it well with the world?
> All's well with the rich!

Among the newcomers to the Active Older Poets, we have Dr. George Walton of Calgary, R. G. Everson of Montreal, and Goodridge MacDonald of the same city. Some of these may be known to a few readers as anything but newcomers: MacDonald has published two Ryerson Chapbooks over the years, and Everson appeared in *Poetry* (Chicago) way back in 1928. But these poets seem to have taken a prominent place in the Canadian picture only recently, and they appear frequently in our poetry magazines, so that their emergence is a phenomenon worth noting.

The peculiarity of these older boys seems to be a somewhat stiff-jointed traditionalism of manner combined with an aggressive awareness of contemporary attitudes and a will to change. They are inclined to be eccentric wits, like Ross; but they can also be serious and tortured behind their mature sophistication of front: Everson and MacDonald write not only of the tragedy of age, but of The Age. All three are also capable of a wise humour and humaneness that sets them apart from their feverish and irritable younger contemporaries. Here is a sample from Everson:

> This May I walk with a caracole child
> Whose blossoms loiter, driven by gales.
> She watches darting slowpoke swallows;
> Her chipmunks flourish otiose tails.
> Jane tears fulltilt through motionless day.
> I pause. I reach—for there goes May.

Over this deft, lighter mood (resembling Ross) these poets may bring to bear the anguished tones of a later generation, as in this fragment from Goodridge MacDonald:

> Better to scramble down funnels far from day;
> Wander with objective misplaced, directions awry,
> This escalator world, then grasp again at sky,
> Clouds, houses, people, glimpsed in another day.
>
> Better, perhaps, these underworld implications—
> Spectre at window of train on the other track.
> This is our private nightmare. Let no illusions
> modify its repetitive impact . . .

The virtues of these poets lie in the intelligent comment of an older generation on the passing crisis. Their defects are in technique, which creaks and relapses into mechanical outworn rhythms, but their independence is clear; and so is their relation to the younger groups. These are poets who, born in an earlier time, are still alive to the needs and pressures of poetry in the present. They have caught on to the movement of the younger people, and are creating their own expression in the new milieu of time. Books by Dr.

Walton and Everson are now in the offing: they will be interesting and, I hope, as widely-read and reviewed as the first books by the college poets. They are usually far better also—redolent of experience, wit, and wisdom. Their authors are the "faters who play ball."

Akin to the above, and variously intersecting other groups, there are some poets who may be described as English Traditionalists, either by education in England, or by conservative upbringing or origin. Not all of these poets are old in age by any means, but since they tend to be unconverted in their methods or their ideas from the boundaries of convention in English poetry, they are clearly related to the older poetry and poets. Among this group I would place Dr. Roy Daniells on the West Coast, Philip Child, George Whalley, R. A. D. Ford, Wilfred Watson, Douglas Le Pan, and Anthony Frisch of Toronto. It is a somewhat miscellaneous group; its traditionalism is no longer the "native tradition" of Carman and Roberts, which still plagued Canadian poetry in the twenties and thirties; it is a traditionalism like that of C. Day-Lewis and Edwin Muir in England, traceable back through Wilfred Owen and Thomas Hardy to the nineteenth century. Here is Wilfred Watson writing about an amateur painter:

> I don't know where he saw them
> The trees and flowers he grew
> But I am not the naturalist
> Of all the things that are
>
> Perhaps he looks into his heart
> Or into his colour pot
> Perhaps he never sees a thing
> Unless that thing is not
>
> Perhaps his observation
> Is rooted in his broom
> And first he sweeps the world away
> To paint it in his room.

A care for traditional metrics is characteristic of such poetry, a high seriousness, and a romantic anguish beneath the surface as the core of meaning. These poets may be inclined to heaviness and dullness. They are also among the most intelligent of the poets, knowledgeable, well-bred, inner-directed gentlemen. They are formidable hostile forces to the troops of the young who want to write with radical new energy, with negative intent. Fundamentally, these traditionalists are our true conservatives.

Canadian critics in the past have been strongly inclined to favour this last group. Criticism is always more conservative than the creative faculty; and in this respect Canadian critics have not been of great help in moving forward with the poetry of the last twenty years. But this point will strike more forcibly when we have looked at the other groups in this survey.

Hardly a separate category, but one illustrating a condition which imposes some uniformity of effect, and which has always had a bearing on the frail growth of a "Canadian literature," is that group of poets whom we might consider as Migrants. Either coming as visitors, these poets remain in Canada for only a few years; or, born here, they leave early to live abroad. In the past, Heavysege, whose principal work, *Saul* was probably written entirely in England, belonged to this category; and, with less damage to their Canadianism, Carman and Roberts. Of the living poets, Robert Service and Patrick Anderson are notoriously borderline Canadians. Others now living abroad include A. J. M. Smith, L. A. Mackay, and Kenneth Leslie (of the Inactive Older Group); Ralph Gustafson, P. K. Page, and R. A. D. Ford of the Forties Poets; Phyllis Webb, Gael Turnbull, and Daryl Hine (temporarily), of the Younger Poets. Norman Levine has spent formative years in England; Peter Miller and Ken McRobbie, exciting poets of recent appearance, have also been educated for poetry abroad.

These geographical contacts are of course highly important and useful in a poet's development. In Peter Miller, the combination of English sensibility with the new acquired attitudes and experiences of Canada makes for a poetry of special gusto. And difficult as it may be to define the "Canadian character" of our literature, it is an unchallenged fact that for those born here living in Canada makes possible a root-nourished development which transplantation abroad either changes or destroys. The poets who have suffered most in their work by removal would seem to be Smith and Page, among our living poets; those who have advantageously changed the core of their poetry by migration are Gustafson, Mackay, and recently Turnbull (a Scotsman by origin, and an American in any case). Daryl Hine, now on a Canada Foundation Fellowship, may test the theory whether travel grants to poets are good for poetry or decidedly harmful: this gifted young poet does not propose to return to Canada in any immediate future. I think a few years abroad is good for the imagination; protracted living, no matter how high the pay, is fatal for the minor talent.

Criss-crossing the chronological and properly literary patterns, the literary magazines have created a certain grouping over the past two decades. Poets often occur in the environment of literary magazines;

and although it is likely, as in the case of *Contemporary Verse* that the existence of a group of poets makes a magazine appear, the reverse also happens. (In modern poetry, the "discovery" of poets by magazines would almost seem to be an act of special creation without which the poet could never have written.) In *Contemporary Verse* in the 1940s appeared Anne Marriott, Dorothy Livesay, Floris McLaren, and Earle Birney in the west; in *First Statement* in Montreal, Layton, the Waddingtons, Souster, and myself; in *Fiddlehead* recently Robert Rogers, Elizabeth Brewster, and Fred Cogswell. All these are regional products of magazine activity. It is rare that a magazine itself establishes a unifying style for such a group of writers, though a common regional quality may be observed. The point to conclude is that at present we need magazines in several regions to cultivate local talents: we need a mid-western poetry magazine, a west coast magazine, and a Maritimes poetry magazine. (Montreal at present has four mags— *Yes, Delta, Prism,* and *Forge*—too many for one region, and none of these seems to be willing to move out.)

We now come to the central design in the Canadian poetry pattern. It consists of three main groups, each of which may be further subdivided into antithetic splinters or individual poets who compose it. These three groups are simply chronological: I will call them the Survivors of the Forties, Les Jeunes of Yesterday, and Les Jeunes of Today. The relations between them constitute the literary activity of the present; and even poets who are uninformed of the recent past are subject to the currents of action and reaction. Eli Mandel, one of Les Jeunes of Yesterday, deliberately fled Montreal and the would-be influence of the Montreal poets; Daryl Hine would seem to have no relation at all to Canadian poetry; but I believe both poets are equally connected fatefully to the activity in Canada since 1940. Our poetry has at least this much organic national integrity: it may not have an obvious Canadian character, but it has a necessary genetic cord attaching it to the native literature and its development.

Of the Survivors of the Forties, one distinguishes those in Montreal from those outside that city. From 1927 (Scott's and Smith's beginning) to 1949 (the date of Reaney's *The Red Heart*), the modern movement was almost entirely centred in Montreal. Apart from the poets already mentioned around the magazine *Contemporary Verse*, the key names in our poetry appeared mainly in Montreal; since 1917 this has perhaps been less true, which would mean that the new poetry has spread more widely to other Canadian regions. (*Delta* today receives good modern poems from Sydney, N.S., from Kirkland Lake, and from the mid-west; so do *Fiddlehead* and *Yes*.) The division, however, between the "Montreal school" and poetry from other quarters before 1947 is necessary to start with.

Outside Montreal, the modernists who began on their own hook possess perforce a great deal of personal vigour, and a certain isolated formidability; they are also more traditional than the Montrealers, nearer to the English Traditionalist Group already discussed. Earle Birney is an individualist of considerable energy; his real father is E. J. Pratt, as one may gather from the method of "Pacific Door" and from the ideas in "Vancouver Lights." Traditional metrics and moral preoccupations are in the back-ground of a well-informed contemporary mind, a poet who knows thoroughly the best English and American contemporary models. Lines such as these are fairly characteristic of Birney:

On this mountain's brutish forehead, with terror of space
I stir, of the changeless night and the stark ranges
of nothing, pulsing down from beyond and between
the fragile planets. We are a spark beleaguered
by darkness; this twinkle we make in a corner of emptiness . . .

Anne Marriott was a much frailer talent; she can hardly be said to have survived. Dorothy Livesay has found the going hard: socialist realism lifted her, like her model C. Day-Lewis, out of the ruck of Georgianism; but having lapsed from political convictions, her poetry has lost power. Ronald Hambleton has shown a similar affiliation and lack of development. Margaret Avison is a more individualistic sport than any of these. She has published very little—one poem, I sometimes think, entitled "The Butterfly"—and her modernism, like Gustafson's, is eccentric, with roots in some foreign exotic soil. She is very much a product of Toronto's tense straitjacket culture, in the same ways that Reaney and Anne Wilkinson are. James Wreford, now silent, was a British colonial settled in Canada, a "modern" poet only in the way that the Orkneys poet Edwin Muir, or Roy Campbell, might be. Modernism in Canada, or anywhere, cannot be an individualistic chance occurrence; it is part of a conscious indigenous movement like the growth of "American poetry" in the nineteenth century, or even like "English literature" in the fourteenth and later.

I have treated somewhat harshly these poets of the Forties outside Montreal in order to underline their doubtful showing as a coherent body and their eccentricity as individuals. ("Eccentricity" may seem to be an odd criterion for criticism, especially in modern art movements; but I would be willing to defend this critical point in a more theoretical discussion. I think that no great art is *eccentric*, although it must be *original*.) By contrast, the Montreal group has much greater consistency of character and sense of common direction. There may be no "school" in Montreal; but the poets of Montreal seem to share a few principles on the social direction and on the experimental direction—toward natural speech—of modern poetry; and in this they must inevitably provide the central drive to the national literature in its movement away from nineteenth century modes.

A. J. M. Smith, being a Migrant (see above), was divorced early in his career from the cosmopolitan-native melting-pot of Montreal. Klein, in his poems of the thirties in the *Canadian Forum*, and Scott, provided the realistic shape and some of the forthright language that was to be characteristic of Montreal. Klein, of course, spoiled his language with rhetoric; and Scott thinned out his message into brittle wit. Scott and Smith, "meticulous moderns," began to chip and polish the first new stones; but a heavy hammer-like stroke is what the Montreal poetry was bound to develop. It was not until Layton appeared, and Souster (from wherever he was stationed with the RAF), and myself, that what was "political" before became truly Canadian and realistic modern poetry; and the language corresponded thereto as Canadian voice and rhythm, not as English metre. (Since Souster appeared in *First Statement*, and has continued his close association with the Montreal poets, I include him in this grouping, as other critics have done.) I would invite a comparison of Souster's *Selected Poems* with Smith's *News of the Phoenix* for use of language and for depiction of reality; or Layton's *Cold Green Element* with Scott's *Overture*; or my book *Europe* with either the Scott or the Smith book, or with Margaret Avison or James Wreford. Here are a few micro-slides:

> A bitter king in anger to be gone
> From fawning courtier and doting queen
> Flung hollow sceptre and gilt crown away,
> And breaking bound of all his counties green
> He made a meadow in the northern stone
> And breathed a palace of inviolable air . . .
>
> (A. J. M. Smith)

> It seems that rifles fire blanks or they're all cock-eyed
> to hell like the kind in shooting-galleries,
> And shells merely nudge you on the shoulder if you've over-
> slept, or jungle your nerves a bit so you get sick-leaves
> for nothing at all,
> And flame-throwers are just pretty little Roman candles that
> give the most wonderful lighting effects after dark,
> And the bayonet comes in handy if the roast beef is a trifle rare.
>
> (Raymond Souster)

Strip for this venture forth, my pretty man.
Props and property are caving in.
The roar of masonry and smothered towns,
Ice cap colitudes on money marts
And four winds out of untested skies—
This is the thunder of the still small voice.

(F. R. Scott)

God, when you speak, out of your mouth
drop the great hungry cities
whose firetrucks menace my dreams;
where Love, abandoned woman, hatless and void,
snares me with her thous and pities;
ambulances pick up my limbs.

(Irving Layton)

The sun upon the snow shows up
a superficial beauty that
coldness underneath the foot
here in the heart may well defeat.

His face, too, lights with seeming fire
and in his eyes the sun shines back
his lips are scarlet but the words
come from a blizzard north, are bleak . . .

(James Wreford)

Where the sea smashes
on the rocks at Bordighera;
simply for pleasure,
like the surf at Sete
alone, for miles and miles
of wind and sea-washed
sand
a strip of land, where there is water on both sides
and a good road running by the sea—
lonely, we stopped and stripped
for the sweet salt surf, the sea
that took us in as though we were nothing . . .

(Louis Dudek)

I hope that I am not setting up, for the wrong motives, what is by
chance the poetry of my friends (and my own) as deserving of
special attention. So little has been written about Canadian poetry
of the last twenty years (most of the critical surveys have stopped with
Scott, Klein, Smith, and Birney in 1940) that the first outright description of what should be quite obvious may appear as a thesis on the
Ego. W. E. Collin wrote a volume of criticism about Scott, Klein, and
Smith before any one of them had published a single book; and E. K.
Brown followed with a second critical study very soon after. Desmond

Pacey's *Ten Canadian Poets* is the third book-length study of these poets, Scott and Smith, who have each of them hardly produced enough to fill one thin book of original poetry in a lifetime of fame. The result is that this first generation of our modern poets has loomed very large. There has been an astonishing lag thereafter to deal squarely with the poets who followed, either the Montreal group, or those since 1949: it is as if the Scott-Smith barrow of criticism were used as a convenient road-block to the recognition of the true poetic style of Canada's new poetry, for the thirties poets were surely only forerunners to the score and more poets who have followed, in a more forthright and uninhibited vein, to explore the reality of the twentieth century in poetry. To describe the groups that succeed the forties poets, it is necessary to assert the central position of the later part of the Montreal movement.

The activity of the forties in Montreal consisted of a fundamental opposition between two groups at that time: the poets of the magazine *Preview* and those of *First Statement*. Of the *Preview* group, Patrick Anderson was the leading member; at his feet sat F. R. Scott, P. K. Page, Bruce Ruddick, Neufville Shaw, and—at some distance apart—on his own *coussin*, Klein. Of this group none have survived but those who were poets before, namely Klein and Scott. (P. K. Page is perhaps a survivor; but her last book, though it received the Governor-General's Award, was a painful imitation of her earlier mannerisms, without any sign of breaking new ground. She was really a poet of the English Traditionalist group mentioned above, a group constantly over-rated by our critics.) Of the *First Statement* group, the three principal poets—Layton, Dudek, Souster—who were characteristically rooted in Canadian life and speech, have continued to grow and write books, whatever their several defects. Hugh Kenner writing in *Poetry* (Chicago) has recently named "the Layton-Dudek-Souster group" in Canada, with several others in England and America, as constituting "the poetry of the 1950s." I am sure that Canadian critics will pop their eyes out—and look under their nose again! But years ago, John Sutherland, the aggressive editor of *Northern Review*, made a similar claim for this poetry in Canada, in his Preface to *Other Canadians*; Sutherland has earned his place as a critic, but his Preface has more or less gone by the board, as most Canadian literary claims do unless approved by someone abroad.

First Statement, which became *Northern Review*, was clearly the channel of a *native* modern poetry of some promise; whereas *Preview* was the engrafted English stock (of Audenism, Day-Lewis, Thomas) of which we have a multitude of withered limbs from way back. As Dr. Lorne Pierce put it, and Sutherland repeatedly printed on the back of *Northern Review*: "No nation can achieve its true destiny that adopts without profound and courageous reasoning and selection the thoughts and styles of another." *First Statement* in the forties had naturalized the modern styles to Canada.

Let us move, then, to the next group in the pattern, Les Jeunes of Yesterday. These are the poets James Reaney, Anne Wilkinson (both of Toronto), Phyllis Webb (of Victoria, B.C.), Gael Turnbull (from Scotland, then USA), and Eli Mandel (from Saskatchewan). Three of these stayed for a time in or near Montreal, but it is clear that they converge from a variety of geographical points. Also, they lack a common centre; they appeared on the scene during that interim when Sutherland had turned against the modern poets and when the Montreal "school" had scattered somewhat. They can hardly be considered part of the Montreal impetus: Wilkinson and Reaney are eccentrics of the kind we have already considered; Miss Webb would also be in this pass, but for a background of political (CCF) activity and some influence from the Montreal group in her poetry. Here is a sample of her nervous manner:

> Whether pain is simple as razors edging the fleshy cage,
> or whether pain raves with sharks inside the ribs,
> it throws a bridge of value to belief
> where, towards or away from, moves intense traffic.
>
> Or, should the eyes focus to cubes and lights of pain
> and the breasts' exquisite asterisks breed circular grief,
> this bird of death is radiant and complex,
> speeds fractional life over value to belief . . .

Turnbull has borrowed something from William Carlos Williams and from the latest French manner in his fantasy-creating. Eli Mandel is important for a new mythologizing style displayed in *Trio*, a style already suggested by Reaney and Miss Wilkinson. But that aspect belongs properly to the last and most recent group, Les Jeunes of Today.

The implication here is that the young of yesterday—Reaney to Webb—were really a digression, or even a regression of a kind; interesting, but not very promising. Reaney was the most sensational talent of the group. His recent book, *A Suit of Nettles*, following the all-edition consuming *Red Heart*, is a crashing disappointment, a pedantic study of metres and an exercise in unnatural comic-allegorical postures. Miss Wilkinson has written some of the most tense and beautiful short poems of the past decade, but she has an undisciplined, hit-or-miss imagination, with little mastery of her emotions or method; her effects are haphazard, and she is not likely to discover a smoothness all her own. She is too nervous and afraid of losing her lucky strokes in a sustained and simplified poetry: she lacks sufficient knowledge of her own process and its direction to make it of general usefulness. These two poets, Reaney and Wilkinson, are, however, the most exciting of the Group of Yesterday; and they are still here. One never knows until a poet is dead.

Les Jeunes of Today are very much alive. They are, some of them, poets of immense talent and individual interest; and they have a consistent relation to the forties poets—sometimes a relation of opposition and reaction—which gives them unity and purpose as a body. To define what this unity is, one would first have to recall some aspects of the forties group which bear on the younger people's predicament, for it is by the absence of the moral and intellectual assurances of the earlier poetry that the recent poetry has to be explained.

The forties poetry, as we know, was utopian in its political idealism (as the poets of England in the thirties were); it was angry poetry, from a sense of frustration in this idealism (*unlike* the Angry Young Men and the San Francisco poets today); it was a poetry of pity, for the oppressed and the unemployed (as may be seen in Spender's early poetry). These attitudes of social idealism, of anger, and of pity, were sometimes damaging, when they led to ideological theses and dogmatizing in poetry; but more important, they channeled the ideal striving which is natural to poets, and they provided a moral and emotional coherence to their poetical expression. They created a spirit of confidence and a drive for discovery and for knowledge. They provided motive for the perfection of technique (the true technique that consists in *skill in achieving a real end*, not just in making a poem); and established the test of poetry as its total effect, even its pragmatic effect, a criterion that, like "popular appeal," can never be a bad test to go by. These characteristics may be found in all the poets of the forties, not only in the Montreal groups but in varying extent in Anderson, Wreford, Hambleton, Layton, Souster, Dorothy Livesay. The loss of these assurances (and that is a familiar story) prepared the predicament of the 1950s. Les Jeunes of Today are the inheritors of a period of political and moral disillusionment; their effort to solve that predicament is the clue to the varieties of imagination they display.

For the young poets beginning to write today, the political ideals of the forties poets have been destroyed in the holocaust of World War II, and what was left of that politics was finally discredited in the emergence of an Organization society based on militarism and efficiency, a society which is accelerating its regulatory and standardizing techniques everywhere around us. "Socialism"—or the Welfare State

—has vanished as an ideal before the reality of mass communications systems serving the New State and the centralized corporations, while an abundance-consumption culture tries to absorb the goods poured out by accelerated and overexpanded industry. (The growth of industrialism is driven by the expanding principle of "faster" and "more"; it cannot at present arrest itself. How far can it go?) Military budgets of astronomical proportions are now a regulatory means (controlled waste) of keeping the machines whirling at maximum speed, while the threat of a devastating war guarantees an unquestioning credulity in the populace, a passivity in the well-informed. Advertising has brainwashed the public intelligence and drained the entertainments almost entirely of the genuine arts. Education is a "preparation" for this life. The future looks even more ominous: societies—soviet or capitalist—will be more "cybernetic" than ever, more mechanically efficient, dehumanized, and unreal, than anything we have dreamed; the free individual, the artist, if he exists, will be a secret misfit, a demented servant, working against the speedy senseless drive and fury of machines.

Perhaps I overstate the case somewhat, perhaps I understate it. It cannot be described convincingly in any moderate, reasonable language: the language of hysteria, as practised by the San Francisco poets, or by the Montreal poets (who anticipated San Francisco and the Angry Young Men) is the only speech we know.

But the newest generation of Canadian poets is not even capable of social anger, or of pity. Social protest has gone beyond these emotions and presents a blank face on all such real issues. The frame of the new poetry is tragedy: the tragedy of life itself, of humanity, suffering an incurable condition. This is the premise I read in the obscure cosmological imagery and the total negation of Leonard Cohen's and Daryl Hine's poetry at its best. The same echoes resound in Al Purdy's poems, in Ellenbogen's, in D. G. Jones, and in the newer poets like Peter Krohn, Moscovitch, and Acorn. Even a few fragments will help to establish the tone and theme:

> In this time of not yet famine
> when children are going mad
> with blood and bone
>   and murder on the parlour rug
> when adults are playing chess
> with guns drums and the young
> and death fails to discriminate
> between colours and flags
> the harvests of the young
> turn grey . . .
>
> (George Ellenbogen)

And we are now the only wonders here
where home's that place years and years behind us,
and a thousand miles from home is where we are.

Past glories cannot pardon present hunger
and a miraculous constellation does not change
passion, sorrow and the threat of war;
only we are different, having lost
the comfort and isolation of our conduct,
those vices which made us proud, indifferent.

In us has died the world when we were children,
the implacable conscience and the swift decision,
so we can wonder which way to go . . .

(Daryl Hine)

A painful rededication, this Spring,
like the building of cathedrals between wars,
and masons at decayed walls;
and we are almost too tired to begin again
with miracles and leaves
and lingering on steps in sudden sun . . .

(Leonard Cohen)

Bloody and stained, and with mothers' cries,
These silly babes were born;
And again bloody, again stained, again with cries,
Sharp from this life were torn.

A waste of milk, a waste of seed;
Though white the forest stands
Where Herod bleeds his rage away
And wrings his bloodless hands.

(Jay Macpherson)

The tragic sense in these poets—paralleled by Layton's recent well-nigh demented poetry—is accompanied in Canada by actual comforts and complacencies that result from a high standard of living and an economy of accelerated efficiency. Hence we have the paradox of an apocalyptic mythological poetry combined with a certain complacent detachment and non-engagement of manner— sometimes even of dilettantism. Yet in these poets, an intellectual disorder (not only in politics, but in morality and in religion) leads to a primitive mythological effort to organize chaos. This, when it is not only a game, proceeds from a state of mind fundamentally disturbed, and bordering on the deeply neurotic, or worse. Poets like Hine, Ellenbogen, Mandel, Cohen, and Purdy, grasp at a confusion of symbolic images, often a rag-bag of classical mythology, in the effort to organize a chaos too large for them to deal with in the light of reason. At the same time, an irresponsibility encouraged by actual comforts and surrounding abundance introduces an element of aimless enervation, sometimes of perverse exhibitionism, which is the psychological compensation for a sense of guilt and inadequacy. (I suspect that this view of the young English-Canadian poets may apply in part also to the young French Canadians published in the Éditions Hexagone and Erta, providing a first connecting link with our French-speaking compatriots. What I have read of them reveals a parallel symbolism.)

Within this range of youthful poetry, where it is hardly possible to say what is permanent, what is ephemeral, there is a division between the poets more entirely committed to the mythologizing method—Hine, Macpherson, Mandel—and those still attached to the method of social realism. The former, who are related to James Reaney and Anne Wilkinson, may be called the surrealist branch; the latter, the political, or sociological. To this latter branch, which is more closely derived from the *First Statement* group of the forties, belong the majority of the recent poets: Jean Arsenault, Milton Acorn, Al Purdy, George Ellenbogen, Moscovitch, Gnarowski, Lachs, D. G. Jones. Some of them may be considered still unregenerate Leftists: but then Acorn, in that class, is in his thirties and is really a remnant, in age, from the older generation. Properly, these new realistic poets express a sardonic bitterness in their social criticism, a realism without any utopian idealism to support it. Their harshness and their rage are more disturbing, and more menacing, than the social criticism of the earlier generation. They are social critics without a cause: one expects at any moment that they will discover their real purpose—is to destroy.

And these social poets are not essentially different from the archetype-seeking mythologists. Both branches of the new poetry suffer from the same deep sense of emptiness, of lies and of aimlessness; of impending ruin, of impending dehumanization; in short, a sense of political and moral demoralization. They express these things either by way of myth, or by concrete illustration and allusion. Their greatest need is a sign of hope, a positive sign. But that sign may have to come, not from any individual, but from without, from the world stage where the tragic drama of despair is being re-enacted—and then, of course, at the right time, from within themselves.

Louis Dudek, "Patterns of Recent Canadian Poetry," *Culture*, XIX, No. 4, December 1958.

GEORGE WOODCOCK

A new magazine always appears in a double guise. It is in one sense the arriving guest, anxious to exert whatever attractions it may possess on its potential host—the particular public to which it has chosen to appeal. But at the same time it sets out to become a host itself, offering its hospitality to writers and their ideas, and ready to welcome to the salon of its pages the most brilliant and the most erudite of guests.

During the past months we have spent much time and energy pressing the claims of *Canadian Literature* as a potential guest of the literary public of our country. We have pointed out that it will be the first review devoted only to the study of Canadian writers and writing. It will—we have added—throw a concentrated light on a field that has never been illuminated systematically by any previous periodical; and we have emphasized the kind of services it will provide for writers, scholars, librarians and—by no means least—the curious reader.

By the very fact of appearing, a magazine renders obsolete such prophecies and projections. It exists, and must become its own justification. But its very existence may have been rendered possible only by the faith of people and institutions who have been willing to become—in one way or another—its hosts. This is the case with *Canadian Literature*. We have been enabled to start publication partly by the support of the Koerner Foundation, which has provided a grant towards initial expenses, and partly by the confidence of the hundreds of individuals who have sent their subscriptions before our first issue even went to press.

Proust's Madame Verdurin thought that the ideal hospitality was that which restricted itself to the exclusiveness of the "little clan." *Canadian Literature* seeks to establish no clan, little or large. It will not adopt a narrowly academic approach, nor will it try to restrict its pages to any school of criticism or any class of writers. It is published by a university, but many of its present and future contributors live and work outside academic circles, and long may they continue to do so, for the independent men and women of letters are the solid core of any mature literature. Good writing, writing that says something fresh and valuable on literature in Canada is what we seek, no matter where it originates. It can be in English or in French, and it need not necessarily be by Canadians, since we intend to publish the views of writers from south of the border or east of the Atlantic, who can observe what is being produced here from an external and detached viewpoint.

As for the subject matter of *Canadian Literature,* the contents of the present number will at least suggest its scope. We welcome the reflections of writers on their own craft with as much interest as the analyses of the critics. Our field is that of Canadian writers and their work and setting, without further limitations, and anything that touches on this subject—the biographical as well as the purely critical essay, the discussion of general literary problems as well as that of individual authors—can expect our friendly consideration.

George Woodcock, Editorial from *Canadian Literature,* No. 1, Summer 1959.

MILTON ACORN

NOTE:

In the letter below the whole new movement in The States, from Olson to Corso, is referred to as "The Beats." There's no beating popular terminology, in the end, and I don't want to.

OPEN LETTER TO A DEMI-SENIOR POET

Dear Dylan:

I think the philosophical root of our disagreement lies in your assumption that there is an inviolate something called "poetry" . . . . That specimens of poetic art can be measured up against an essential standard and accepted or rejected on the grounds of whether or not they fit the definition "poetry." I'm against that. "Poetry" is only a convenient label for a kind of creativity with words. A poem can be judged only on the basis of whether it is *something* or *nothing at all,* not on whether or not it is "poetry."

To me, this is inseparable from the idea of freedom.

I know, a while ago I was telling everyone who'd listen that poetry was indubitably speech. I went farther and said that as far as I, the poet, was concerned, poetry was "direct speech." In time I found myself writing stuff which while still speech, was far from direct. What was I to do? Snip off a finger here? A brain-lobe there? (A DVA doctor once offered to arrange the brain-lobe job for me—I'd be so peaceful!) By snipping get myself back into proper definitional shape? I decided to ignore the definition for a while, and concentrate on the poetry . . . Tho I always kept my mind on communication.

And in fact I've read fine poems by Eli Mandel, and one by Phyllis Gottlieb, which were hardly speech . . . And now I've come across good poetry—stuff that has a message—by Charles Olson, which is not speech by any possible definition.

Yes, Olson . . . That's the itchy spot. To you he is an offender against your Sacred Goddess Poetry. To me he is an innovator in the science of poetics . . . The first to deeply analyze—in modern times—the poetic line as spoken, not printed. Also, as noted above, he has made advances in another type of poetry; that which literally cannot be spoken. His work, in the spoken aspect, has been carried forward magnificently by the whole Beat movement, from Creeley to Corso.

Creeley's poetic touch, his emotional surety, is a wonder to behold . . . tho, like nearly all of them, he's a bit short on the top end. Ferlinghetti has a simple and marvellous sense of imagery, tho again his thinkpiece is rather sloppy. Corso publishes a great deal of very bad stuff, but we shouldn't lose sight of the fact that when he's good he's superlatively good. He has a very strong sense of dialectic, not a contrived dialectic such as we find in Ginsberg—good as he is—but a true artist's knack of looking squarely at contradictions and allowing them to work themselves out in his poems. Let's remember he's quite young.

These Beats have it. They're the true heirs of Sandburg and Fearing, the poets with large American souls. If their work is often ugly blame that on the ugliness of the present-day America.

Just the same I'm discombobulated—as Pogo would say—to admit I agree with much of your criticism of them. They carry their revolt (all of them except Eigner) as far as an attack on Promethean Man —man in his logical and materially creative aspect. This I unreservedly damn. In practically all of them except Olson and Levertov, there is philosophical and scientific ignorance . . . a prol know-nothingism. It is just to call much of it brain-washed poetry.

What I find mean and unforgivable is the monopoly they've established in the American little magazines. In issue after issue of practically everything not put out by the academies—except *Migrant*—you find the same darn names over and over again. The editors show little discrimination. They publish everything they get from these *big boys* . . . excellent; good; bad and awful. The little fellows don't get in at all . . . This is why *Moment* has opened up a bit to these younger American poets, at least for a while.

I see bad and good in them, but don't allow anything to blind me to the fact that they are an important movement . . . Perhaps the most important to come on anywhere since the war. Equally I don't allow their importance to blind me to the worth of Canadian poetry, which doesn't divide nearly as neatly into "schools", which progresses

more evenly . . . alert to the new—even helping create it as Layton,
Dudek and Souster actually helped create the Beat school—but rarely
losing sight of tradition. I think Canadians have much to learn from
these Beats, and the younger American poets could learn much from
us. Not that I'm too hopeful they will . . . after all Canada hasn't
got a large enough army for the Yanks to pay much attention to her.

Milton Acorn, "Open Letter to a Demi-Senior Poet," *Moment*, No. 4,
September 1960.

ALAN BEVAN

The title of this magazine suggests its purpose. It is hoped its contents will reveal evidence of a search for new ideas and their expression by the individuals in our modern society who are actively resisting the insidious influences which depress and deform its levels of Art
and Culture.

These influences are formidable and terrible, and seem endemic
in any society organized for profit. Mass education has resulted in
the unexpected consequence of a lowering of sensibility and a chaos
of ideals; mass advertising and propaganda have sanctified fear and
made it a sales gimmick, and, through means which do not even
faintly defer to human intelligence, influenced great masses of people;
the prevailing economic and political systems are blatant corruptions
of fine ideals which, in reality, prove only as effective as the people
who are supposed to safeguard and implement them; the vicarious
and easy entertainment offered by Television has all but paralyzed
the individual's capacity and will to indulge in the experience of life,
and has served up images of man with which he can pleasurably
associate himself and select and discard as and when he so wishes
or is advised to do so by the demons who motivate his character
and his conduct. Apathy and indifference, fear, complacency and
shrill hysteria lie like a great weight over the human potential for
understanding and creative endeavour. Only rarely do there appear
people both willing and able to give back to life at least as much as
they have taken from it. Among these rarities, the creative artist
figures prominently.

Evidence Magazine, like the aforementioned ideals, can only be
as good and vital as the works animating it. And, if there are no
suitable works submitted for publication, there can be no *Evidence*.
It is just as simple as that. Because the editors have faith in the
eventual triumph of what William Faulkner calls—"the old verities

and truths of the heart, the old universal truths (lacking which any story is ephemeral and doomed)—love and honour and pity and pride and compassion and sacrifice," out of which stem the fronds of all progress, they feel that essentially well-motivated stories, poems and essays will always be forthcoming. Authors are invited to submit work in any literary or poetic form provided that they have regard for the highest standards of idea and expression. Experimental writing which merely exhibits a desire for something new, or is designed simply to shock and astonish is clearly not acceptable. On this point, the editors have some very definite and fixed views.

The validity of experimentation rests firmly upon the premise that the experimenter is fully aware of the nature and character of the things he is experimenting with. A writer uses language and, to experiment with it in any intelligent and creative way, he must necessarily have a mature awareness of its potentialities and limitations. To a greater or lesser degree, this maturity is gained through familiarity and usage of language over a long period of time, or during a shorter period of intense concentration. It is not a gift, but an intensely hard-earned acquisition. Milton earned it, so did Wordsworth, Joyce and Henry Miller. The fullest application of every creative resource of mind and body go into its making.

Involved in, and at the basis of appreciation and mastery of language, are the ideas and emotions it communicates. To make language "live" demands very special powers of imagery and expression. It follows then that the experimental writer must also possess a fine sensibility, a great fertility of ideas, and a deep and vivid experience of life: the inevitable raw material of literature. Only by being thus endowed can he know in which direction to experiment and whether his "new" ideas are, in fact, new, and, if they are, whether they require a new and radical re-arrangement of language to fully express. Experimentation takes time, and time is what a serious writer can least afford to waste.

Though there will always be serious experimental writers, the need for writers to "experiment" is no more pressing today than it has ever been. It is not necessary or desirable that literature produce new models each year in the same way that the automobile manufacturers of Detroit turn out re-styled cars—not necessary, that is, unless Art has already become the servant of Fashion, a fickle and disastrous profession, and writers the guilt-ridden and ambitious remnants of people whose native and developed talents were really for design and decoration. What is necessary is that young writers bathe unashamedly in life and discover that the human mind is still capable of elevation without the aid of gross and violent stimulants. Ideas and passions articulated intelligently in prose or poetry will prevail no matter how decadent the society around becomes. They will illuminate and perhaps even arrest the decadence. Attacking decadence in forms which themselves constitute a decay or corruption of language and thought, and are therefore equally as deplorable as the things they attack, is the surest way to commit artistic suicide.

It appears unmistakable that there is a trend among a great number of young writers to "experiment" with the materials of their craft in the hope that something of value might accidentally turn up. The years of what should be a writer's rigorous apprenticeship are frittered away in this purposeless and frantic game. Some of the avant-garde magazines published in the United States are full of works exhibiting the consequences of this addiction. In vain one looks through them for writing which reveals an author's preoccupation with life, celebrating its joys and penetrating beyond the superficial causes of discontent to their much less sensational but far more significant origins. Poetry, possibly the most difficult and exacting of the Arts to practice, and yet that which, to those lacking a true understanding, is often, one suspects, only taken up because it has the misleading character of a short, easy and sensational sprint as opposed to the more obvious grind of, say, the long-distance novel, abounds, punctuated by absurdities and riddled through by the malignancy of hate, bitterness and self-pity. The effect of this sort of work can only be bad. It alienates men of sensibility and corrupts the writers themselves, often beyond help.

Evidence magazine was born out of the conviction that there is a good deal of serious writing being done for which there is no adequate outlet in Canada. It is designed to provide this outlet. The Editors sincerely hope the magazine will gain the support of serious, energetic, aggressive writers, and an audience appreciative of these qualities, and with an abhorrence of ugliness in whatever form it becomes manifest. Mr. Irving Layton, long a fighter against decadence and its attendant evils, has been active in urging writers to contribute to *Evidence,* and the Editors wish to acknowledge their debt to him.

Alan Bevan, Editorial from *Evidence*, No. 3, Fall 1961.

MILTON ACORN

Because, among other things, of the small size of the Canadian Army, Canadian poetry gets little recognition on the international scene. When Creeley was in Toronto he spoke publicly of Irving Layton, and in terms of the highest praise. Little reflection of this shows in critical works south of the border. The Beat movement, with its monumental faults as well as its virtues, has inundated all but the academies . . . To whom nobody listens.

North of the border, in Vancouver, we have the Tishites who—at this stage of the game—have taken the Beat philosophy, with its emphasis on creative freedom and imagination, and transformed it into the most rigid and sterile dogma you could imagine. They too remain deaf to Canadian poetry, including what has been done in their own locale, and to mention the Montreal Miracle would no doubt throw them into saliva-spraying fits of doctrinaire rage.

Yet the miracle continues, and whether time will recognize it or bury it remains a side issue. It *is*. In an English small town buried in a French city, with an undigested mixture of national origins and a truncated class structure, a vital independent poetic tradition has originated and revivified itself in each generation. A. J. M. Smith and Frank Scott kicked off the ball forty years and more ago. A. M. Klein carried it on. Layton and Dudek in the fifties. Purdy and Acorn got their essential training there.

It isn't ending today. Henry Moscovitch seems most times like a caricature of a Montreal poet, but has produced work of value. Leonard Cohen . . . And today when new poets spring to life everywhere, Avi Boxer, Gertrude Katz, Stanley Nester, are only three among the names we might mention. The tradition has maintained its identity. The Academic reaction of the forties and early fifties never had an impact in Montreal—or if it did the nibble was so slight it has been forgotten. The much more vital Beat movement has had little effect. Two characteristics distinguish Montreal poetry from all that has come and gone: (1) it doesn't think the square world can be abolished by ignoring it; it remains in the midst, socially conscious, socially critical; unlike *Tish* it doesn't reduce poetry to a contraceptive plaything: (2) *The poets learn their trade!*

This issue of *Moment* features the poetry of K. V. Hertz, one of the younger Montreal poets. The faults of the poetry are obvious, but they are faults of growth. Here is a poet occupied *too* intensely with metre and the subtleties of voice. These are good faults, they show he is learning his trade. A line such as "I nightmared torn dragons" is twisted and tortured efforts to get the last drops of meaning out of language. This again is a good fault, be-speaking well for the future.

Above all—and this is no fault at all—these are poems involved in the world. The most dangerous tendency I can see in them is that they are all too much on the blue side. At present K. V. Hertz has not learned to *celebrate* as well as blame. What's the use of mourning about damnation if there is no salvation?

This is enough of talking down over the bridge of the nose. The good poet is good in an embryonic way even when he isn't good yet. The essential thing is that he has something to say, and even in his earliest and worst poems he says it. These are far from being the earliest and worst of K. V. Hertz's production. Listen to what he says. That's important.

One thing is certain. Despite all the dogmatic *Tish* talk about "commitment to voice" (What an abysmal degradation of that good old word "commitment") their examples fade, like a sordid dew, before the work of a poet who is genuinely committed . . . To voice and to far more than voice.

Milton Acorn, "The Montreal Poets and K. V. Hertz," *Moment*, No. 7, *ca* Summer 1962.

GEORGE BOWERING

To me, the most remarkable thing about *Tish* has been that a newsletter created by a passel of young poets should emerge as something more responsible than a blurbing of self-indulgent romanticism. In fact, most of the adverse criticism has come from young romantics who feel that *Tish* poetry has been unemotional and academic, the two terms somehow thought of as interchangeable. Academic it has not been, except occasionally. George Hitchcock calls Olson, Creeley and Duncan academic poets, though, so at least among our correspondents the term washes out somewhat.

Let me explain what I mean by young romanticism. Nietzsche was asked about the poets, and replied, "The poets lie too much." This is my main objection against romanticism. The *Tish* poets have striven for accuracy and clarity, and have turned their attention upon the factual things that make up the world, men included among them. The young romantics (chiefly from Eastern Canada and in the U.S., New York and California) don't seem to have the desire to work for accuracy. Instead of communicating they fall back on some intensity of feeling, hoping to inundate the reader with expressions of their own superhuman soul, interpreted by themselves. They scoop a lot of slush into the space between themselves and natural phenomena. They think they have to *put* poetry into things; they don't have the sense and determination to find the poetry that is already there.

Often they think it isn't poetry unless they are wailing and screeching about some injury done to themselves. They regard nature as a personal enemy or at least a personal insult. They want to reconstruct the great chain of being, with themselves at top.

Happily, over the past year and two-thirds, the *Tish* poets have resisted that kind of auto-advertisement. If they have too often proclaimed their Black Mountain forbears, that is more forgiveable than enshrining themselves as modern Rimbaud-type juvenile delinquents of the poesy game.

Frank Davey is moving to Victoria. Fred Wah is moving to New Mexico. James Reid promises to leave the continent. Lionel Kearns is going to lock himself in his writing room for a year. I'm moving to Calgary. That leaves Dave Dawson as the new editor of *Tish,* of which I approve heartily. He has a cordon of fresh working poets around him. That's what made *Tish* in the first place.

George Bowering, "The Most Remarkable Thing About *Tish*," *Tish*, No. 20, August 1963.

FRANK DAVEY

The intent of many a little magazine is altruism, but this could never be said of *Tish*. Writer conceived and directed, *Tish* was from the beginning selfish and pretentious. To the reader it could easily have appeared as a monthly exhibition, but it was never so to the editors.

For them *Tish* became the nagging and insistent mother of almost all their writing. The more whimsical of them, myself especially, were glad of the controlled demand it placed on their energies, although the mechanical and editorial burdens were always somewhat discouraging.

The increase in writing output was something the editors had anticipated when founding the magazine, but other dividends were entirely unanticipated. For instance, the improvement in writing skills which came to each of the editors with regular exposure to a critical audience. And, equally important, the friendship and advice of other writers, both beginning and established—and contact with book publishers and magazine editors.

Would such results come to any writer-edited mag? *Tish*, at its founding had for its editors people who were already writing almost enough to supply a regular magazine. They had been meeting at parties, in classrooms, cars, and pubs to argue about questions of literary or critical theories for the previous two years, and had gained the confidence of Warren Tallman, someone who was to encourage, supply beer, and finance during all the nineteen issues. This accumulated stock of latent literary energy was what propelled *Tish* until now. It was far more valuable than money (although more of the latter would have helped) and to me is essential to the success of any "little magazine."

Now that careers are leading four of the original editors away from Vancouver and *Tish,* the chances of *Tish's* survival rest on the amount and definition of the energies of those who are taking it over. David Dawson, the new managing editor, has been with *Tish* since the beginning, and Warren Tallman will remain to give advice. To me *Tish's* future rests with the new members of the editorial board, all of whom have been in the near foreground of Vancouver writing for some time. If they can sustain self-interest and camaraderie in the face of the terrifying *Tish* printing press, the magazine may continue to be Vancouver's most popular literary magazine for many more issues.

Frank Davey in *Tish*, No. 20, August 1963.

FRANK DAVEY

Every schoolchild learns that "rhyme" involves the correspondence of terminal sounds of lines of poetry—"masculine rhyme," the correspondence of the sounds of final and accented syllables, and "feminine rhyme," the correspondence of the sounds of two syllables, the first heavily stressed and the second final and weakly stressed. Or that it denotes a poem which is built on metered lines bound by a pattern of corresponding terminal sounds—such as the quatrained "Rime of the Ancient Mariner."

Except for blank verse, almost all of English poetry up until the twentieth century has been based upon these definitions of rime. To many "men of letters" poetry almost *was* rime; especially adamant in asserting this have been the classically and traditionally educated who forgot both the extreme flexibility of Shakespeare's mature blank verse and the fact that little of classical Greek or Latin poetry was ever rimed. Even today these men who hold the forts at Yale and at the offices of *Alphabet* and of *Canadian Poetry* will glance at a piece of poetry, note the absence of regular meter and of end rime, and toss it aside as "another bit of chopped prose."

What in many cases is offending these men, however, is not the absence of rime, but the absence of rime as they know it. Contemporary poets had come to the traditional resources of English poetry and found them arbitrary and unfruitful. Figures of speech, meter, assonance, alliteration, parallelism and end-rhyme had deteriorated to little more than embellishments through which any professorial greybeard could twist stale thoughts into complex "poetry." Although there were standard forms, such as the sonnet, there was no uniting theory of form or technique; worse, there was no theory joining form to content. End-rhyme itself had grown from possibly a mnemonic device in the middle ages, to a patterning device in Provençal, to a decadent toy in medieval French poetry (such as the "Chanson de Rolande"), to finally in English an arbitrary way of turning sentence patterns into poetry.

Clues existed even at the turn of the century that rime as the correspondence of terminal sounds of lines might not be an essential of poetry. Whitman had managed to abandon "rhyme" and still write what was recognized as poetry. Hopkins had completely submerged the rhyme-schemes of his sonnets by the use of run-on lines and a welter of alliterative and assonantal devices suspiciously similar to "rhyme" which were more important in creating pattern than the rhyme-schemes themselves. Shakespeare had been acclaimed for three-hundred years as the language's greatest poet largely on the basis of blank verse plays. It thus seemed obvious to some writers that end-rhyme might not be a requirement of poetry, and that perhaps behind the actual conception of rhyme as the correspondence of the terminal sounds of lines lay a more basic principle.

Sometime during the 1950s the American poet Robert Duncan leafed through his OED for the etymology of *rime*. The word was an adoption of O. F. *rime* (*ridme, ritme*) or an adaptation of Latin *rithmus* (*rythmus*) both of which were adoptions of the Greek ῥυθμός which meant "measured motion, time, proportion." According to the OED, the term "rime" was first applied to poetry in the phrase *rithmici versus* which was used to denote accentual in contrast to qualitative verse (*metra*). Apparently, as the correspondence of terminal sounds of lines was a common feature of accentual verse, the *application* of rithmus eventually became narrowed to this particular characteristic.

However, Robert Duncan decided to ignore the alleged history of the meaning of the word *rime* and re-interpret logically the application of a concept of measurement to the correspondence of sounds. *Rime* to him, then, has virtually the same meaning as its Greek ancestor *ρύθμός*: proportion as a measurable distance between correspondences, or the instinctively measurable sense of recurrence or of non-recurrence that is possible at the opposite ends of a continuum of resemblance. *Rime* could involve the correspondence of almost any two or more things: themes, images, syntactic units, phonetic units.

Rime in sound, number in sound, is derived from our possible awareness between total disresemblance of sounds and total resemblance.

Before considering the implications of Duncan's theory, one should note that it is on the surface a wishful one—that it does not agree with the best evidence available on the actual history of the word *rime*. Whereas the OED claims that the present application of rime is a narrowed version of the word used to denote measured, rhythmic verse, Duncan would want the medieval poets who first used *rime* for the correspondence of terminal sounds of lines of poetry to have had in mind its etymology and to have been considering end-rhymes as crude attempts at measured, patterned verse constructions. The etymologist and the historian would both claim that in the first "rhymed" verse the only measurement consciously attempted by the poet was in the kind and number of feet, and that "rhyming" sounds were considered embellishments separate from the attempt at "measured" verse. The long series of repeated end-rhymes in the "Chanson de Rolande" would support this position in that their rime is clearly an embellishment—a gimmick or a toy. But Duncan would feel that in the original urge to use patterns of tonal resemblance the first users of what has come to be called "rhyme" revealed a wish to provide proportions, lengths, and distances, and to make poems which were measurable constructs.

In such a consideration as Duncan's, etymology is not enough. The fact that the word rime originated rather accidentally and illogically from the Latin name for rhymed or unrhymed accentual verse, or that today it tends to mean merely the correspondence of terminal sounds, does not prevent a poet such as Duncan from pointing out that the attempt in the use of tonal rime is as much measurement as is the attempt to build lines of poetry of a set number of determined feet. When Duncan points out that tonal rime need not consist merely of total resemblance but can run all the way down a scale to complete disresemblance, and that this scale can be worked out according to a phonetic classification of vowels and consonants, he is merely intellectualizing something that poets with good ears have hitherto known instinctively—so that, as Duncan puts it, a poet will "know what he is doing."

Etymology, however, can still throw some interesting light onto a consideration of *rime*. *Rhythm, rime* (and its variant *rhyme*) both came originally from the Greek *púθμόs*, and until the seventeenth century were spelled identically as *rithme, rhyme,* or *rhythme*. Thus a close connection between *rhythm* and *rime* must have been felt by any speaker of English before this time—a connection that could not be written off as simply as it is by the twentieth-century etymologist, as stemming from the earlier corruption of the Latin *rithmici versus*. Even today the confusing etymology of *rime* cannot prevent a thoughtful person from noting that rhythm is essentially the repetition or riming of certain stress patterns, and that regular rhythm is at the total-resemblance end of the scale of rime and irregular rhythm (what some might call the "unrhythmic" as much an impossibility as the concept of "unstress") near the total-disresemblance pole.

When word of Duncan's re-definition of rime as the measurable distance between two corresponding elements, whether they be phonetic units, stress patterns, images, or whatever, reached Vancouver in 1960, local poets immediately tried to utilize it. Most, however, were unfamiliar with the international phonetic alphabet which Duncan used to illustrate the possibilities in tonal resemblance. And of the other possibilities for rime which he suggested—theme, image, syntactic units, gender—only rimes of image seemed practical. Rimes of theme appeared possible only in long works, rimes of gender seemed esoteric, rimes of syntactical units seemed an awkward way of expressing the ideal of parallel structure. The first Vancouver poet to write a poem based on Duncan's "rimes of image" was Lionel Kearns; his poem "Subversion" appeared in the May 1960 issue of *Delta*:

> I can't stand smoking
> Vowed the reclining nude
> A smouldering cigarette
> Protruding from her vulva
> And a thin line of fumes
> Coiling around her leg.

Here is illustrated the potentially grave error that local poets made on hearing of Duncan's theory: that riming images, sentence patterns, genders, et cetera were new to poetry. And that these "new" gimmicks would merely take the place of conventional end-rhyme. Why should any rime occur at the end of a line? Merely because tonal rimes have traditionally been placed at the ends of lines of English poetry, did Kearns have to place his "riming images"— "smoking," "cigarette," "fumes," and "nude," "leg," "vulva" at the ends of lines?

This poem, of course, represents a primitive stage in Vancouver's understanding of Duncan's rime. The rimes of syntactical units (parallelism), rimes of sound (assonance, alliteration, and conventional rhyme), rimes of image, rimes of gender, had been used before in poetry but had never been unified under one theory for conscious application. Now that they were, we find Kearns confusing them all with the only one he was familiar with as rime—tonal end-rhyme.

Duncan's concept of rime as being any degree of resemblance, from total to none, can be applied to any characteristic of poetry and can be used anywhere as the poem requires. Particular vowels can be permitted to recur and recur; front, mid, or back vowels can dominate a passage, round or unround vowels, and the recurrence of one of these characteristics in a later passage of a poem can set up a further pattern of resemblance. The distinctions among the consonants—voiced and voiceless fricatives and stops, or bilabials, labiodentals, alveolars, or velars—can be utilized in the same way. Also the recurrence of certain sentence patterns at key places can be used, as well as similarities and dissimilarities of stress pattern.

All of these possibilities are possibilities in rime, and, used in conjunction with Creeley's theory of organic form, can give patterned individuality to any poem. Hopkin's theory of inscape, where a poem gains the personality of a work of art through fusing assonantal, alliterative, and syntactic techniques, might well be considered an instance of good use of rime. As I mentioned before, the sonnet form of Hopkin's sonnets is often incidental; a multitude of other riming devices gives the poem its unity and conveys to the reader the sense of a crafted, measured, artistic construct.

Rime today can be used for many purposes. Rimes of stress pattern —i.e. careful interplay of degrees of resemblance and disresemblance—can be used to give mellifluous continuity that will *propel* the poem on from line to line despite burdening complexities of thought. Tonal rimes seem to me best used on heavily stressed syllables within lines to knit the poem phrase by phrase together by resemblance and/or contrast. Rimes of image work best at the level of association, providing that sense of recall—again resemblance and/or contrast—that so often strikes us in our daily living. The best rimes of image are those that *occur* to the poet, and not ones that he has searched for. These guide the poem by a natural law, as it were, of incidence or coincidence. Rimes of theme are more thoroughly in the hands of the poet. Stretching over series/sequences/years of poems, these only reveal themselves if the poet has a unifying vision of his world and his relation to it. Rime is structure; reflects order. Only so much as the poet's vision is ordered by his own sense of occurrence and recurrence, by a sensitivity to the rhythms/rimes of the natural world, will he be able to give rimes of theme.

We speak freely of the rhythm of the seasons, of the tide, of the planets, of the stars, of the life-cycle, of the menstrual period, of the wind, of the mountain stream, of the breath, or of the heart-beat. Rimes surround us, make the world meaningful, make language possible. "Without rime or reason" we say of something we cannot understand. Rime is the first assumption of scientific endeavour, is the means of the world communicating with us; it is what allows us to see proportions, meanings, structure in nature, to draw conclusions, to take measure of our world. In poetry it should have the same freedom that it has in nature. In neither can there be any fixed "rhyme schemes." The poet must have an intuitive sense of the resemblances and disresemblances possible in language—an ear for language—and must try to develop this on a conscious level so he can know what he has done and its value. Only then will each of his poems have memorable, individual, and engaging beauty and form, and be able (as Charles Olsen advocates in discussing the importance of the rhythms of the human breath in poetic utterance) "to take its place alongside the things of nature."

Frank Davey, "Rime, A Scholarly Piece," *Evidence*, No. 9, *ca* Winter 1965.

RAYMOND SOUSTER

Whether you believe it or not, the sub-title of this book, *The New Explosion in Canadian Poetry* is neither a publisher's gimmick nor emotional excess on my part. For I contend in all seriousness that within the covers of this anthology is the most exciting, germinative poetry written by young Canadians in the last hundred years of this country's literary history.

To start at the beginning: the most important fact for Canadian poetry has been that Canada is situated on the northern border of the United States of America. But until the early 1940s, no one would have been remotely aware of this given the poetry written before that time. In that decade two or three Canadian poets began to read and be influenced by the work of certain modern American poets, most notably Ezra Pound and William Carlos Williams, and several others to a lesser degree. This forward progress was negated almost entirely by developments in our literary situation in the 1950s, but by the end of this largely reactionary period had begun slowly to recover its initial impetus. Since then it has never looked back.

Leadership in this strong new influence, which had been generated by poets in Eastern Canada, shifted to the West coast at the beginning of the 1960s. *Tish,* the Vancouver-based "poetry-newsletter" which spear-headed the new direction, was poorly mimeographed, but there was no mistaking the freshness of the poetry or the stubborn serious-ness of its editors. Names like Frank Davey, Lionel Kearns and George Bowering began to appear more frequently in print, and provided much of the drive to the English-Canadian section of *Poetry 64* (Ryerson Press). But that anthology, limited in space and concept, only suggested the real strength of the West coast move-ment. This collection, by the inclusion of Daphne Buckle, David Cull, David Dawson, Gerry Gilbert, Robert Hogg, James Reid and Fred Wah, gives at last the true dimension to that scene.

Like all good movements, this "West coast" influence has spilled over beyond its borders, and such Eastern Canadians as Victor Coleman, William Hawkins, Barry Lord, Roy MacSkimming, David McFadden and Scott Davis have been influenced and encouraged in varying degrees by their fellow British Columbia poets, while still maintaining their own distinct individuality.

Three of the poets in this volume, however, have arrived by a far different path. Not native-born Canadians, their backgrounds, when brought into contact with a new environment, have given their work a distinct, personal flavour. Who can doubt but that Canadian poetry will continue to be enriched by contributions such as we find here from E. Lakshmi Gill, George Jonas and Michael Ondaatje?

Beyond this I only wish to say that I believe every one of these poets has something to say to their generation, indeed, to all of us; that they say it with grace, wit and precision, throwing aside in the process most of the barriers erected between the modern poet and his audience. This is a book to read and to enjoy, to re-read and to learn from. This is Canadian poetry after one hundred years of our history, at last vigorous and very sure of where it is going.

Raymond Souster, "About This Book," Preface to *New Wave Canada*, ed. Raymond Souster (Toronto: Contact Press, 1966).

Acknowledgments

Grateful acknowledgment is extended to the following for permission to use material:

A. J. M. Smith: and *Fortnightly Review* for "Contemporary Poetry"; and *Canadian Forum* for "Wanted: Canadian Criticism"; and Oxford University Press for excerpts from the Introduction to *The Oxford Book of Canadian Verse* (1960); and *Canadian Literature* for "A Rejected Preface." F. R. Scott: and *Preview* for "A Note on Canadian War Poetry"; and McGill University Press for "The Poet in Quebec Today," from John Glassco (ed.) *English Poetry in Quebec* (1965); and Macmillan of Canada for Preface to *New Provinces* (1936). Robert Weaver and *The Tamarack Review* for "John Sutherland and Northern Review." Northrop Frye: and *Canadian Forum* for "Canada and its Poetry"; and Canadian Broadcasting Corporation Publications for "The Keys to Dreamland" and "Verticals of Adam" from *The Educated Imagination* (1963). Neufville Shaw and *Preview* for "The Maple Leaf is Dying." Louis Dudek: and *First Statement* for "Academic Literature"; and *Contact* for *Où sont les jeunes?*; and Contact Press for the preface to Dudek's poems in *Cerberus* (1952); and *Canadian Forum* for "The State of Canadian Poetry" and "The Role of the Little Magazines in Canada"; and *Culture* for "Patterns of Recent Canadian Poetry." P. K. Page and *Northern Review* for a letter to the editor. Irving Layton: for Foreword to *A Red Carpet for the Sun*, reprinted by permission of the Canadian publishers, McClelland & Stewart Ltd., Toronto; and Contact Press for preface to Layton's poems in *Cerberus* (1952). Raymond Souster: and Contact Press for Preface to his poems in *Cerberus*; and Contact Press for "About This Book" from *New Wave Canada* (1966). Earle Birney: and *Here and Now* for letter; and Ryerson for Introduction to *Twentieth Century Canadian Poetry* (1953). Estate of Robert A. Currie and *CIV/n* for "Don't Blame This on Bliss." Desmond Pacey and *Culture* for "English-Canadian Poetry, 1944-1954." Eli Mandel and Ryerson for Preface to *Poetry 62* (1961). Michael Gnarowski and *Culture* for "The Role of 'Little Magazines' in the Development of Poetry in English in Montreal." Joan Finnigan and *The Globe & Mail* for "Canadian Poetry Finds its Voice in a Golden Age." Courtesy *Time*, copyright Time Inc. 1964, for "The Private World of Raymond Souster," and copyright Time Inc. 1965, for "The Purdy Pigment." Jean-Charles Bonenfant and *Culture* for "L'influence de la littérature canadienne-anglaise au Canada français." George Woodcock and *Canadian Literature* for an editorial. Alan Bevan and *Evidence* for an editorial. Milton Acorn and *Moment* for "The Montreal Miracle and K. V. Hertz" and "Open Letter to a Demi-Senior Poet." James Reaney and *Alphabet* for an editorial. Frank Davey: and *Tish* for a statement; and *Evidence* for "Rime, A Scholarly Piece"; and *Canadian Literature* for "Anything But Reluctant: Canada's Little Magazines." George Bowering and *Tish* for "The Most Remarkable Thing About *Tish*." Irving Layton for "A Note on Layton," first published in *The Improved Binoculars*, Selected Poems of Irving Layton (Jargon 18, Jonathan Williams, publisher, Highlands, N.C.), copyright 1956 by Jonathan Williams. By permission of New Directions Publishing Corporation, Agent for Mrs. W. C. Williams. Robert Fulford and *Maclean's* for "On Raymond Souster: A Good Toronto Poet Never Discovered." Every effort has been made to trace copyright ownership; if anyone has information we lack, we would be most grateful for it.